TAROT AND PSYCHOLOGY

Spectrums of Possibility

TAROT AND PSYCHOLOGY

Spectrums of Possibility

Arthur Rosengarten

PARAGON HOUSE
St. Paul, Minnesota

First Edition, 2000

Published in the United States by
Paragon House
1925 Oakcrest Avenue, Suite 7
St. Paul, MN 55113

Manufactured in the United States of America.

Library of Congress Cataloging-in-Publication Data

Rosengarten, Arthur, 1950-
Tarot and Psychology : Spectrums of possibility / by Arthur Rosengarten.
p. cm.
Includes bibliographical references and index.
ISBN 1-55778-785-9 (cloth). — ISBN 1-55778-784-0 (pbk.)
1. Tarot–Psychological aspects. I. Title.
BF1879.T2R67 2000
133.3'2424—dc21 99-44720
CIP

10 9 8 7 6 5 4 3 2

For current information about all releases from Paragon House,
visit the web site at http://www.paragonhouse.com

For my loving family,

Sangita, Alexander Sky, and Maia Lena

Credits for Illustrations

Illustrations from New Palladini Tarot Deck reproduced by permission of U.S. Games System, Inc., Stamford, CT 06902 USA, Copyright © 1996 by U.S. Games Systems, Inc. Further reproduction prohibited.

Illustrations from Universal Waite Tarot Deck reproduced by permission of U.S. Games System, Inc., Stamford, CT 06902 USA, Copyright © 1990 by U.S. Games Systems, Inc. Further reproduction prohibited.

Illustrations from Tarot of Marseilles reproduced by permission of U.S. Games System, Inc., Stamford, CT 06902 USA, Copyright © 1996 by U.S. Games Systems, Inc. Further reproduction prohibited.

Illustrations from the Alrister Crowley Thoth Tarot reproduced by permission of AGM AGMuller, CH-8212 Neuhausen, Switzerland. Further reproduction prohibited. © AGM, Switzerland / OTO, USA.

Illustrations from the Röhrig-Tarot deck copyright © Carl-W. Röhrig, published by Bluestar Communications under the title The Röhrig-Tarot Deck.

Contents

List of Charts and Illustrations

Acknowledgements

I am indebted to many wise friends who have shown their generous support and guidance for this book. I thank Nicolee Jikyo McMahon for her tremendous counsel and belief in me throughout the many stages of this project. Ed Buryn and Mary Greer were great catalysts for the inception and initial mapping of my thoughts. The eminent Jungian analyst James A. Hall, M.D. has offered tremendous feedback and encouragement, and has honored me with his friendship and experience. Professor Victor Mansfield and Dr. Hall were particularly eloquent masters of synchronicity theory and Jungian ideas, and early supporters of the Tarot Research Project. Tarot historian Robert V. O'Neil, Ph.D. along with my dear friends Howard Rossman, Ph.D. and Barry Shea, CEO of Caminar/CLC in Menlo Park, provided especially helpful critical feedback for the refinement of my focus and writing style. Pal Bhasin offered his expertise in statistical concerns. Wald Amberstone and Ruth Ann Brauser of The Tarot School in New York published three excerpted articles in *Arcanum* for which I am very thankful. And, of course, without the ongoing support and patience of my lovely wife, Dr. Sangita Bhasin Rosengarten, none of this would be possible. Special thanks to Laureen Enright at Paragon House for her great facilitation and support.

I owe a large debt of gratitude as well to my loyal students of the Tarot Circle in San Diego who have over the years provided me with the sincere and intelligent audience I've needed to develop and apply my unique approach to Tarot and Psychology. In particular, I wish to thank Bob Lloyd (Director of Homepeace), Yvette Lyons, Arnell Ando (creator of the Transformational Tarot), Ellen Johnson, Nicole Gigger, Sue Silva, Sheila Washburn, Linda Gail Walters, Sue Shorey, and many others who have explored with me many spectrums of possibility with depth, good humor and enthusiasm. I also wish to thank my friend and colleague Lon Milo DuQuette for his abounding scholarship in Western occult traditions and his recent collaboration in the Tarot Circle.

Acknowledgments

Preface

To speak at once of the exotic realm of Tarot card divination *and* the vibrant professional muscle of contemporary psychotherapy—would seem similar to placing Jesse "The Body" Ventura in all candor into the same heavyweight ring as Mohammed Ali. The match-up appears more farcical than feasible (and rather messy besides), though ironically, in some circles of thought, arguments will no doubt linger on through the night over which of the two combatants is the true Goliath, and which the true David.

By all appearances, I have endeavored to take just that foolhardy course, evidenced by the book's ambitious title: *Tarot and Psychology*. But let it be known that my motive is more one of professional obligation than underdog bravado. I have witnessed far too much of the stunning psychological elegance and insightfulness stimulated by the Tarot Method to simply and quietly ride off into the metaphysical sunset, selfishly hoarding, in effect, my precious satchel of therapeutic gems that might otherwise bestow great benefit to others. In the pages to follow I have elected instead to put my cards on the table, as we say, in order to lay out what I believe to be the important groundwork, both philosophical and practical, for serious usage of Tarot in the service of enhanced psycho-spiritual exploration.

But pitting these two great vehicles of consciousness against one another (as I have done above) is a terribly mistaken metaphor. Much to the contrary, Tarot and Psychology should be understood not as dueling enemies but as fighting lovers. Their essential compatibility is a central theme throughout this book. In part, my task is to facilitate a troubled relationship in the capacity of (brave and a tad unconventional) marriage counselor. The initial phase of this treatment has now officially begun, though of course, due to the enormity of the task at hand I rather suspect by termination the work will remain largely unfinished. For our purposes, however, the dialogue and the process itself should be enough.

Admittedly, I have taken this case with a bias towards propping-up and making more accessible the tremendous, underactualized strengths, talents, and potentials of Tarot. But I do this with a certain respectful deference and affinity for Psychology as indeed I make my living as a psychologist and family therapist. The clinician in me knows his primary responsibility is to treat the relationship itself, or "nonrelationship" as the case may be, comprised of two richly deserving, mature, though incomplete (and I might add, slightly paranoic) parties. I am convinced, however, that a happy and prosperous marriage between these two strange bedfellows is not only desirable, but in fact indispensable for the emergence of a new standard of mental health and "wellbeingness" in the 21st century—a standard which must deeply and adeptly strive to integrate spiritual and psychological dimensions into whole spectrums of human possibility.

In the short forewords that follow, two highly esteemed contributors in these respective areas have written generous and illuminating introductions to this book. I am much indebted to Lon Milo DuQuette and James A. Hall, M.D. who have encapsulated their own friendly interludes between Psychology and Tarot, but who have found their way to the party from distinctly opposite ends of the spectrum.

A.R.

Foreword

Lon Milo DuQuette

Promise me never to abandon the sexual theory. That is the most essential thing of all. You see, we must make a dogma of it, an unshakable bulwark…against the black tide of mud…of occultism.

—Freud writing to Jung, 1913

I knew that I would never be able to accept such an attitude. What Freud seemed to mean by 'occultism' was virtually everything that philosophy and religion, including the rising contemporary science of parapsychology, had learned about the psyche.

— Jung's reaction to Freud's statement

For at least five centuries the Tarot has tenaciously survived the condemnation of church, the persecution of state and the ridicule of academia. Long the instrument of fortune-tellers and persons of dubious if not felonious character, the Tarot enters the new millennium still in the guise of a fallen angel. However, unlike Milton's rebellious protagonist, the Tarot now hovers dangerously close to redemption. I am pleased but not at all surprised to learn that these ancient and evocative images are now attracting the serious attention of modern mental health professionals. Foremost among these is Arthur Rosengarten, Ph.D. whose provocative and thoroughly readable work is the subject of these brief words.

Since the mid-nineteenth century, adepts of Western Hermeticism have attempted to demonstrate that the Tarot is constructed in strict conformity with the fundamental principles of Hebrew mysticism known as the Kabbalah. They asserted that images of the Tarot, especially those displayed on the 22 trump cards, are visual personifications of various aspects of Deity which had been categorized with anal retentive zeal by unnamed Hebrew sages at some time in the distant past.

The ancient Hebrew philosophers built upon the scriptural premise that man was created in the image of God. Later esotericists, observing the phenomena of repeating patterns in nature and remembering the Hermetic axiom "as above, so below" tended to agree, albeit with less parochial bias. They reasoned that if the images of the Tarot were metaphors of aspects of divine consciousness then, it followed, they also must be reflected on the human level as key components of the psyche—archetypal citizens of the mind which each of us share with our fellows.

While I do not presume to speak with any measure of authority on matters relating to the field of psychology, I do feel somewhat qualified to speak on matters touching on Kabbalah and Tarot. It is clear to me that the "mystical" concept of the archetypal images of the Tarot is identical in essence with those of Jung's Universal Collective Unconscious. Moreover, I firmly believe that under certain circumstances the images of the Tarot can trigger, activate, subdue, direct or empower the specific dynamics these archetypes represent.

Regrettably, few professionals are aware of the practical potential of the Tarot. Fewer still are as yet willing to risk the condemnation of colleagues by embarking upon a course of study that would enable them to skillfully employ this tool in a therapeutic environment. A master of both disciplines, Dr. Rosengarten remains somewhat immune to such concerns. He is a pioneer in the purest sense of the word. Not only has he courageously ventured into uncharted territory, he has lingered along the way to break ground and erect landmarks for the benefit of those who will inevitably follow.

Ironically, the antagonism, real or imagined, that exists between the Tarot and Psychology parallels in many respects the fundamental differences between Eastern and Western mysticism. The Eastern mystic, by tradition (and perhaps because of temperament), is taught to quietly plunge inwardly to meet the myriad facets of self on their own turf. Furthermore, to overcome the distractions of mind which hinder this inner self-communion he or she strives with ruthless meditative fervor to virtually assassinate the harpies of thought, creating as it were a vacuum into which pure illumination will theoretically pour.

The Western mind, on the other hand, prefers to deal objectively with subjective matters. We want to reach in, personify them, pull them out, throw them down in front of us and have it out with them here and now. But dealing objectively with internal realities is impossible if one is unable to recognize and engage them as such. For what more perfect tool could one ask than a deck of colorful archetypal images that can be manipulated at will in nearly infinite combination. As the author points out:

> In a typical ten card spread, the chances of reproducing an exact duplication are simply staggering when one calculates the probability from a deck of 78 highly differentiated cards. But with Tarot, a transpersonal commonality is equally brought to bear upon human individuality and difference. This perhaps is why Tarot's light shines through all quadrants of the psychological universe and may be applicable in varying degrees to diverse theoretical persuasions.
>
> The symbolic language of Tarot compacts multiple levels of meaning into each card illustration and synchronistically one soon learns that there are no accidents in Tarot (or life), or put differently, accidents themselves are inherently meaningful. Universal themes of human experience unfold within original permutations of the Tarot matrix, reflecting countless variations on common myths, such as the perennial stages of human suffering and attainment, the psychological tasks and demands of human development, and the mysteries and potentials of the human spirit.

Rosengarten's landmark work spans the abyss that yawns between Psychology and mysticism. Remarkably, it does so without diminishment to either art or science; indeed, both are immeasurably enriched by his unique contributions. It is obvious that this is a work written primarily for the continuing education of mental health professionals. (Certainly its meticulous notes, exhaustive references, bibliography and heroic index set it apart from nearly every book on Tarot ever published.) Nevertheless, we of the Tarot/metaphysical community should welcome it with particular gratitude and interest for it offers us a rare and entirely new look at an ancient tradition.

—Lon Milo DuQuette, Newport Beach, California, 1999
Creator and author of *Tarot of Ceremonial Magick*

Foreword

James A. Hall, M.D.

I have been aware of Tarot since my adolescence but considered it simply a method of fortune telling. During my studies in Zurich, I first appreciated its deeper meaning. Jung was interested in many divination systems—astrology, geomancy, *I Ching,* and Tarot — and asked some of his inner circle to undertake studies of them. Linda Fiertz choose to study Tarot. After her death, her son Heinrich, a psychiatrist, carried on her studies. While at the Jung Institute, I arranged to take a private tutorial course on Tarot with Dr. Fiertz.

It opened my eyes to the deeper symbolic meaning of Tarot. The Major Arcana or trumps seem to be nothing less than an outline of the usual individuation process itself—so far as it can be outlined. Laying aside two cards (No. 1, The Magician, and The Fool, which is 0), the Major Arcana can be laid out in numbered sequence in four columns of five rows each, revealing an overall developmental pattern as well as a logical movement within each row. For example, Row 1 begins with the High Priestess, card 1, the very beginning of psychological development. In the popular Rider-Waite deck the robe of the High Priestess can be easily imagined as the origin of the river which is seen in other trumps. Next is The Empress, card 3, taken psychologically to be the emotional awareness of change. She is followed by card 4, The Emperor, signifying that the change is now a conscious thought. Last in this first row is trump 5, The Hierophant, who knows the thought well enough to proclaim it: He knows that he knows.

Similar developmental movements can be found in other rows, as well as other meanings that suggest an overall symbolic outline of the course of psychological development that begins with The Magician and ends with The Fool. These beginning and ending images are both profoundly ambivalent. The Magician has on the table before him symbols of the four suits analogous to Jung's four functions:

Cups = Feeling
Swords = Thinking
Pentacles = Sensation
Wands = Intuition

The Magician can be seen either as the conscious ego responsibly adjudicating the proper proportion of the functions or as the heroic ego trying to manipulate to achieve his/her own conscious goals, while ignoring the unconscious call to wholeness rather than perfection of the dominant function. The very best view of The Magician is to envision him as a conduit of force from a higher realm traveling through the wand in his upraised right hand to a lower realm to which his left hand points. Likewise, The Fool can be imagined either as a foolish dreamer unaware that he is about to step over a precipice or as one who has integrated the four functions to such a degree that everything works to protect him. Even his dog pulls him back from a misstep.

For three decades this understanding of Tarot served me well in my private life. A Tarot reading, like other projective devices such as sandtrays, could make me rethink my attitudes, allowing for unconscious or tacit factors I had neglected. In addition, Tarot carried the overtones of some mysterious transpersonal force that might be at work. In my practice, though, I used Tarot images only in amplifying dreams and sandtrays. Not until I read Dr. Rosengarten's manuscript was I aware of the potential of Tarot. If I were still in practice, I would certainly try using it. I held back before for fear of creating a shamanistic transference, implying that I, like a card reader, was in touch with occult forces.

Rosengarten discusses this problem (p. 40), pointing out (p. 86) that

> when a reading is particularly meaningful, the therapeutic process itself is elevated, at least for the moment, to a level of transcendence that can only be described as an almost mystical reverence shared by client and therapist alike for some unseen intelligence at work.

This is congruent with the recent tendency to view transference/countertransference as a transformative field which, if effective, changes both analyst and analysand.

Tarot is probably the parent or the child of our familar deck of playing cards minus the 22 trumps and the four Knights. "As many people know," explains Dr. Rosengarten, "modern playing cards are intimately tied to Tarot cards, both structurally and historically, and there has been a chicken-or-egg controversy for years over which came first." The use of the two decks is vastly different. "In Tarot, the game is your life as a whole, or stated more subjectively, your self." Interestingly, the author explains the deletion of the Tarot Knights — "...a few scholars have conjectured this omission [of the Knights] was likely due to their dangerous associations to the Knights Templar, a controversial secret society of religious mercenaries which flourished during the Crusades" (p. 12).

Several impressive case examples illustrate the author's incorporation of Tarot in his clinical practice. I find particularly striking his description of how a group Tarot reading revealed hidden conflicts in a well-established group of women. Although there is doubt that mantic methods are demonstrable scientifically, the author makes a brave attempt with perpetrators and victims of domestic violence. The author makes one innovation in the classic Celtic Cross spread, adding an 11th card called 'gift and guide' drawn by the therapist.

In his summary, the author enumerates advantages of incorporating Tarot in many psychotherapies. In discussing one advantage, he quotes well-known Tarot researcher Cynthia Giles: "The querent doesn't usually put up defenses against divination the way a patient puts up defenses against therapy"(p. 42). There is no blindness though, to the disadvantages or even prohibition of using Tarot in some cases. As always, the psychotherapist must use his/her clinical judgment. In certain clinical situations, contrary to Giles' suggestion, Rosengarten has found:

> Tarot may actually be more threatening to a client than traditional therapy. For those clients who are in great need of mothering, for instance, or who have strong dependency and transference issues, no matter what special insight the cards may provide, such individuals will still likely prefer the

> parental attention and approval of a surrogate object in the guise of a flesh and blood therapist over any transcendent or divined source. (pp. 42-43)

Even in suitable cases, the method should be used sparingly ("I, for instance, typically will bring Tarot into a course of psychological treatment no more frequently than three or four times a year"). What are suitable times to introduce Tarot into the therapy process? The author offers this guidance:

> The most favorable times for introducing Tarot come when ordinary attempts to resolve or understand a problem have been unsatisfactory, a plateau period over many sessions has brought stagnation, deeper and more dynamic objectives are desired, the number of available sessions is inadequate to access underlying themes, or finally, future goals and vision are sought through a non-ego-mediated source (that is, beyond the known frames of reference of client and therapist alike). At such times, the Tarot method can serve to forward the process nicely. (p. 45)

Among the three schools of Jungian thought that have thus far evolved—classical, developmental, and archetypal/imaginal—this use of Tarot will seem more compatible to classic and imaginal therapists rather than those emphasizing a developmental paradigm, which relies heavily on the analysis of transference/countertransference. Moreover, the use of Tarot (or any mantic method) calls attention to a growing-edge tendency to conceptualize the two persons of the analyzing dyad as contained within a transpersonal field that effects, contains but is superordinate to both of them.

Were I still in practice, I would test for myself the integration of Tarot (and other mantic methods) into analysis, something this book has given me courage to attempt. I realize that this would be part of a larger question that may have no rational answer, or rather, a rational answer that depends on previous irrational assumptions—where do you choose to draw the line dividing psychotherapy and life?

—James A. Hall, M.D., Dallas, Texas, 1999
Author of *Jungian Dream Interpretation* and *The Jungian Experience*

Where there is no vision, people perish.

—*Proverbs 29:18*

Introduction

An unseasonably warm October evening on the North Shore of Chicago found me sitting on a large hotel ballroom stage among 20 or so of the nation's leading Tarot experts. We were assembled for a panel discussion that would launch the first World Tarot Congress, a three-day conference sponsored by the International Tarot Society. The upbeat gathering of several hundred seemed set for the prospect of awakening or, at least, bucking the fates. The room was rich in red carpet, soft chairs, and flowers everywhere. A colorfully-clad audience of men and women hailing from some 40 states and three continents comprised what would become in the year 1997 the first ever Tarot event of this magnitude.

Frankly, as the only clinician on the panel it hadn't yet dawned on me how misplaced I would feel through much of the weekend, especially given the floral scents and the aureole lights of the crystal chandeliers that lifted the large hall. That is, not until the moderator asked each expert to comment on the following question: "*Is Tarot primarily reflective or predictive?*" It was our surprise topic for debate. As other panelists began their intelligent elucidations, my own brain neurons apparently stopped firing. That I was deeply ensconced in a writing project over the past year addressing this very topic (the book, in fact, you are reading now) was of little help.

I fumbled through an answer when the microphone reached my hand, referring to my pet Husserlian notion of the "possibilizing and diaphanizing" of experience, but I was clearly dissociated from my own response. Apparently obvious to the others, the question seemed utterly paradoxical to me. I ruminated philosophically. Reflective or predictive of what exactly? I felt stuck in that troubling intuitive quandary, certain the answer was as close to my thoughts as my nose yet I was unable to see it. I tried to organize my mind. Reason was usually good for such things. Was the question referring to behavior, cognition, emotion, narration, the unconscious, the lived moment, karma, libidinal object-seeking, all or none of the above? Could not Tarot be both reflective *and* predictive simultaneously, I wondered, plus a few other things besides? Like 'creative' for instance, in the sense of bringing new possibilities into focus. Was this perhaps so obvious it required no further comment? Had my brain simply stopped, or was my sudden mental density a product of its over-working?

Disregarding its absurdity, I tried to imagine how different it might be if the same topic was discussed before an assembly of psychologists and related clinicians, say at the annual APA Convention. Experimentalists, I figured, would quickly define the parameters within which prediction could be measured and studied. Cognitive-behaviorists would insist that divinatory effects were caused by the Tarot card's stimulus of cognitions and core assumptions about self. Dynamic therapists would specify predictive "for its activation of internalized object representations," and Jungians would emphasize reflective "of compensatory oppositions between ego and archetype." Settling nothing, I continued to hold court. Humanists, I noted, would likely insist upon individual uniqueness and forego prediction altogether in favor of reflection, followed by the constructivists quickly reminding us that both predictions and reflections were intrinsically self-narrative fictions. Lastly, the phenomenologists, still fresh in my mind, would reframe the question to emphasize the individual's *experience* of Tarot itself, independent of its reflective or predictive properties.

The reverie became my private leitmotif on through the busy weekend. I sensed that any such change of venue would not appreciably relieve my confusion, but if I had to choose I'd probably lean towards the phenomenological solution. What exactly was the experience of Tarot anyway? Everyone seemed to be talking about it, but no one had quite taken the bull by the horn. The idea comforted me, even afterwards on my flight back to San Diego, that is, until the other shoe dropped. I thought I had left it in my hotel closet. Now somewhere high above Denver, it wasn't the plane's descent that brought me tumbling down to earth, but rather the casual conversation that had ensued with the professionally-dressed passenger sitting to my right.

"Business in Chicago?" he asked.

"Sort of," I replied, "I was presenting at a conference."

"Oh really, what do you do?" he asked.

"I'm a clinical psychologist in private practice," I said.

"No kidding. What was the conference on?" he asked, turning his body more in my direction, like he cared.

"Tarot." I say.

"What?" He looked puzzled. "You mean eh…."

"That's right, Tarot cards." I over nodded, and then blurted out. "You know, those little cards used for fortune-telling?"

There I said it myself, shame on me! I suppose I was simply trying to make it easier to put together, but once again I was reminded of the awkwardness and mystification that seems to follow my restless commitment to blend these strange bedfellows, Psychology and Tarot. *That* was the real problem as far as I was concerned. How to explain Tarot to those who would use it properly for the greatest good—individuals who desired greater spirituality in their lives, including the benefits of psychological insight and depth, without the baggage of affiliation that invariably accompanies any single set of beliefs. Tarot, they will soon find, operates on many levels of profound meaning from a purely non-affiliated platform in the truest sense. Tarot makes accessible to awareness a full spectrum of psychological and spiritual possibility with little preference for its user's qualifications or beliefs. Rather magically, one might say, Tarot captures the heartbeat of experience. This fact alone should make the deck of human possibility, as I call it, immediately relevant to helping professionals who deal with the heartbeat of experience daily.

Most Tarot books today, however, are devoted primarily to tracing the historical development of the deck or to describing the interpretative significance of the cards. The use of Tarot as an oracle for creating awareness and gaining insight into particular symptoms, problems or questions—i.e., Tarot divination—is often mentioned as an afterthought, alongside other meditational exercises and alternative spread configurations. Yet in the 20th century, the vast majority of individuals who have discovered the wonders and mysteries of Tarot have done so through experiences of divination. Card reading, without a doubt, is Tarot's most beguiling and potentially beneficial enterprise. Why dance around the magic? Yet for Tarot to continue to evolve into the 21st century (and beyond) it must have a stronger application emphasis, that is, it must be relevant, accessible, and meaningful to the changing contours of people's lives. It must resonate with all who seek greater meaning, creativity, and awareness, not simply with small segments of the New Age.

Back to my faux pas over Denver, I would soon discover this slip had served its own purpose. I vowed then and there to redirect my writing efforts to therapists, analysts, counselors and other helping professionals who were themselves navigating the mercurial currents of a service industry in significant turmoil. They, I felt, were most like myself—dismayed by the corporatization of psychotherapy and eager to reinvigorate the excitement and intellectual challenge that once brought them into the field to begin with.

Next I would address those intelligent students of life and the so-called "human experiment" who continually desire more understanding and insight into their own inner workings. I hoped that an in-depth exploration of Tarot presented by a practicing psychologist grounded in more conventional means might coax them a little closer to a realm often derided as "New Age" or occult. I believed as well that serious researchers, philosophers, and scholars interested in the emerging science of 'consciousness' might discover in Tarot certain unique and compelling examples of a transpersonal intelligence readily accessible through a method that capitalized on, of all things, random selection and synchronicity.

Finally, I wanted to offer some new ground to those seasoned tarotists, hermeticists, artists, mystics, magicians, and sundry esoteric thinkers who were interested to learn more of Tarot's psychological and therapeutic properties and possibilities. Psychology, I would show them, is intrinsic to both the structure and the method of Tarot itself.

As we shall see in the chapters that follow, our subject matter will sway in the gentle breeze that flows between theory and practice. Its ground will be thickly covered in the green mosses of human imagination where it will seek strong and healthy roots in the dynamic landscape of contemporary psychotherapy. May we proceed through this burgeoning "forest of souls" in good faith.

—*Art Rosengarten*

Encinitas, California, 1999

PART ONE

THE TAROT OF PSYCHOLOGY

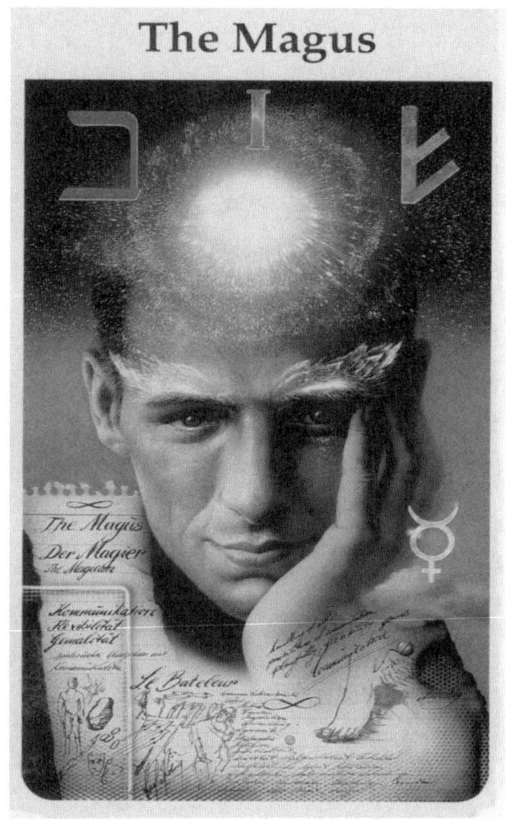

Chapter I

THE DECK OF POSSIBILITY

By asking for the impossible, obtain the best possible.

—*Italian Proverb*

The Wheel of Tarot

In my therapy office is mounted a very large spinning wheel. It's a quieter version of those glitzy Wheels of Fortune one finds in gambling casinos. This wheel too was designed for spinning in some game of chance or 'luck'. From its steel hub at the center are long, alternating, black and white rays that extend outwards to the periphery where formerly was pasted a full deck of 52 playing cards around the outer ring. A brief hypnotic effect is felt in the wheel's turning, accompanied by rapid clapping sounds reminiscent of the sweet pattering of baseball cards fastened to the spokes of a child's bicycle. The faster the spin, the more triumphant the patter. At the top of the wheel, bordering my ceiling, a plastic red pointer marks the 'winning' card upon completion of each rotation. Years ago, my wife found this marvelous contraption hanging in a local bookstore, presumably there as some interesting art piece, and managed to persuade the store owner to sell it to us.

Like some crazed pirate of metaphysics back to his lair, I at once took great pleasure in methodically replacing the pasted playing cards with a deck of Tarot cards. A little glue made the correction completely operational in no more than an hour. Unfortunately, however, there were only enough spots on the original wheel to accommodate 52 cards, that is, merely the Lesser Arcana of Tarot (minus four cards). The elitist in me quickly judged he could survive quite nicely without those servile young Pages adorned in their natty Elizabethan plumes and summarily excused all four from their 'wheel-duty', thereby downsizing to the standard 52. As many people know, modern playing cards are intimately tied to Tarot cards, both structurally and historically, and there has been a chicken-or-egg controversy for years over which came first.

Playing cards are roughly equivalent to the Minor (or Lesser) Arcana of Tarot. Both have the familiar Ace to Ten progression in four suits, with Tarot adding a Knight to each standard court trio of Jack (or Page), Queen, and King. The Knights of Tarot were inexplicably removed from modern playing cards sometime during their 600-year history, though a few scholars have conjectured this omission was likely due to their dangerous associations to the Knights Templar, a controversial secret society of religious mercenaries which flourished during the Crusades, and to this day continues to stimulate intriguing speculation over its true (hidden) agenda. Tarot history, however, is not a subject matter this work explores in any depth.

But, returning to the matter at hand, we might say that playing cards are Tarot cards devoid of symbolic significance. The Suit of Diamonds in playing cards, for instance, corresponds to the Suit of Disks or Pentacles in Tarot; Hearts correspond to the Suit of Cups, Clubs to the Suit of Wands, and Spades to the Suit of Swords. That each of these suits and cards are symbolically encoded with profound spectrums of spiritual and psychological meaning is lost, however, on modern card players. The card player sees in his cards one-dimensional *signs* of numeric value signifying known and established quantities. Three of a kind, for instance, always exceeds two pair, just as two 8's are always 'higher' than two 7's. The card reader, on the other hand, sees in his 'hand' multidimensional *symbols* of personal meaning that point to mysterious possibilities of experience. There is no competition per se in cartomancy (divination by cards), nor are higher and lower values immediately discernible.

In addition to the 56 cards of the Minor Arcana there is a second set of so-called 'power cards' in Tarot. These comprise what is termed the Major or Greater Arcana, and consist of 22 essential 'keys' or 'trumps'. Their obvious correspondence in Psychology is to the archetypes of Jung's collective unconscious. Trump cards, as they are called, are sequentially numbered and descriptively titled from Trump I (The Magician) to XXI (The World). Of this second set, only the un-numbered *Fool* card (accounting for the 22nd trump) has survived in modern playing cards under the guise of the lowly and unappreciated Joker. Together then, the Minor and Major Arcanas combine to form the complete Tarot deck of 78 cards.

The Game of Your Self

In this book I will lay the groundwork for approaching Tarot as a tool of significant psychological and spiritual usefulness and discuss its relevance to contemporary psychotherapy. Though I use Tarot quite sparingly in my own clinical practice, as much and often as the situation allows, I have witnessed on countless occasions Tarot's fantastic therapeutic properties firsthand. I mention my converted Tarot Wheel because the wheel itself serves as a fitting metaphor for the Tarot. Tarot is the Wheel of Life and the Wheel of Fortune, the Native American Medicine Wheel and the Buddhist Dharma Wheel. It is the wheel of your mind and the wheel of all human possibility. Its evolving and unfolding nature captures the circularity and dynamic turning of the seasons, the cycling and spiraling of change, and the 'roundness' and indeed the wholeness of the human psyche and its potential.

The actual spinning contraption in my office described earlier, in principle, operates along the basic rules for random selection that Tarot usage requires. Instead of shuffling the cards ten times or more (what mathematicians have demonstrated necessary to fully 'naturalize' a deck of 78), here one simply takes a spin. The procedure is direct and simple: ask a question such as "how should I attend to x," then empty the mind of distraction, make a random selection from a large set of meaningful possibilities, apply the given answer to the original question, and see (attend to) what you get. [To insure reliability, I've had my handyman install two new well-lubed, deluxe, pillar bearing-blocks so that no flawed mechanical effect would be detected in the wheel's rotation.]

Loosely speaking, this is what is meant by 'divination' and is how the Tarot method is set in motion. It requires, contrary to an habitual Western mental reflex (challenged later when we examine casusative vs. Synchronistic preferences of psychological explanation), the placing of supreme trust in the natural intelligence that collects momentarily around events, thereby awakening a non-linear mode of perception through what I respectfully call 'sacred' or 'empowered' randomness. Rather than seeking to determine above all else the 'cause' of a given effect, asking why or perhaps 'how' did such and such occur, instead one is encouraged to openly explore spontaneous patterns and simultaneous occurrences, asking in effect "what is reflected?" in this event. In Tarot, the blind selection undertaken with the intent to see and understand more clearly and expansively, i.e., "empowered randomness," opens the doors of perception to many new and interesting spectrums of possibility.

But with such talk of spontaneous patterns, spinning wheels, and playing cards, some readers may conclude that Tarot is rather like a game, and in fact, in certain respects it is. Tarot is a game inasmuch as life is a game, unfolding through a process of choices, strategies, random events, discoveries, victories and defeats. Conventional games are often effective tools of learning and are themselves no strangers to the serious enterprise of counseling and psychotherapy practice. Therapists are familiar with well-designed play therapies involving games which are often essential in the treatment of children and adolescents. For adults, therapeutic games cover an assortment of role-playing exercises and the like, such as psychodrama, guided imagery, expressive arts therapy, and sandtray therapy. Games are also used in many well established assessment tools like the Wechsler Adult Intelligence Scale (WAIS) that measures IQ by utilizing puzzles, math and word games, etc., and the Thematic Apperception Test (TAT) which uses ambiguous photographs to stimulate projective storytelling.

When introduced into a clinical setting, quite a few other techniques as well are structured as games and require a client's gamesmanship. Game-related activities develop important abilities and attributes such as creative imagination, problem-solving, self-expression, plotting strategy, competitive tasking, skill and coordination, planning, risk taking, storytelling, spontaneity, winning and losing, and even a little humor as well. Unlike games based strictly on competition or entertainment, psychological games have the underlying purpose of cognitive or emotional development and assessment. In Tarot, the game is your life as a whole, or stated more subjectively, the game is your self. The game board is the 'spread', and the 'pieces' are the 78 cards themselves. The object is not winning, but learning.

Interestingly enough, one of the more intriguing (though outdated) myths regarding Tarot's historical origins suggests that its gaming appearance was a deliberate diversion by its original makers. The theory is attributed to the 19th century Spanish-born physician, Theosophist, and Kabbalist, Dr. Gerard Encausse, better known as Papus. According to Papus, writing in *The Tarot of the Bohemians*, the secrets of Tarot were deliberately obscured by its creators who ingeniously hid them in the form of an alluring popular game for public consumption, thus slyly employing this tactical maneuver to preserve Tarot's longevity, believing as they did in the game's enduring appeal when compared to religious practice. Ascribing Tarot's authorship to the ancient Egyptian priesthood as was the fashion of his day, Papus thus speculated:

> At first [the priests] thought of confiding these secrets to virtuous men secretly recruited by the Initiates themselves, who would transmit them from generation to generation. But one priest, observing that virtue is a most fragile thing, and most difficult to find, at all events in a continuous line, proposed to confide the scientific traditions to vice [i.e. gaming]. The latter, he said, would never fail completely, and through it we are sure of a long and durable preservation of our principles. This opinion was evidently adopted, and the game chosen as a vice was preferred.[1]

Today from a postmodernist perspective, however, we see that speculations such as these, whether convincing or conflated, rest ultimately in the mental constructions of their authors, not necessarily in the events they describe. But this alone is not sufficient cause to dismiss their psychological merit and interest. Human imagination need not conform to historic fact or physical reality for its validity when put in the service of man's soul or psyche.

While at times troubling to intellect, surely the sublime creations of the artist, from Blake to Van Gogh, and the otherworldly visions of the mystic, from Ramana Maharshi to Teilhard de Chardin, inspire us beyond our intellects to ever deepening levels of psychic reality, for abstraction and symbolism have a timeless quality. But they hardly confer any satisfactory measure of reason or usefulness in regards to our knowledge of the physical world or the historical record. Carl Jung once wrote:

> When we consider the history of humanity, we see only the dim mirror of tradition. What really happened escapes historical research, for the real historical happening is deeply hidden, lived by all and perceived by none. It is the most private, most subjective, psychic life and experience. Wars, dynasties, social revolutions, conquests, and religions are all the most superficial symptoms of a secret psychic fundamental attitude in the individual, unknown to him and therefore not recorded by any chronicler. The great events of world history are in themselves of small importance. What is important in the final reckoning is only the subjective life of the individual.[2]

Papus' theory of deliberate obfuscation, deemed unlikely today because no physical evidence whatsoever supports Tarot's Egyptian roots, opens us to another more palatable and interesting possibility of psychological meaning regardless of its factual error. When taken as an imaginative construction of a 19th century occultist, rather than any historical truth *per se*, in the least we glimpse upon a subjective archetypal theme running through Tarot itself, that is, the paradox of gaming, gambling and the myth of 'luck' (Fortune).

The phenomenon points as well to a central and related theme of postmodernist psychological theory known as the principle of 'foundationlessness.' Constructivists believe we do not view the world 'as it is' but only as a product of our cognitive operations. That is, we impute meaning to our perceptions rather than apprehend pure impressions or sensations. Because we add meaning to our perceptions, there is no knowledge free of our presuppositions. Our beliefs in all cases are without foundation in themselves, but point instead to the cognitive structures which construct subjective meaning from experience. More will be said of this notion in the chapters to come.

A Tool for Self-Exploration

In the construction of this book, Tarot is viewed not simply as a game but more importantly as a powerful tool and method for psychological exploration. Its modern resurgence, as witnessed by as many as 300 different decks commercially available today, has been spurred mostly to facilitate creative discovery, the intuitive arts, and diverse spiritual practices. Particularly over the past three decades, by so entrusting themselves to this unusual and admittedly strange-sounding procedure, many people throughout the world have rediscovered Tarot's unique wonders, wisdom, and mysteries. If Tarot's uncanny knack for mirroring subjective experience remains its most potentially beneficial enterprise, as I believe, then unquestionably the 78 cards themselves, these magical little creatures of imagination—extraordinary systematized symbolic pictures which claim to contain the countless variations of human choice and possibility—are Tarot's heart and soul.

Yet for all the minor fascination this arcane tool has evoked, its correct message has not been adequately communicated to those who would put it to greatest use. For Tarot to evolve on any meaningful scale into the 21st century (and beyond) it must have a stronger application emphasis, utility, and accessibility; that is, it must speak compellingly to people's lives. In this regard clinical usage would seem a natural context for a technique which, as we shall see, offers so many psychological opportunities and benefits.

Unfortunately for Tarot, however, it has often lacked the sophistication, precision, empiricism, training, and code of ethics that have served modern psychology and related disciplines well. In this laundry list of Tarot's professional shortcomings, however, I stop short at any attempt towards 'standardization', as the thought itself is abhorrent to the essential vitality and versatility of this intuitive art, and would surely more stifle than guarantee its effective implementation. That is why I prefer to think of the cards as carrying "spectrums of possibility" based on sound philosophical and psychological grounds that allow Tarot to maintain its matrix of great diversity, creativity, and universality. This framework is a central theme of this work.

To the mainstream psychological provider today, increasingly under toe of the scientific imprimaturs of academic research and the shifting market forces of clinical practice, Tarot card reading has carried a dubious aura of association with storefront fortunetellers, European occultists, psychic hotlines and New Age faddists. This is an understandable, but nevertheless unfortunate, development. The correct message has not gotten out. And the problem cuts both ways.

In the compartmentalizing and downsizing trends of the 1990's, serious Tarot practitioners have in turn often steered away from the institutions and professions where their efforts might otherwise contribute to the society at large. Both sides, it seems, have grown either oblivious or suspicious of the other, and perhaps unconsciously, each has tended to re-emphasize the more mutually alienating aspects of their differences. Psychology has tended to rededicate its drive towards experimentation, symptom relief, pharmacology, the brain, the medical model, and corporatization. Tarot has tended to branch out into specialty schools of exotic spiritual, feminist, occult, commercial, offbeat, mythological, and artistic imagination. In many ways the gap seems to be widening, not lessening. The biggest loser should this trend continue, is undoubtedly the human imagination in search of psychological meaning and depth.

This book attempts to bridge the gap by removing from Tarot its misappropriated gypsy garb and occultic forays through psychological territory. Those things may be well served for particular small segments of enthusiasts, but in themselves they will never bring Tarot the larger recognition and application that it needs and it richly deserves. The message that is presented in the chapters that follow is concerned particularly with the Tarot method, insights, and implications that have emerged from extensive readings, study, research, and experimentation over the past 25 years of personal and clinical practice.

It is my hope that new generations of psychological explorers will be inspired to pick up the Magician's baton, so to speak, and run with it wisely. I also feel confident this method will appeal to the swelling appetites of a good many of my intuitively eager (and undernourished) contemporaries in the transitioning psychotherapy arts. I claim no final word on any of the matters discussed; but to the contrary, I only hope to initiate a more serious investigation of Tarot's psychological possibilities. In many respects I am no more than a Tarot novice myself, without years of advanced training in other related divinatory and hermetic arts such as astrology, alchemy, *I Ching*, magick, or arguably Tarot's closest esoteric ally, The Holy Kabbalah. Certainly expertise in such studies will deepen a tarotist's perspective and execution, but then again, so will graduate study of mythology, world history, Western and Eastern philosophy, art, anthropology, language, literature, mathematics, physics, psychology, psychiatry and religion. Nevertheless, my experience over many years has made it quite clear to me that one need not master these profound subjects before deriving significant value from Tarot, particularly in the practical realms of self-knowledge and human service. What is far more valuable for the beginner is his or her genuine enthusiasm and sincerity, ability to suspend disbelief, and courage to experiment.

The Talking Cure

Psychology, of course, in the largest sense, is a subject which applies to us all, whether therapist, client, or as we in the trade say lovingly, "normaloid." You are right now, for instance, perceiving, understanding, imagining, processing, investing, defending, storing, retrieving, smelling, touching, eating, judging, hating, desiring, anticipating, dismissing, resisting, or absolutely resonating to the words on this page entirely through the operations of your individual psyches. Try as we may, there is no escaping Psychology short of death, and even there we don't know for certain. Being concerned with the deep study of human nature, as Theodore Roszak (1995) points out, the field of psychology itself "is inherently speculative…with no choice but to work from hunches, inspired guesses, and intuition."[3] This is certainly the case with *Tarot and Psychology* as well, especially as ancient models of wisdom are presented within modern and postmodern parameters for which few real precedents are known to exist.

Though the nature of the material under consideration lends itself quite naturally to the Jungian/analytical approach, I will be arguing essentially for an integrationist stance (eclecticism) which will be presented in Chapter IV. Given my humanistic roots, I tend to shy away from a heavy-handed reductive analysis of psychopathology, as it often tends to eclipse a fair and humane profile of the whole individual. Nor do I believe that ponderous scholarly amplifications involving curious historic connections to psychological content are especially helpful in typical counseling situations. I prefer to think in terms of awareness, obstructions and possibilities, though in this study encouragement is given to students and practitioners of all theoretical backgrounds. I ask all to consider the Tarot from a vantage point that is both comfortable and consistent with their own clinical preferences.

But before we can take our discussion much further and do justice to our aspiration—the blending of Tarot and Psychology—it will first be helpful to picture some real life examples of Tarot in action, particularly for those who are entirely new to the subject. In the following chapter, therefore, I will present three introductory vignettes as representatives of Tarot when used in a healing context.

Notes

[1]Giles, Cynthia, *The Tarot: History, Mystery, and Lore;* Simon and Schuster (Fireside) New York, 1992, p. 35.

[2]Jung, C. G. *The Collected Works* (Bollingen Series XXVII); Trans. R.F.C. Hull. Princeton University Press, p.55

[3]Roszak, Theodore, Gomes, Mary E., Kanner, Allen D., *Ecopsychology: Restoring the Earth/Healing the Mind;* Sierra Club Books, San Francisco, 1995, p. 14.

Chapter II

HEALING CONTEXTS: THREE VIGNETTES

Turn your face to the sun and the shadows fall behind you.

—*Maori proverb*

What follows are three vignettes of Tarot divination when utilized psychotherapeutically. They were selected from potentially hundreds of examples mostly because they continue to stick with me after so many years, and each I believe captures a distinct and familiar flavor of the process. But as we shall come to appreciate, every Tarot reading is an original event unto itself, non-replicable *per se* in its particulars, and can be judged as valid and meaningful ultimately only through the subjective experience of its recipient. In this way it is not different than a human relationship, a spiritual experience, a flavor of ice cream, or a work of art.

Yes!

A Women's Support Group

Several years ago I was invited to speak to an ongoing women's support group about Tarot. I wanted to discuss the conditions under which experimenting with divination were most opportune and offered to make a small demonstration of the cards. The ladies seemed receptive to anything I might offer and gladly consented. The group was comprised of 12 to 15 college educated, mostly middle-aged, affluent, professional women who had been meeting monthly for some three or four years. Meetings rotated between members' homes and typically followed a potluck dinner.

Few had experienced Tarot first hand, but everyone appeared curious.

What then took place was typical of the Tarot process, and I think instructive of its natural therapeutic agency when used in groups. Members sat in a circle around a coffee table and were given the preliminary task of formulating an agreed upon question, itself of course, three-quarters of the battle. Then they were encouraged to meditatively empty their minds of all expectation and distraction, shuffle or cut the cards mindfully as we passed the deck around the table, and with the help of several volunteers to randomly select four cards from the face-down, fanned deck, without turning them over. I placed these four unseen selections in their spread positions on the table. In the brief reading format utilized, only the 22 trumps were used; four were picked, and the fifth was determined by the numeric addition and then reduction of the first four cards, a common convention of this ancient artform. The fixed positions of the Five-Card Spread were: (1) What Is Working *For* Us, (2) What Is Working *Against* Us, (3) What We Know, (4) What We Don't Know, and the final position, (5) What We Need.

After a productive ten minutes of sorting through individual query ideas, it was not hard to determine the most compelling question of the bunch: *What is the future direction of this group?* I explained that after turning the first two cards in the spread (Working *For* Us/Working *Against* Us) I would begin by giving a brief explanation of each card's established spectrum of meaning, including the dynamic tension existing between cards, and then ask the group members for their own personal associations to each card in the context of the question asked and the spread position in focus. What happened next was entirely unexpected by group members (though perhaps quite familiar to tarotists).

The very first card turned was Death reversed. To say the least, not the most tactful way to launch a reading, particularly as the invited guest. But what made the selection even stranger was the fact that it fell in the predesignated position: 'Working *For* Us'. What, I wondered aloud, might this mean? I should emphasize that responding in this way is itself instructive of the proper approach to be taken towards a divination, directing one down quite a different road of inquiry than if one were to more authoritatively ask "is this true or false?" or exclaim "this means x." The former attitude directs the endeavor towards introspection, a sense of mystery and possibility, the latter towards conscious evaluation, review, judgment and conclusion. Though sometimes helpful, the latter attitude narrows the spectrum of possibility.

I then suggested to the rather baffled ladies that Death's reversal occurring paradoxically in this favorable position pointed to some significant inner change that was emerging in the group's unfolding. Furthermore, I noted that the card was primarily concerned with endings and new beginnings, and its reversal suggested either some denial or resistance to such change, or else (vertically speaking, as we shall learn later) the transformation alluded to was operating internally within individuals, and referred more to a subjective dimension, i.e., an "ego death" of sorts. The group mulled this over with little comment.

Moving next to the second position—'Working *against* Us'—I turned The Empress card. Here I briefly described the 'earth-motherly' attributes of The Empress—emotional support, fertility, unconditional love, passion, healing and so forth, and explained the positioning had curiously suggested that such qualities were apparently *not* working so well for this group's future direction. In fact, according to the reading, they were approaching something of a disaster. *What might this mean?* Again I deferred back to group members. Up to that moment, I must say, the energy in the room had been genuinely quite friendly, supportive, accepting, and welcoming (that is, remarkably *Empress-like)*, as one might expect from a group of warm and bright women who had been meeting together in this way for years. Now, after two measly Tarot cards, hot steam and dragon fire began erupting like Mt. Saint Helens. Tarot, it seems, had presented an opportunity to air certain grievances, apparently quite atypical of this group's normal functioning (I was later to learn).

One woman flatly announced she was planning to leave the group but had been waiting for months to find the appropriate opening to announce her intention. People were shocked to hear it. She was obviously responding to the cards, but made no mention of them. Another woman said she resented the tendency of "certain members" to tacitly promote "only safe and nice interactions" while often leaving her feeling like an ogre in her less composed side. She, though, declared outright—"I sometimes feel smothered by that fat, doting Empress. Frankly she makes me sick!" fuming as her finger aggressively poked at Trump 3 on the table.

The hostess was visibly bothered by the comment and countered defensively, "I think that's *your* choice Mary, the space is there and has always been there." A brief debate ensued. Another woman broke out with the admission of having just been diagnosed with breast cancer, claiming apologetically, "I wasn't planning on saying anything" for fear that such news would cast a pall over the evening. A sad indictment, I thought, for a support group that didn't seem safe enough for such important news. "But that's why we're here," another woman was quick to respond; "I can't *believe* you would feel that way." I felt like I'd stumbled into the murky undercurrents of a major family conflict (which clearly and unapologetically I helped to precipitate). I knew, therefore, we were hitting important ground, a therapeutic "bulls-eye" so to speak. Instinctively, from years of practice, I simply stayed out of the way for at least the next 20 minutes of lively disclosure that heated the ambient living room.

Two opposing camps were coming to the fore, while a third group of "undecideds" looked on, anxious and a little amused. One camp was expressing a long held (and previously unshared) dissatisfaction with the group's tacit agenda of positive support at the expense of direct confrontation and difference of opinion. They complained that the group held no place for dissension within ranks. This was the 'Death reversed' camp, as I could now formulate it rather succinctly through the card. The other camp, the 'Empress' camp, much to the contrary, upheld and defended the group's status quo, referring regularly to the affirming virtues of the great goddess who rested there on the table. "We've all got enough negativity in our lives," echoed one distinguished Empress-camp spokesperson; "this is a place where we open our hearts and grow together." "That's why I come," reiterated another, even as the troublesome positioning of the cards themselves suggested quite a different destiny for the group's unfolding. The problem was becoming more clearly defined.

I then advised that we move on to the next two cards representing 'What We Know' and 'What We Don't Know' regarding the stated question pertaining to the group's future direction. In position three ('What We Know') I flipped over trump 1, The Magician card. In unison, everyone sighed. Ahhhhhhh! You might have thought it was Santa Claus, or perhaps in a slightly different circle of women, a surprise visit from the likes of Wayne Newton or Alan Alda. Group members seemed greatly relieved to behold this magical fellow, especially given the tensions that had just flared in the room. By contrast, The Magician appeared cuddly and comforting in this context; *He* was easily associated with the group's own established charter vis-à-vis personal growth, transformation, and personal empowerment. My brief interpretation brought little response, as the card's relevance seemed transparent and required no further explanation.

This often is the case with certain cards in a full reading and reflects Tarot's confirming and diaphanizing (clarifying) properties of what is consciously known. When a card is greeted by a quiet nod and requires little further explanation it is not unlike some high and holy sage taking you aside, placing his compassionate hand upon your shoulder and whispering gently into your ear: "You know how you've always felt about x? Well you were quite correct to feel that way. Nice work, keep it up!" When a card diaphanizes what we suspect to be so, our mild suspicion is raised to formal acknowledgment and a new measure of confidence in the matter is consciously achieved. Here the timely appearance of The Magus seemed a fitting reminder of the known reasons for why we were here; to gain a higher vision of the group's future direction.

The next card however was a little less mellow. In the fourth position ('What We Don't Know') came trump 10, The Wheel of Fortune, but reversed. As it was positioned to point to the unknown, I interpreted the card as suggesting some group difficulty around issues involving change, cycles, rhythm, and timing. "The laws of change are impeded in their natural flow," I said, "and there seems to be confusion over the matter of right timing pertaining to this cycle of the group's evolution." Furthermore, I asserted, the positioning now encouraged greater attention should be paid to this unseen and hindered dynamic.

Then once again I deferred to group members for their personal associations, and almost on cue, once again the two opposing camps instantly reignited. The woman with breast cancer complained that the group was rigid and not responsive to her real needs. She wanted change but didn't know how to ask for it. Her anger was now on the surface. "I need to be with real people who can talk about real things like suffering and pain without trying to fix it!" she bitterly complained. She preferred less magic, she said, and more hard core reality in her life. Another woman objected, saying she was hoping for quite the opposite—"less of the crap that drags us down in our lives and frankly a little more magic and wonderment would be lovely!" Still another woman shared feeling oddly "out of synch" with the last several meetings and didn't know why. Something no longer felt right to her. Others shared similar impressions. One woman commented, "maybe this is just part of the cycle of any group's evolution?" Indeed. I said nothing. The cards were so much more eloquent.

I sat quietly as the process unfolded away from the reading in progress. This is usually a good sign that the divination is taking hold. Someone even apologized to me for getting off the topic of Tarot, to which I simply laughed and said, "this is often the way it goes." Group therapists are well familiar with the pure process quality of these spontaneous, flowing interactions, and in fact, covet them. Now the issue of decision-making and agenda-setting was hotly debated, polarized, of course, between the Death reversed camp and The Empress camp. Several members in fact applauded the level of intensity and open expression, observing that this was all fresh and new for the group. Others said they were not comfortable with the chaos and emotionalism. I was asked to comment on what I saw in the reading thus far, and briefly acknowledged what seemed to be an unspoken tension among members needing more group cohesion versus more room for individual expression. I said that change and difference seemed uncomfortable issues to discuss in this group, but were important issues nonetheless.

I then suggested we move to the final card in the fifth position, determined by a numerological reduction of the first four cards. Thus I added Death (13) plus The Empress (3) plus The Magician (1) plus The Wheel of Fortune (10) to determine the fifth position, 'What Is Needed'. The answer (as often occurs) was both startling and confirming, in this case being none other than trump 9, that lantern bearing and austere monk himself, The Hermit. "What might this mean?" had by now become the mode of response reflexively asked by every group member, sweet oracular music to my ears. What was needed for the group's future direction, I said, was greater individuality, spiritual focus, self-reflection and introspection. And absolutely more permission for individuality and difference, with less concern for approval or agreement. At least, this is what the Hermit himself would tell you.

Trump 9, I explained, was foremost an agent of individuation, and therefore he must follow tenaciously his own inner direction regardless of external pressures. Of course, I was simply interpreting the card the way I always interpret it, within the context of the query, the spread position itself, and the querent(s)' personality. I was sure The Wise Old Man's strong showing in the final position had made The Empress camp quite uncomfortable to say the least. Fortunately for me, a willing victim through the years of many misplaced therapeutic outbursts (an important part of the job), these reactive transferences would now be directed at the message itself, and not the messenger. Therapeutically, a great opportunity is thus presented for working through the transferential content. In many ways the confrontations stimulated by a nonpersonal authority figure such as The Hermit of Tarot become less easily projected onto the person of the therapist, thereby fostering a cleaner encounter with a client's wounded past while freeing up the therapist to occupy a gentler and perhaps more helpful proximity to the pain. One is left to consider the so-called "luck of the draw" in both a literal and symbolic sense.

Not for this reason alone have I long ago learned never to

hedge an interpretation. The 'luck of the draw' is a naked truth of life itself. It's how we choose to assemble ourselves around the luck of the draw that counts. As a Tarot reader I implicitly trust that each selected card is always accurate (or relevant), however baffling or unpleasant it may seem at first, particularly when it is honored with the open and at once humbling attitude that inquires: "what might this mean?" What lessons and possibilities might be here for me to explore? What of myself is mirrored in this card? It is properly left to us, as readers and questioners, to discover exactly where and how such meaning is best served.

Our group, however, had appreciably quieted down at this point, becoming (how else to put it?) notably contained and subdued, reflective but intense, inner-directed and clearly introspective, that is to say, distinctly *Hermit-like*. I could feel both camps seriously digesting His implications for themselves personally and for the group's future as a whole. In fact, there was little left to say. The Hermit now carried the moment, the seeds were planted, and He was perhaps his own best spokesman. The prognostication was now over, and rather quickly the group began to disband. The ladies politely made their way over to my seat, thanking me for a fascinating evening, before making their private and unceremonious exits. I don't know how the group was to continue after that evening, but I am confident that the Tarot had done its job. On the following page a visual layout of this Five-Card Spread is presented.

Q: What is the future direction of the group?

Five-Card Spread

3.
What We Know

1.
Working For Us

5.
What Is Needed

2.
Working Against Us

4.
What We Don't Know

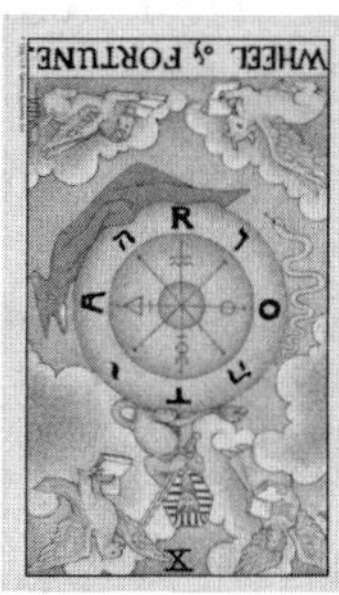

A Man Dying of AIDS

Before AIDS was so termed, an early victim of this incurable virus came into therapy to prepare for his death. Diagnosed with "Kaposi Sarcoma," his mysterious lesions continued to spread throughout his body; he had lost 40 pounds, was weak and chronically fatigued. The experimental chemotherapies undertaken at Stanford Hospital in Palo Alto had done nothing to improve his condition. David, age 55, a Ph.D., a retired school principal and life-long educator, to his credit had accepted that he was dying of some mysterious illness and now desired to psychologically ready himself (and his lover) to this tragic fate.

After four or five couple's sessions over previous weeks we had worked through much of his relational loose ends, the couple often weeping together in my office, but remaining remarkably dignified under the stress. I was struck by their ability to hold together. David now wanted to center himself emotionally and spiritually for his immanent death. His doctors had given him perhaps only a few weeks more to live. I suggested we might use Tarot; he was unfamiliar with the cards but receptive to the idea.

Under the circumstances, predictive divination seemed meaningless as David's fate sadly was all but sealed (short of some medical miracle), and there was little interest in this sort of future-viewing. David was agnostic regarding his beliefs about death itself and was not particularly interested in religious bromides. Reflective divination seemed somewhat futile if it meant merely a reflection of his present circumstance. There was little left to reflect upon. He was in incredible pain, his days were literally numbered, and he felt reasonably complete with the significant relationships in his current life. He had appropriately contacted his few remaining family members in New York and felt sufficient closure. He could no longer work, and he was bed-ridden and nauseous for most of his days over the past months. What David needed was to find himself in his last hours. He wanted to put the meaning of his life into some discernible order, most of which resided now in his tangential memories of the past. His present thoughts, beliefs, reflections, and the inner places that touched him were for the most part overwhelmed by the stressors of his condition. However, even under the most severe and ghastly conditions, as Frankl wrote of the Nazi concentration camps in *Man's Search for Meaning*, it is basic human nature to seek a sense of coherency and meaning to one's circumstance. Tarot is a natural facilitator of this need.

I suggested that my AIDS patient select a deck from several available that most appealed to his emotions, that spoke to his heart. He chose the Aquarian Deck as the colors and imagery had a soothing effect which he liked. Then I placed the full set of 78 cards on the table, in no apparent order, and face up so that each card was in clear view. The process was quite simple, and remarkably meaningful to him. I asked that he slowly scan through all the images and pull out every card that touched him in some way without being stingy with his feelings. It was not important that he know a card's designated meaning, only that it spoke to him, tickled his imagination, or touched his emotions. He relished the task, and slowly sifted through the images, picking out perhaps three quarters of the deck, one by one. I believe anyone given the same task under normal conditions would likewise respond positively to the intrinsic evocative properties and possibilities laden in Tarot images.

I then laid out all the selected cards, and asked David to arrange them in some meaningful groupings that made sense to him. Whatever felt right to him and connected to his own sense of organization and meaning. After a few minutes spent rummaging through the cards, this task too was rather quickly comprehended and actualized. He designated three groupings of cards: those he liked, those he didn't like, and those he found mysterious and intriguing. I then asked him to choose which of the three he preferred to explore first. He chose "the cards I don't like." Besides fostering coherency and personal meaning, the process was designed to empower a sense of personal choice, something there was precious little of in the wake of a deteriorating terminal illness.

The other two groups were removed and I placed only the aversive cards on the table, again face up and in no particular order. David was encouraged to further order these in any way that made emotional sense; there was no "right way." After only a few minutes he had made three more sub-divisions which he called "childhood and adolescence, adulthood, and my present life." Within these three sub-categories I asked whether certain cards belonged together, felt interconnected, or else seemed more singular or isolated, and again asked that he make further arrangements to reflect these distinctions.

Of the 18 cards David did not like, seven belonged to childhood and adolescence, six to adulthood, and five to the present. His criterion for selection was that in some manner each card triggered feelings of guilt, regret, or despair. From a structural Tarot standpoint they revealed no apparent rhyme or reason, though each grouping made remarkable emotional sense to David. "This group here is related to my mother," he said, "this group to my sexuality," and so on. The task was designed to allow David, rather quickly as time was of the essence, to sort through and organize the themes of his life. The cards were like symbolic magnets drawing together the bits and pieces of David's overwhelmed psyche. The process was for the most part non-verbal and required no analysis or interpretation. Only David could make those determinations.

Through tears and laughter we spent the remainder of the session free associating and recollecting from the stimulus of the cards. I encouraged David to release what he could of the cards he didn't like, and make peace, if possible, with the rest. Under the circumstances, simply identifying and emotionally connecting to these symbols was perhaps the needed work itself. Time was very short. At the session's close I handed David the stack of cards from his second sub-group—'what I like'—to take home and explore for homework. We would do a similar process with this grouping on the next day.

On the following morning David returned notably more calm and relaxed. He had spent much of the previous evening with his partner exploring the cards that he liked. He said the experience had been "very therapeutic" and life confirming. He had cried, laughed, and recounted many wonderful parts of his life. I asked what was learned. He said he had loved books, his work with children, and teaching primarily. Certain cards had triggered such memories much as projective techniques are used to stimulate unconscious contents in psychological testing for diagnosis and assessment. The exercise helped to stimulate positive images and emotions connected to his former healthy and productive self, now all but subsumed in the chaos and distress of current circumstances. Tarot cards, through their imagistic power, often aid in suspending and preserving visual representations of past experience regardless of current or transient emotional states.

At the close of the session I then handed David his third stack of cards, those which he found "mysterious and intriguing." I invited him to explore these over the weekend, as with the other groupings, and return again early the following week. The next time I saw David in my office would be the last time. The illness was taking its turn for the worse and he died a week afterwards. Our session that day however was powerful for the two of us. I was touched by the receptivity of a person so near the end. What David had found most intriguing was the entire Major Arcana itself. Each trump card brought a different fascination and sense of hope, he said. Their universality had rekindled memories of his early studies of philosophy as a young man, most of which he had forgotten. He was now grateful to reconnect to larger principles beyond his own suffering. And he was reminded of the illusory and dreamlike nature of ordinary reality itself, his "reactive mind" as he called it, not to mention his illness. The experience had had a tremendous calming effect. He was now ready, or at least willing, to approach the larger mystery of his dying.

Beyond Couples Counseling

John was an affable and easy-going 48 year old typesetter. He had survived five marriages and five divorces, two grown kids, and 18 years of sobriety after an otherwise impressive career as an alcoholic, heroin addict, and polydrug abuser that began from the precocious age of 11 up until 'hitting bottom' by the toppled age of 30. His three marriages that came (and went) after he stopped using had each followed a self-described familiar pattern: "they asked for more than I could give, it got too hard, I split." His first two marriages, from which two children were born, had been simply too chaotic and drug-infested for him to clearly recall.

Now, however, and for the past three years John had found happiness with Julie, a different breed of woman than he had previously known. Julie was 12 years younger, a survivor herself of one divorce and a briefer stint with alcoholism, though now with seven years of sobriety as well. As expected, both had come from alcoholic families. Both had benefited from AA. But as for the relational situation now, Julie was clearly the more worried of the two. She, unlike John, was a go-getter and a self-asserter. She was completing her Master's degree in counseling and worked in several high-powered treatment facilities. She was the doer of the pair, but he was the nurturer and emotional anchor. She valued these qualities in a partner tremendously and was convinced they would not be found in another.

Compounding matters, Julie now desired to be married with children. In fact, she had made up her mind; it had been her lifelong dream, and she was not to be denied. This development was more than a little anxiety-provoking for John. He, to the contrary, had suffered through the trenches of child-rearing, was now pushing 50, and shared little of her enthusiasm for 'daddying up' once more. What were they to do?

They had tried every maneuver of problem-solving they could muster. For the past year, both had tormented over the problem, searching their souls for guidance. They had tried praying for clarity and resolution. They had tried discussing the issue almost daily with each other. She tried brief therapy. He tried the power of positive thinking. They both tried couple's counseling. All to no avail. They even tried breaking up (for about a week), but it wouldn't last. There was only one thing left they figured—move in together and become engaged (the wonders of the rational mind!). They found a new apartment and changed zip codes. They even set a wedding date. They were encouraged by their guru. They were still terrified.

Friends and family had given up trying to persuade them otherwise. From the outside it appeared like madness: he was too old, his track record spoke for itself; she was too headstrong and uncompromising; they were moving in different directions, the combination seemed doomed. However there was no denying it—their hearts wanted to be together—even as their heads saw the ruin and damnation written on the wall. Perhaps the clearest sign of their painful and chronic ambivalence was the four times they had set up, canceled, and then rescheduled his reverse vasectomy. That's ambivalence. Even the surgeon was growing suspicious and began to question the advisability of the procedure. I suggested that perhaps it was time for a Tarot reading. They agreed. What was there to lose?

They came to my office the following week. "So, are you really ready to cast the fate of your relationship to the gods of Tarot?" I kidded them, as the nature of our rapport made it possible for such jests to be made half seriously. Nervously they laughed, but obviously they were aware of the agenda. I felt equal to the task as well, having grown to trust the veracity of Tarot under such complex circumstances, knowing full well that whatever emerged in divination would likely be eminently workable and relevant (even if uncomfortable at first). And also time-released. Sometimes weeks might pass before the true implications of a reading became fully conscious, but in the least, important seeds would be planted in the unconscious today.

Unceremoniously, we prepared the cards together and I then asked, somewhat rhetorically, if a question had been formulated for the reading. Their answer was quick and to the point: "*Should we get married?*" exclaimed Julie, of course, but with slight trepidation detected in her voice. At this point, there was little else that mattered to them. This familiar and exceptional circumstance—being at the end of one's rope—as all diviners know, often marks the perfect station from which to embark upon a Tarot reading. An intervention outside of one's conscious control is thus called for.

I instructed the couple in their own sequential drawing of the cards, rotating between his selection and hers, so that responsibility for what is received falls squarely back to the querent(s) themselves. I find this increases the subject's ownership and interest in the prognostication. Additionally, I have made a practice of myself blindly selecting a final (11th) card called 'gift and guide.' This last modification serves two functions in an extended reading: (1) it points to interventions and influences that occur outside the subject's own sphere of causality (i.e., an encounter with the 'other'), and (2) it creates a place in the reading where linkage is established and acknowledged between reader and readee, thus underscoring the co-created aspect of the reading. Tarot divination, unlike astrological charting or psychological testing, requires the here/now relational field between reader and querent. In this way it is closer to psychotherapy and ballroom dancing.

We then spent the remainder of the therapy hour reading the cards, exploring both his and her personal associations and their implications to each card, along with the oracular message as a whole. If nothing more, the procedure encouraged a calm, thoughtful and much needed dialogue over issues that often became unmanageable when pursued under the heavy artillery of premarital warfare. On the following page is an interpretative summary of the spread broken down into clusters (discussed in the next chapter). Card phrases are taken directly from Appendix A. After each cluster grouping, I have written the most salient comments that were conveyed (through the interpreter) by the cards themselves.

Interpretation by Cluster

(Should We Get Married?)

- (1) *The Core*

Present Situation: 9 *of Wands—"Power and victory; strength in opposition; creative power; psychic alignment."*

Obstacle: 2 *of Cups—"Emotional reciprocity—coming together on heart level; falling in love; union, the loving relationship."*

Author's Comment: While there is currently much creativity and energy in your commitment to proceed, the underlying connectedness of your union (which has previously been your great strength) is currently blocked and must be attended to first.

- (2) *Above and Below*

Goals: 8 *of Swords—"Self-imposed ego; cognitive distortions; to be bound and blinded by one's own negative thoughts."*

Foundation: *Knight of Pentacles reversed—"Dense, unrooted, expedient, overidentified with appearance."*

Author's Comment: Your ability to set positive future goals for the marriage, to visualize and invest in your future together, is severely hampered by worry, negative thinking, cognitive distortion. This negativity is

Modified Celtic Cross Spread

Question: Should We Get Married?

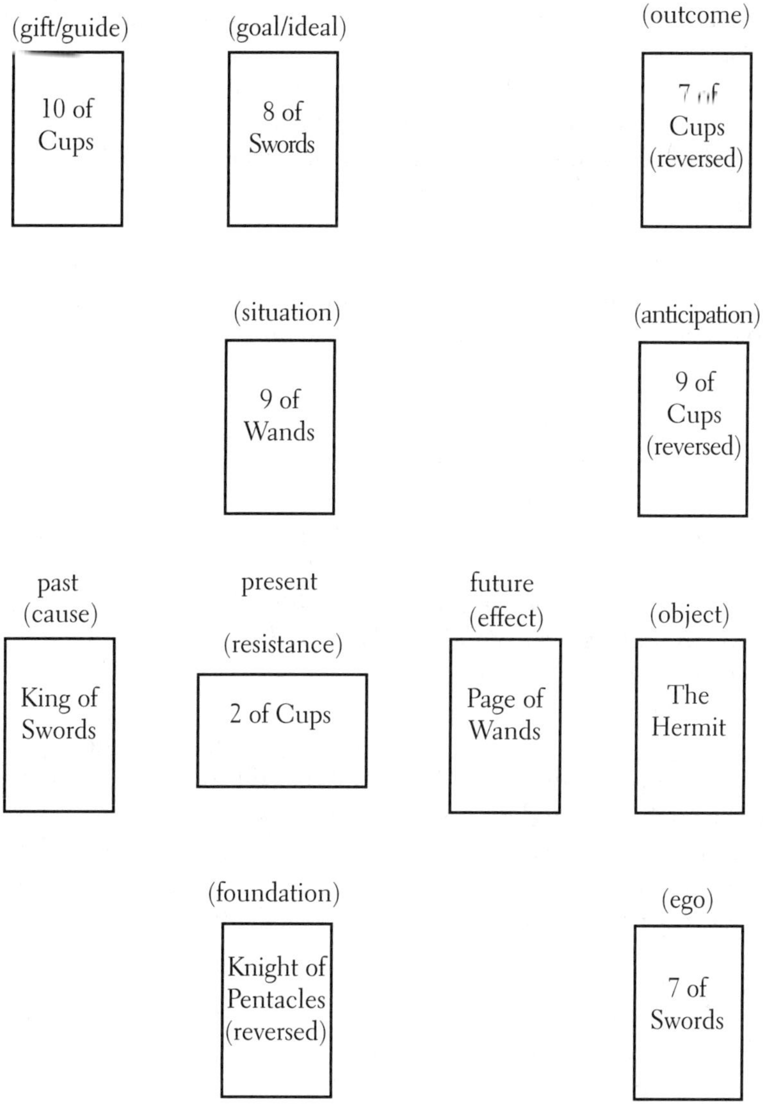

(gift/guide)
10 of Cups

(goal/ideal)
8 of Swords

(outcome)
7 of Cups (reversed)

(situation)
9 of Wands

(anticipation)
9 of Cups (reversed)

past (cause)
King of Swords

present (resistance)
2 of Cups

future (effect)
Page of Wands

(object)
The Hermit

(foundation)
Knight of Pentacles (reversed)

(ego)
7 of Swords

founded upon too great a concern for security and material appearances at a time when you indeed are somewhat unrooted and ungrounded.

- (3) *Cause and Effect*

Past Cause: *King of Swords— "Impartial and objective knowledge; the judge at court—makes unbiased judgments based on objective facts and presented information; command and authority."*

Present Obstacle: *2 of Cups*—[same as Cluster 1]*"Emotional reciprocity—coming together on heart level; falling in love; union, the loving relationship."*

Future Effect: *Page of Wands reversed—"Fear of commitment, inadequate personality, or Magician's apprentice."*

Author's Comment: There was an important time in the past when you saw yourself and the world around you clearly and objectively. You took command of your life and saw the errors of your ways. You must now bring this same objectivity to what currently impedes your heart connection, hasten to restore the loving aspect of the relationship, and together examine your shared fears of commitment.

- (4) *Self and Other*

Ego Identity (How we see ourselves?): *7 of Swords—"Carrying a conflict at the expense of a friendship or relationship; martyrdom and betrayal; scheming while in confusion."*

Object (How others see us?): *The Hermit—"Wisdom seeker/spiritual journey; fiercely independent and determined; archetype of The Wise Old Man; cares little for outside approval; values aloneness; 'seeks his own salvation with diligence (Buddha)'; path of individuation; introspection and self-containment, strong sense of self.*

Author's Comment: You see yourselves as divided between your current conflicts and the loss of some former trust or friendship in the past. Issues of martyrdom and betrayal now fill your 'self talk' and need to be confronted and expressed directly to each other before they can mend. Others view you two as extremely independent, committed to your spiritual beliefs, and in little need for outside approval or social conformity. They may not understand your mission, but they respect it.

- (5) *Anticipation and Resistance*

Fears and Hopes: *9 of Cups reversed—"Overindulgence, consumption, and addiction, or self-satisfaction."*

Present Obstacle: *2 of Cups*—[Same as Cluster 1 and 3] *"Emotional reciprocity—coming together on heart level; falling in love; union, the loving relationship."*

Author's Comment: The current strain in your relatedness has to do with fears around previous addictive behaviors. There is also hope this relationship can provide great physical pleasure and emotional fulfillment. Indulgence, however, must be differentiated from over-indulgence. You will need to discuss and resolve these concerns soon to restore the current critical tension in your heart connection.

(6) *Resolution and Wisdom*

Outcome: *7 of Cups reversed—"Lack of options, failure of imagination, or else active awareness of subpersonalities."*

Gift and Guide: *10 of Cups—"Falling in love; intoxication, bliss, larger than life (inflation); 'rainbows in the sky' (impermanence)."*

Author's Comment: You will need to be more imaginative in resetting the possibilities available to your relationship. You have a tendency to spin your wheels without making forward progress. There are many different parts to your personalities, and you will do well to develop many aspects of your selves not simply in your relationship, but in other aspects of your life as well. This will help bring a proper balance to your lives. You should trust the power of your feelings for each other and view them as both a gift and a guide. The intoxication will not last, however, but it is an indication of the strength of your attraction, a testament of your love.

It should be noted that each comment above is extrapolated directly from the card's spectrum of meaning within the context of the question and spread position. Making such determinations precisely and consistently will be discussed in detail later in this book. As is often the case, this reading did not so much reveal new material as confirm what was already felt, sensed, believed, avoided, and denied by the questioners. The fact that such information arrived through a purely random means underscores its importance to the subject. This fact should not be underestimated. The reading's manner of communication was notably absent of blame or exaggeration, as its source was nonpersonal and transcendent. Of course the full-bodied style and presence of the reader, and the unique interactive field established in divination between reader and querent(s) are purposely omitted in this third vignette so that we may explore properly the Tarot Method in the following chapter.

How Tarot did this, that is, by what strange "twist of fate," luck of the draw, or magic has this particular complex feedback arrived—will be closely examined when we turn later to the theories of synchronicity and nonlinear time. The skeptic, naturally, will attempt to debunk the reading as being so general and universally applicable that it arises less from divined intelligence than from divined hucksterism. He should be reminded however that a myriad of radically different comments would naturally issue forth from any different set of cards. The skeptic, too, will be properly addressed in Chapter IX. For now, it is perhaps enough to know that John and Julie were greatly relieved by the Tarot's message, and grateful for the experience. A clear sorting through of the issues had taken place, and an agenda to foster continued exploration and communication was established. I myself was left with the distinct impression that their next appointment with the urologist would be their last.

Six weeks after the reading the following announcement arrived at my office in the mail:

> When John and Julie fell in love,
> God said, "Thou Shalt Not Part."
> Now they joyfully ask you to attend,
> Their wedding of the heart.

I expect this couple will consider returning for follow-up Tarot readings, as they say, *after the honeymoon.* As we can clearly see, the Tarot Method certainly provides a shared window of reflection and exploration for intimate partnerships. Hopefully, these three quite different vignettes have each in their way given the newcomer to Tarot an initial impression of its application in psychotherapy. We are now ready to examine the Tarot Method more closely, which will be the subject of the following chapter.

Notes

[1] Arrien, Angeles, *The Tarot Handbook: Practical Applications of Ancient Visual Symbols,* Arcus Publishing Company, 1987, p. 20.

[2] Giles, Cynthia, *The Tarot: History, Mystery, and Lore*, Simon and Schuster, 1992, p. 133.

[3] Ibid.

Chapter III

THE TAROT METHOD

> It is as hard to see one's self as to look backwards without turning around.
> —Henry David Thoreau

Risks and Benefits

The rich imagery and intriguing methodology of Tarot will ordinarily bring to the clinical atmosphere a more open and interesting ambiance, often serving to soften resistance to the traditional clinical format while increasing client participation in the process. It is my belief that Tarot can be integrated into an experienced therapist's bag of tricks, especially in this age of brief treatment, and pulled out occasionally when its particular usefulness is called for. Of course, at those times the risk of introducing a spiritually-based instrument into a psychotherapeutic setting must be weighed against the risk of remaining so clinically static as to become no longer a reliable agent of change but rather a predictable proponent of psychologism. Clinical eclecticism, few would argue today, has become the logical destination of seasoned practice, in contrast to a rigid adherence to any one treatment approach for all problems and people. Perhaps more than anything, the preponderance of therapist jokes that swirl through popular culture reflects this lifeless tendency towards predictability experienced in what often goes as psychological treatment.

The ritualized self-focus in both psychotherapy and Tarot is seductive in itself and lowers barriers which ordinarily separate conscious and unconscious knowledge. Cynthia Giles in her excellent book *The Tarot: History, Mystery, and Lore* suggests that Tarot work and therapy have something else in common: "Each offers a space and a time for the querent or the patient to study his or her own myths."[2] The Tarot situation in many cases may actually have an advantage over conventional therapy in that it is less threatening, language dependent, predictable, and hierarchical. At times it brings clinician and patient to share their co-transferences, not so much towards each other, but towards a neutral, and perhaps wiser, oracular voice that touches (and occasionally perplexes) them both. Notes Giles: "The querent doesn't usually put up defenses against divination the way a patient puts up defenses against therapy."[3]

However should the Tarot card be implemented, as it were, a clinician must have a mature and sensible relation to divination or run the risk of appearing unprofessional and/or unethical. He must likewise guard against what might be termed a 'shamanistic transference', that is, the projection of special magical powers onto the personality of the therapist himself. The unique dimension of awareness that is gained through the symbolic and synchronistic agency of Tarot is certainly facilitated by the skilled therapist/reader, but it can hardly be attributed to any particular talents or abilities unique to his or her own "magical powers." The therapist should make this point abundantly clear to the client from the outset lest the true purpose and meaning of divination be saddled by a mistaken understanding of its workings and teachings. Both therapists and Tarot readers are professional agents of psychic change and awareness, not magistrates of truth or power.

There will also be some contraindicated situations, as well, where introduction of the Tarot would be counterproductive, offensive, or potentially harmful to a client, and therefore not recommended. In certain clinical situations, contrary to Giles' suggestion, Tarot may actually be more threatening to a client than traditional therapy. For those clients who are in great need of mothering, for instance, or who have strong dependency and transference issues, no matter what special insight the cards may provide such individuals will still likely prefer the parental attention and approval of a surrogate object in the guise of a flesh and blood therapist over any transcendent or divined source.

In general, it will be important for the therapeutic relationship to first establish a sufficient level of trust and rapport before Tarot experiments can be appropriate. A client or patient will need time to express and explore his or her areas of difficulty through conventional means first before applying this unconventional approach. Without question, like any special technique, Tarot can be over-prescribed so that its effects cannot be properly absorbed and its efficacy declines. I, for instance, typically will bring Tarot into a course of psychological treatment no more frequently than three or four times a year.

While a series of elapsed readings are often preferable to a single event, they should be spaced sometimes over months to allow the necessary time for reflection, assimilation, and integration. In other situations, however, it will not be uncommon for one experiment to naturally demand another immediately, as the psychic dimensions of a client's query have been adequately revealed and now beg for further exploration. The timeliness of such follow-up readings should be left to the judgment of the therapist who must weigh all relevant factors in determining the best course of treatment.

There are also clients, often character disordered and intractable, who will be threatened by the strength and unmalleability of an oracular authority and will become uncharacteristically timid before it. In the pilot study presented later in this book, noncompliance to experimental Tarot readings has suggested that subjects with higher degrees of sociopathy will likely become more threatened, not less, by Tarot divination than by traditional methods. As we shall see, I suspect this effect may be owing to the sociopath's perception of less opportunity for manipulation, deception, avoidance, and denial of core issues when face to face with a personless, oracularly-conceived tool not otherwise found in the normal therapist/client set of interactions and expectations. Indeed, often it is less easy to manipulate, resist, or dismiss a Tarot card, and the person of the therapist seems the more dispensable and dismissible.

Finally, other contraindicated situations for Tarot in therapeutic

settings would include for obvious reasons: actively psychotic schizophrenic and bipolar patients, paranoid and obsessive-compulsive patients, clients without capacity for insight or inadequate ego strength, and persons of fundamental religious beliefs who may hold Tarot as evil sacrilege or pagan devilry. Adolescents often do not have the necessary level of insight to work effectively with symbolism but may enjoy the therapeutic incorporation of Tarot symbols in group therapy activities. I have known latency age children to find benefit from playing therapeutically with the cards (there are some decks which are well suited for this, like the *Tarot for Cats*), and my own son Alexander at age six is a gifted storyteller before any random sequence of these appealing and mysterious images.

Nevertheless, the "normal neurotic" range of clientele generally gains tremendous insight and motivation when exploring with Tarot. Couples, families, and groups will also find Tarot uniquely helpful in reflecting interpersonal dynamics. The author has additionally found effective applications with high level borderline and narcissistic patients, recovering addicts and alcoholics, as well as those suffering from a wide range of depression, anxiety, adjustment, and post traumatic stress disorders. Ironically, skeptics or non-believers themselves make excellent candidates for divinatory experiments provided they are sincere and genuinely willing to suspend disbelief and give it a go. No previous experience, belief, or understanding is necessary to gain value from a Tarot reading; however, any coercion of the procedure is simply poor practice. I would never give a Tarot reading to someone who has not freely chosen to receive one, and I hold that as a general law.

Such precautions and contraindications should not intimidate the therapist from taking the necessary measures of study and training which will eventually make this tool available to his or her practice. The potential therapeutic applications for Tarot are wide and quite exciting, and will be discussed in more detail in later chapters. Whatever the level of application, an appreciation of the following key ingredients of Tarot reading will then greatly aid the clinician in his or her efforts.

Preliminaries

Unlike other therapeutic techniques, the Tarot method requires placing supreme trust (as opposed to 'belief') into the process of execution itself, almost to the exclusion of all previous and parallel sources of information. This unquestionably challenges the normal *modus operandi* of psychological treatment. The therapist's expertise and authority during a Tarot session must take a backseat to the 'divined' authority. Often it is best that the therapist knows less, rather than more, about specific background data surrounding a particular client's query as such preferred ignorance adds focus and intensity to the process itself, whereas competing information dilutes and diminishes the concentration required.

The therapist will need to suspend ('bracket') much of his previous knowledge of the client, particularly during the preliminary stages of card shuffling and selection, attempting instead to refocus attention and concentration onto the moment at hand. The therapist will also need to empty the preoccupations bumping about in his/her own mind in order to generate his/her most sincere and undivided attention to the task at hand. In Zen, such focused openness is referred to as "beginner's mind." Preparing the cards for divination requires both reader and querent to achieve a certain "beginner's mind" during the process.

The timeliness of such an experiment depends upon a number of factors, including the level of rapport established between therapist and client as well as the particular phase of treatment or life context the client is in. More will be said about therapeutic applications, risks and contraindications for treatment in the following chapter. However, in general, the most favorable times for introducing Tarot come when ordinary attempts to resolve or understand a problem have been unsatisfactory, a plateau period over many sessions has brought stagnation, deeper and more dynamic objectives are desired, the number of available sessions is inadequate to access underlying themes, or finally, future goals and vision are sought through a non-ego-mediated source (that is, beyond the known frames of reference of client and therapist alike). At such times, the Tarot method can serve to forward the process nicely.

Configured Patterns

Whether one reads Tarot for oneself, another individual, a couple or family, a group, the boardroom or staff room, an entire community, a special population, or even more abstractly, the world as a whole, consultation typically takes place within a prefigured pattern called a *spread*. A Tarot spread can be thought of as a complex "field of presentation" designed to contain the constituent parts of an inquiry. It is itself neutral and static, perhaps analogous to the therapist's open engaged attention in free association, or the empty sandbox in sandtray therapy. The selected 'pieces' that are placed within each container (or 'holding object') are what gives psychic life. In Tarot these pieces, of course, are the symbolic resonances of the randomly selected Tarot cards.

Spreads invariably have a certain formalism attached to them; they are made up of constants called 'positions' which are specific placement locations with preassigned meaning values, such the 'present situation' position, the 'hopes and fears' position, or perhaps the 'hidden factors' position. Configurations are varied in size and complexity as we saw in the first chapter, and can range from simple two or three-card spreads signifying, for instance, 'Past, Present, Future', or 'Body, Mind, Spirit' to more elaborate patterns which theoretically might include the entire deck of 78, but in practice usually fall short of 22 cards.

Sequence of selection and physical placement of the cards are figured in as well, so that a spread is viewed in the particular shape of its layout, typically some symmetric or geometric pattern. This facilitates easier contemplation of the whole network of thematic interrelationships. A variety of spreads are commonly used, and each will carry the specific organizational structure and pattern sought for analysis. A ten-card (Celtic Cross) spread is by far the most traditional, popular, and perhaps owing to its complexity and versatility, most effective of all Tarot spreads. When later we move into experimental cases, a modified version of this spread will be used. It should be also noted that a ten-card spread can usually be completed within the confines of an hour session.

Despite their ingenuity, however, one should not become too

fascinated with the great variety of spread styles available in Tarot texts, just as the model type, body color, leather upholstery and all those alluring bells and whistles, practically-speaking, are of secondary importance when buying a car. The main point in either case is to get the ride, presumably for travel to desired locations, and most Tarot spreads like most automobiles will (more or less) accomplish this task. Whatever the vehicle, individual parts function as the necessary structural components of the machine's functionality. Whatever the size or shape, consultation will generally involve the random selection of a series of cards from a fully naturalized deck. Selected cards are then sequentially placed within their targeted position. Interpretation relates the card meaning to the position it occupies, and afterwards to interactions with other spread positions.

Typically, once the cards are turned over and made visible, the subject will immediately start to react to the numinous press of the archetypic content of the images, often non-verbally and unconsciously at first. One can easily imagine that even a few selected cards placed in their respective positions create a rather complex stimulus to the question in focus. Dynamically, given the multiple levels of symbolic meaning within a single card (which will be explored later in Chapter V), the rich matrix of a full 10- or 11- card spread is something akin to a game of three-dimensional psychological chess: syncretic, holistic, and multi-dimensional patterns are presented that capture both vertically and horizontally an intricate web of interrelated possibilities and strategies. Indeed, the allusion is echoed by the famed artist of the Thoth Deck, Lady Freida Harris, who said

> The Tarot…could be likened to a celestial game of chess, the Trumps being the pieces to be moved according to the law of their own order over a checkered board of the four elements.[1]

A spread can be interpreted in great detail, broken down into smaller pieces, or quickly and intuitively scanned like a topographical map for brief impressionistic glances over a veritable "field of dreams." Only with Tarot, the dreams have been captured, framed, and systematized, in fact—'suspended'—one could say, in a deep-freeze museum for our careful study, each offering a unique, complex, and unmeltable snowflake of the inner human context and condition.

In this vein stands another enchanting feature of a Tarot spread, namely, the enabling of a complex system of inter-relationships to be presented for extended periods of attention much as a map or work of art. Typically, when receiving information we are accustomed to the mode of cognitive processing that comes through speech, through words on a page or screen, through frames on a reel or sounds on a disc or tape, each of which is essentially sequential, point-referenced, and fleeting by nature. Processed in the left hemisphere of the brain, they are experienced as self-vanishing bits (or bytes) of information that will momentarily be added to the towering stockpiles of memory, much as when observing from the vantage point of a moving train, to use the endearing example in J.W. Dunne's classic *An Experiment with Time*: "*From the windows of our railway carriage we see a cow glide past at fifty miles an hour and remark that the creature is enjoying a rest.*"[2] Dunne calls such viewing "serial perception," which describes our conventional linear manner of processing the world.

By contrast, a Tarot spread 'suspends' a train's motion before the observer, leaving open a viewpoint that is outside the conventional flow of serial time. As a right brain function, such "glance access" is perceived before an unmoving, holographic field facilitating for the viewer an interactive and intuitive experience of the object. The cow will regurgitate before our very eyes for as long as we can stand it. Or in a more human example, perhaps we are minutes away from visiting a sick uncle in the hospital. Our state of mind is swirling and it's hard to put our finger on 'why' such anxiety. To center ourselves, perhaps over coffee in the hospital cafeteria, we decide a quick reading might be helpful, and so from a miniature deck tucked away in our pocket (appropriate for such occasions) three cards are randomly drawn. We have designated the three spread positions: past/present/future (using the Universal Waite deck).

Suppose, for argument's sake, the Ace of Swords is selected in the 'past,' the 5 of Cups in the 'present' and The Empress in the 'future.' Linear time is now amplified through symbolic resonances which themselves have arrived through non-linear means (synchronicity). As is typical of the process, a channel of associations to each card immediately ensues (quite possibly unrelated to the visit itself), new emotions may be triggered and forgotten memories may jump back, leaving one feeling subtly stimulated and entranced by the numinosity of the images. Without knowledge of intrinsic meanings, such projected associations will nevertheless begin to forge a rational point of departure to an otherwise chaotic multiplicity of thoughts, feelings, sensations. A narration of one's immediate story is easily constructed. The moment is now marked, as it were, by symbolic guideposts and can be returned to for reflection well after the visit (or the uncle) has passed.

Past/Present/Future Configuration

Ace of Swords (Past)	5 of Cups (Present)	Empress (Future)

In the simple case above, the Ace of Swords in the 'past' position returns the subject to a lost memory of his youth: from its suggestion of clarity and primacy, he recalls a brief interlude of great lucidity while strolling across his college campus some 20 years earlier. A transient and formless experience (like most of what constitutes "inner life"), it was a momentary impression never consciously referred to again, until now, of course. But what relevance to the hospital visit? The subject studies the card for several moments, noting his current surroundings, until an intuition issues forth: "the reality of death." To the outsider this response seems a reach, but internally, the synchronicity has restimulated a profound inner moment: the remembrance of his first conscious encounter with mortality. He now wonders: Was the reality of death to be the visit's lesson?

Next the 5 of Cups is considered in the 'present' position. With cups, an entirely different elemental base instinctively turns the subject's focus to the feeling function. To his surprise, he now finds stimulated a fluttering of unresolved pangs inflicted by a former lover's betrayal. He hadn't thought of 'her' in years, either. But why had this come up in the 'present' he wonders? A stream of thoughts and memories are triggered by the question and context. The sick uncle, ostensibly the precipitant of the reading, is recalled to have suffered a grueling divorce himself many years earlier due to similar romantic transgressions. Momentarily, the subject feels a special kinship with the uncle, even though their relationship has been neither close nor intimate. The subject's anxiety has significantly lessened now, perhaps owing to the unearthing of such connections. The timeliness of the third card, The Empress in the 'future' position, offers the soothing possibility of ultimate healing and healthy return. The subject is comforted by Her nurturing presence and now feels ready for the visit.

Could such a slice of 'hidden' psychological experience come so swiftly and reliably by other means? The whole procedure here takes no more than three or four minutes. The effect is achieved without 'expert' interpretation, coming rather through the direct perception of the cards themselves in their spread positions. Even in this modest example, deeper interpretation and interplay between themes could obviously extend onto many levels of meaning. But as we are dealing at this point merely with hypotheticals, for the sake of demonstration, suppose a troublemaking little pixie has preyed upon our better judgment to 'doctor' the sequence. Of course 'switching' like this is typically frowned upon in real life readings as it can harm and confuse the sanctity of the divination. But for argument's sake, suppose The Empress instead should now appear in the 'past' position, the Ace of Swords in the 'present', and the 5 of Cups is placed in the 'future' position.

Switching The Sequence:

Empress (Past)	Ace of Swords (Present)	5 of Cups (Future)
	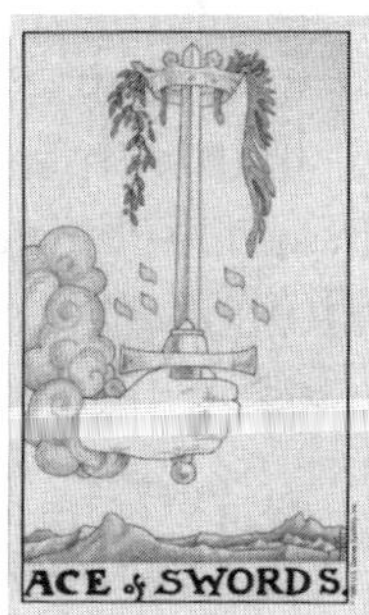	

Now imagine the same uncle, the same hospital visit, the same subject, but a different card sequence. The Empress in the 'past' no longer is seen to represent "healthy return" but instead is quickly associated with his mother, who is also his uncle's sister. He now wonders about his mother's health, something she rarely talks about. He notes how well she takes care of herself. He considers her other Empress-like qualities, her passion for life, her earthiness, her warmth and so forth, and is struck by the realization that she is unaware of this visit. The impetus had come solely from within himself, though clearly it was something his mother would greatly approve of. The card gives pause to consider his own mothering qualities, something not normally thought of as such.

In contrast, the Ace of Swords in 'the present' now appears stern and unchallenged; it conjures an impression that some defining moment has arrived. He wonders whether it has to do with the visit itself. Will he be able to "cut through" the formalities and really make contact? Could it be signaling some decisive downturn in his uncle's health? Or is it more about his own present moment? What meaning had this visit brought to his own life? With a smattering of such possibilities and foreboding, he is left more sensitized to the immediacy of the moment. But then the 5 of Cups appearing in the 'future' position inadvertently triggers spontaneous tears of sadness. He senses loss and grief in the overturned cups, and considers that his uncle may be dying. If not now then soon, as assuredly death will come to his mother as well, and for that matter, to himself and to all living creatures. The insight is tempered by the two remaining cups that stand behind. They remind him that life and death continuously recycle, that a period of grief is natural, that with loss comes gain. He is now ready to proceed to the hospital elevator.

Stephen Karcher and Rudolf Ritsema, eminent *I Ching* scholars and authors, note the following observation about divination:

> The idea that words, things, and events can become omens that open communication with a spirit-world is based on an insight in the way the psyche works—that in every symptom, conflict or problem we experience there is a spirit trying to communicate with us. Each encounter with trouble is an opening to this spirit, usually opposed by the ego because it wants to enforce its will on the world.[3]

In our vignettes above, it is the event of the hospital visit itself that brings the subject's "encounter with trouble." This is what precipitates our nephew to consider the cards. In both instances, a clear case is given for the presenting symptom or 'trouble' to serve merely as a jumping off point to a 'spirit' within. This is crucial to therapeutic application and must be underscored. Presenting problems or stated questions will likewise serve merely as such points of departure for deeper exploration. On the Tarot journey, spread positions provide a framework and orientation to such trouble. In the second example, we see how quickly an interpretation can vary by framework, yet cover not entirely unrelated territory due to the inherent terrain contained within each card.

Because this 'train' ride has now been suspended in the Tarot picture frame, review is easily retrievable and sustainable. The message has been photographed, so to speak. Later on, when our nephew returns home, the three cards may themselves be revisited and reconstructed for greater insight and integration. Of course, repeated study reveals not so much changes in the spatial field *per se*, as it does alterations in one's own "present time" perception. It is we who are perpetually changing, not our Tarot cards.

Fortunately, from its inherent kindness, Tarot offers up a forgiving branch for us to grasp onto from *our* own side.

The Spread Cluster

As in all walks of life, experience teaches certain practical techniques of a craft which are not necessarily taught in one's original training, so-called *tricks of the trade* that nonetheless become exceedingly useful in practice. Along these lines, when reading Tarot cards I recommend that one learns to appreciate the power of the *cluster*, a method of subdividing spread configurations into constituent parts similar in effect to the sub-scaling implemented in other psychological tests (e.g. Minnesota Multiphasic Personality Inventory and WAIS).

In Psychology, the term 'cluster' is associated with the statistical operation of factor analysis; a cluster is a group of variables which have higher correlations with each other than with other variables. More generally the term is used to suggest any group of objects or events which seem, subjectively, to belong together, that is, to form a natural grouping. In Tarot, by cluster is meant specific two or three card interfacings (or subsets) within the larger spread which carry essential structural and dynamic information when grouped together. As significant parts of the whole, they can aid handsomely in the organization and conceptualization of a full-bodied interpretation. Of course ultimately, all positions are interdependent and interrelated, all carry important and interconnected aspects of the whole person. This crucial theme of interdependency will be taken up in Chapter VIII.

The specific dynamics and intent of a given spread will determine the most useful cluster groupings for a reading. To demonstrate clustering I have chosen the widely-used "Celtic Cross" spread which I have modified slightly to be more applicable to the therapeutic context. On the following page, a skeleton of this spread's configuration is presented. The numbers inside each box designate the selection sequence and physical placement of each card. Afterwards is presented a brief description of these six clusters by name and function that bear special attention.

Celtic Cross Spread

(gift/guide) 11.

(goal/ideal) 5.

(outcome) 10.

(situation) 1.

(anticipation) 9.

past (cause) 4.

present (resistance) 2.

future (effect) 6.

(object) 8.

(foundation) 3.

(ego) 7.

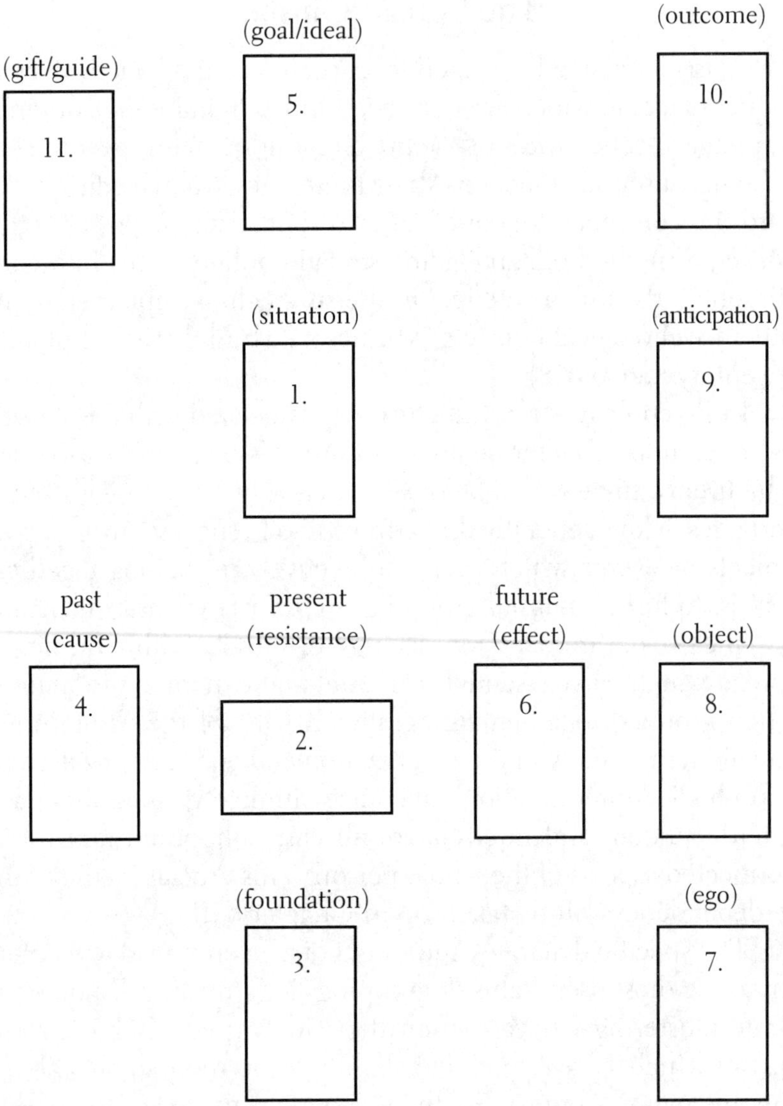

Celtic Cross Spread Clusters

(**Note**: the numbers appearing after each cluster title point to the card positions interfaced; see previous chart.)

Cluster 1: *The Core (1-2)*. The first two cards selected define the actual nature of the querent's issue and, as its name suggests, this cluster marks the central dynamic of a reading. It examines the interface of the **'situation'** and **'obstacle'** and reflects the presenting problem or symptom of the client. Cluster 1 may also help to reframe the question of the initial query into greater precision and specificity. A reading typically should not proceed until the two cards of Cluster 1 are clearly established with meaningful referents for the querent. The reader must be flexible and careful to correctly identify where these cards are relevant to the query. This cluster is equivalent to the formation of a "therapeutic contract" between clinician and client in the early phase of treatment, one that identifies the areas and issues to be worked on.

Cluster 2: *Above and Below (5-3)*. Extending the vertical dimension, this cluster interrelates the air (mental) and earth (motility) elements at the poles. It examines the interplay between **'goals/ideals'** and **'foundation/ground'** respectively, pointing to potential imbalances of energy (whether top or bottom heavy) in these areas. It may also be seen to differentiate consciousness (above) from the unconscious (below). Extended in this way, a vertical axis is now more fully established, one that positions Cluster 2 at the poles and contains Cluster 1 at the center. This vertical line represents the querent's "psychological space" with analogous "body centers" (chakras, points, meridians, etc.) in a metaphorical sense, from top to bottom, signifying: head (goals/ideals), eyes/mouth (present situation), heart (obstacle), and legs/feet (foundation). Cluster 2 describes the 'body' or corpus of the querent's relation to the query.

Cluster 3: *Cause and Effect (4-2-6)*. Movement from left to right, past to future, cause to effect, i.e., linear progression, temporality, and causal relationships, are examined in this cluster. Cluster 3 describes the 'process' dimension of the reading. Illustrated in this horizontal axis is a symmetry and reversibility in temporal progressions where constructs such as **'past and future'** and **'cause and effect'** are ultimately seen to be not so fixed as we conventionally believe despite the "arrow of time." Cluster 3 additionally shows continuity and discontinuity in the process dimension. Past and future are viewed causally as conditional constructs relative to the observed present situation. Card 2, the obstacle at the 'heart' of the reading (first addressed in Cluster 1), bares a central determining influence in this cluster as well, as indeed it will become equally crucial to several other clusters as well.

In the logic of the spread, 'past cause' must transit through the present 'obstacle' in order to arrive at the 'future effect' (4**→**2**→**6). In this way the spread focuses heavily on the present troubled condition, the implication being that how one relates to difficulty (pain) in the present, whether through proper alignment or resistance, acceptance or avoidance, will become a strong determining factor of its future effect. The logic is reminiscent of the Buddhist doctrine of karma (as stated by Padmasambhava: "If you want to know your past life, look at your present condition; if you want to know your future life, look at your present actions"[4]) which accords primary responsibility to each present moment. Linear versus nonlinear theories of time and psychological explanation will be explored further in various contexts throughout this book.

Cluster 4: *Self/Object (7-8).* The structural personality components of **'ego identity'** and **'object representation'** are examined here. 'Ego' is defined generally as the 'I' or 'self', the organizing center of the conscious personality (as distinct from the 'archetypal self'). 'Object' can be thought of either perceptually and cognitively as an aspect of the environment of which one is aware, or psychoanalytically, as a person, a part of a person, or a symbol representative of either, towards which behaviors, thoughts and desires are oriented. Given this spread position that addresses the vast and overriding concern of modern psychoanalytic schools, some readers may breathe easy and 'decathect' to learn that we are merely seeking in these positions a cursory set of navigational coordinates. 'Ego identity' in this context describes how one sees oneself in the situation at hand and can be interpreted horizontally and/or vertically. 'Object representation' ('others') applies particularly to significant others related to the situation in focus, and likewise may be interpreted horizontally and/or vertically. Often Cluster 4 helps to differentiate one's identity and object relations from the situation in its entirety, that is, from the situation itself. In this regard it has a supervenient relation to the spread as a whole. In our case studies that come later, this cluster is particularly revealing.

Cluster 5: *Fear/Obstacle Axis (9-2).* The fifth cluster shows the relationship between **anticipation** (traditionally, 'hopes and fears') and psychological **resistance**, a relationship which is invariably interdependent and reciprocal. Here 'anticipation' is defined as "a preparatory mental set in which one is primed for the perception of a particular stimulus." Resistance, in the psychoanalytic sense, is viewed to be caused by unconscious factors as opposed to a conscious refusal. The cluster as such shows the psychological tugs between conscious expectation and unconscious counterforces. Experience has shown that quite regularly a reciprocal relationship operates between these two positions. As one accepts and aligns with Card 2 (the obstacle), anticipation tends towards its positive pole, hopefulness. Conversely, the more one resists Card 2, the more likely a negative expectation will be filtered and informed through fear and anxiety reactions. Solutions to obstacles are often to be found through examination of one's conscious and unconscious relationship to anticipation.

Cluster 6: *Resolution and Wisdom (10-11).* Tarot philosophically reflects both determinism and free will, karma and liberation, prediction and reflection as functions of awareness. In this cluster, predictable outcomes are postulated through causation mediated by conscious choice and transcendent guidance, as expressed by the convergence of '**outcome**' and '**gift/guide**' positions. Normally, with insufficient awareness of the multiple hidden forces operating within a presented problem or symptom, one is likely to repeat or "play out" a pattern that is unconsciously predetermined and predicted. The addition of the 11th position, deemed 'gift and guide', is designed to offer some agency of support that falls outside the querent's own sphere. Its classically 'oracular' appearance (i.e., external to the will of the subject), coupled with the card's innate symbolic multidimensionality, ensures an emotionally enriched receptivity within the subject. It is the one card not selected by the querent himself, but (blindly) by the reader. The 'gift/guide' when combined with the 'outcome' ultimately returns responsibility to the querent, who now with the benefit of this rich dynamic assessment, is given both the means and the ends to achieve a degree of conscious participation with the trouble at hand. This approximates the intelligence of true wisdom.

Reading Styles

Finally, we now turn to the art of reading itself. Although we have so far identified the purpose and structure of spreads and spread clusters, we have not allowed for the fact that practitioners will vary in approach and style. In the next chapter we will go into greater detail about how diverse psychotherapeutic systems may adapt interpretative styles in accordance with varying philosophical and practical beliefs. Here we will explore general interpretative approaches which can later be tailored to specific techniques.

Leading Tarot author Mary Greer (1988) has differentiated four interpretative styles of Tarot reading, noting that highly skilled tarotists are likely to integrate all four methods in a comprehensive reading.[4] As we shall see, therapists typically will be drawn more to styles one and two (Analytic and Therapeutic) while one-time readers, spiritual and psychic counselors, artists and writers, or highly intuitive therapists will often experiment more freely with style three and four (Psychic and Magical). I have found this distinction quite useful in my own work and will borrow directly from Greer's research.

(1) *The Analytic Style*: Based on analysis and correspondences, it assumes that everything in a spread stands for something in the individual psyche, not unlike Gestalt dreamwork and related

approaches which assume everything appearing in a dream stands for some aspect of the dreamer's personality. This style typically takes each card and symbol, one at a time, and analyzes its multiple levels of meaning before an overriding synthesis is offered. Those details which seem most germane to the client are particularly noted and personal associations will be encouraged. Interpretation typically involves the horizontal and vertical symbolic levels (discussed in Chapter V), is insight-oriented, and allows for reversals. When an analytically-based reading is given, the querent will come away with much information which will require further contemplation and introspection not immediately grasped during the session. This style will be less effective for querents of limited intellectual understanding or capacity for insight.

(2) *The Therapeutic Style*: Based on reflection and perception, in this style the reader becomes primarily a supportive mirror who facilitates personal associations and feeling-responses of the querent for the purpose of self-discovery. The reader's role is like a client-centered therapist's—to listen and amplify, to reflect the querent's response back to them, and to offer support, self-disclosure, and guidance when called for. The reader may inquire about the card's interior importance to the querent. The reader may offer his own personal sense of the card when appropriate. Traditional meanings are discouraged, and personal connections to the imagery reinforced. As a mostly non-directive approach, the therapeutic style will not push for insight as will the analytic, but will offer the safe and supportive container for the client to explore at his own pace. The method can be utilized with children as well, and is particularly effective for clients in the throes of emotional crisis, or when needing help in sorting out and problem-solving.

(3) *The Psychic Style*: Based on psychic intuition, in this method the reader uses the cards as springboards for inner 'sight' and subtle sensory 'feelings'. Whether they acknowledge it or not, most therapists use their intuition regularly and abundantly in counseling situations, whether consciously or unconsciously. In the psychic method, readers are encouraged to go with their

hunches or 'felt-senses' that are triggered by the divination. As mentioned above, this style is less practiced in a clinical setting, with the possible exception of group therapy, where a single card may stimulate in members important intuitions regarding the state of group process or cohesion. True psychic or intuitive readers (I use them interchangeably here) tend to turn all the cards upright at once, and after glancing at them, will direct their attentions more to the perception of subtle energy fields or impressions (expressed usually through internal images, sound, bodily sensations or speech) that surround both the querent and/or themselves.

Psychic readers may scan for one minute detail within the card that stimulates their own internal 'guides', which they will then assume is somehow relevant to the querent, trusting such clairvoyant signs through years of experience, often to the baffled amazement of both client and conventional tarotist alike. Refining such impressions through a variety of sensory channels including those offered by Tarot, the talented intuitive reader will convey subtle observations and insights without necessarily pinpointing them in the cards at all. Interestingly enough, most of the leading scholarly and practicing tarotists today, to my knowledge, do not consider themselves to be psychics but 'diviners' (conduits), whereas those who specialize in psychic readings using Tarot cards tend to consider themselves technically not tarotists, but clairvoyants.

(4) *The Magical Style*: Greer's fourth suggested style is based on positive affirmation and conscious intent, and encourages the querent to focus on the very highest potential in every card (and position) through positive affirmation and creative visualization. Related techniques have for decades supplied both the Human Potentials movement and curiously, behavioral therapy, which utilizes visualization, desensitization, implosion, etc., to reinforce behavioral change through deliberate image replacement. In this context, 'magic' is defined as "the art of changing consciousness at will," and can be thought of as the application of creative will and conscious intent. Reversals are not utilized, nor are levels of meaning especially relevant. The use of card illustrations serve as

meditational aids to the visualization process. Again, this style is not typically used in the therapeutic context but may be found useful for some specific applications.

Naturally, it goes without saying that each style can be misused or unskillfully managed, but such is not our discussion here. Again I must emphasize that apart from an individual's particular talent or interpretative preference, ideally each of these reading styles will in various ways be integrated into one effective, comprehensive, and indeed elegant consultation. The reader must always guard against his own inflation as the process is indeed numinous and will stimulate powerful emotions in both reader and client. As with any art form and technical skill, experience and practice shall lead the way.

(5) The Global Method: I have taken the liberty to add this final category to Greer's list because it offers for the first time a procedure which gives Tarot divination a potential application for experimental research. The "global method" can be implemented utililizing any of the styles discussed. It attempts to abstract to the many from the results of the few. It is a way of using divination on a larger scale not simply for assessment, reflection, clarification, prediction (or future-viewing), but for a comprehensive analysis of the dynamic forces and underlying psychic structures that comprise a particular targeted population of study.

Of course, conventional research methods commonly attempt to study and generalize their findings across populations, but they are typically limited by measuring instruments that can only register physiological effects within a narrow spectrum of access, or else they fall reliant on reported experiences and anecdotes mediated through a subject's (or observer's) presuppositions, defenses, and conscious awareness. Using the global method, Tarot is potentially able to gather information that may remain otherwise inaccessible or hidden to conventional measures. In Chapter VIII a pilot study of domestic violence using the global Tarot method will be presented in depth, followed by two case studies.

However, to complete our initial study of the Tarot of Psychology, it will be necessary to compare and contrast the Tarot method with other accepted methods of psychotherapeutic treatment. It may remain unclear to clinical practicioners exactly how Tarot can be implemented in the therapy hour. In the next chapter I hope to make a strong case for Tarot's most outstanding assets in psychological usage, namely, its great versatility and adaptability. The reader who has no particular interest in the field of psychotherapy may prefer to move to the second section of the book, where Tarot's unique psychological properties will be explored and precise lexicons of card meanings will be constructed.

Notes

[1] Crowley, Aleister, *The Book of Thoth: A Short Essay on the Tarot of the Egyptians*; York Beach: Maine, Samuel Weiser, Inc., 1969 (Originally published in 1944).

[2] Dunne, J.W., *An Experiment with Time*; Faber and Faber Ltd., London, 1927.

[3] Ritsema, Rudolf and Karcher, Stephen (translators), *I Ching: The Classic Chinese Oracle of Change*; Element Books Limited, Great Britain, 1994, p. 10.

[4] Greer, Mary K., *Tarot Mirrors: Reflections of Personal Meaning*; Newcastle Publishing Co. Inc., 1988, pp. 34-39.

Chapter IV

TAROT AND SYSTEMS OF PSYCHOTHERAPY

> I see it as a kind of building of doorways, opening conduits, and making channels, like a giant bypass operation, throwing in all kinds of new tubings so that things flow into each other. Memories, events, images all become enlivened.…That's one thing therapy can do.
>
> —James Hillman, *We've Had a Hundred Years of Psychotherapy and the World's Getting Worse*[1]

The Politics of Self-Preservation

The intuitive and spiritual vision gained from Tarot divination and related methods remains even to this day outright suspect to the spiritual establishment, to say nothing of the world of mainstream psychology. The established religion asks: Why is there need for these methods when we have already spelled out everything so clearly? Who can be sure that people channeling their own spiritual insight won't go their own way? The established psychology asks much the same rhetorical question, only laces it with concern over "good practice" and statistical verification. David Steindl-Rast, author, Ph.D., and monk of the Mount Savior Monastery observes:

> One way or the other, the same plot is acted out repeatedly on the stage of history: every religion seems to begin with mysticism and end up in politics.… Fortunately, I have not yet come across a religion where the system didn't work at all. Unfortunately, however, deterioration begins

> on the day the system is installed.... Our social structures have a tendency to perpetuate themselves. Religious institutions are less likely than seed pods to yield to the new life stirring within. And although life (over and over again) creates structures, structures do not create life.[2]

Though Steindl-Rast's subject is religion, he might just as well be addressing psychology. Provincialism and territoriality are long shadows stalking the bright brass bodies of earned knowledge, though embodied with a good deal less candor in those representing divinity, human ethics, wisdom, mental balance, and the healing arts. New vision is rarely sought by those who claim already to see, nor is it easily shared or received. However, unless any philosophic, religious, or psychological school of thought grows irreparably stale or stultified within its own dogma and tradition, finding its last refuge of hope dwindled to the politics of self-preservation, like all living organisms it must continue to adapt and evolve to the changing demands of each age. As a simple matter of common sense, the closer an organization is to the lived heartbeat of its constituents, the more likely its survival. And neither should this fact be lost on Tarot itself; to the contrary, Tarot practitioners must continue to creatively use Tarot's own wisdom and method upon itself in order to adjust to the changing demands of this age and the next.

Similarity and Diversity: Approaches to Treatment

In this chapter we will explore Tarot's relevance and applicability to existing systems and schools of psychotherapy. Insofar as there are currently estimated as many as 400 schools of psychotherapy,[3] we will attempt to cover only a representative smattering of major trends in the field. If nothing more, the glut of therapeutic schools reflects the great exuberance of the 100-year discipline of psychotherapy, and given our topic, can only be compared to the estimated 300 or so diverse Tarot decks that are now commercially available. Of course, Tarot decks *per se,* however fascinating a subject, are hardly the focus here nor is equating them with therapy schools a particularly fair comparison. The great profusion of new decks over recent decades, however, from Arnell Ando's *Transformational Tarot* to *Zolar's Astrological Tarot*, quite on a par with psychotherapy's zestful proliferation, is perhaps a testament to the creative fervor that both disciplines have inspired in the modern age.

But the comparison between Tarot decks and psychotherapy does in fact allow for one important parallel: namely, that despite significant heterogeneity within both, in each case the sizable variance and diversity of approaches, oddly enough, all seem to achieve roughly comparable results (though arguably with slightly different emphases). To date, for the broad range of problems that clients bring to psychotherapists there is still no convincing evidence that one system is any better than the others. The same can surely be said for decks of Tarot.

According to Jerome Frank in his highly regarded *Persuasion and Healing*, four features are shared by virtually all approaches to psychotherapy: (a) a relationship in which the patient has confidence that the therapist is competent and cares about his welfare, (b) a practice setting that is socially defined as a place of healing, (c) a rationale or "myth" that explains the patient's suffering and how it can be overcome, and (d) a set of procedures that require participation of both patient and therapist and that both believe to be a means of restoring the patient's health.[4] It is within these same professional confines that I wish to introduce Tarot as an adjunctive tool and technique in psychotherapy.

Versatility, as previously noted, is perhaps Tarot's great virtue, as the universality and archetypal foundation of its symbolism carries the breadth and depth necessary to sufficiently accommodate the technical language and constructs of most therapeutic approaches. Wisdom is never so provincial as to be intelligible in only one language exclusively, and in the Confucian sense, Tarot is endowed with the advantage of the "thousand words" each picture is worth. In practice, Tarot is easily adaptable because it is inherently neutral and doctrinally foundationless; it carries no particular allegiance to any system of belief which posits an exclusive claim on truth or reality.

In this regard, it would seem quite naturally to fit within the more open-ended narrative and integrationist (eclectic) theoretical camps. Yet paradoxically, and seemingly contrary to constructivist theory, Tarot does indeed posit the pre-existence of underlying core psychic structures or 'archetypes.' In this regard, we might say that although Tarot is conversant in all subjective languages of experience, it additionally comes stocked with a preformed mind of its own. As Jungian analyst James A. Hall suggests:

> To my mind, the *a priori* existence of archetypes does not preclude the construction of hypothetical archetypes including even constructs of 'self.' 'I' is certainly a construct as are 'shadow' and the 'syzygy of anima/animus.' But we must not think of the ego as the only constructivest. There may be a center of subjectivity in the collective unconscious that constructs the self that constructs the ego. It reminds me of Escher's drawing of hands drawing hands.[5]

Psychoanalysis

Any discussion of modern psychotherapy must begin at the beginning, and so we briefly commence with Freud, and his famous epigram, "Where id was, there shall ego be," which perhaps best captures the central goal of psychoanalysis as proclaimed in his later writings.[6] Based on Freud's topographical model, it suggests the proper aim of classical psychoanalysis: to make the unconscious conscious. This to a large degree is a key function of Tarot as well, that is, to make possibilities conscious. Tarot cards either clarify, interconnect, or amplify what already exists in consciousness, or else they bring unconscious possibilities into conscious awareness. That is, they 'diaphanize' or 'possiblize'.

How might Tarot operate in classical analysis? It wouldn't. But for argument's sake, suppose we could establish a quasi-classical situation that would admit of such an auxiliary tool. This is not so far-fetched if we recall that Freud himself was a dabbler in Kabbalah, a metaphysical system believed by many to be the basis of Tarot. Bakan traces the historically neglected influence that the Kabbalah and Jewish mysticism played in Freud's early thinking:

> Participation in the B'nai B'rith in Vienna was one of the very few recreations that Freud permitted himself—among his recreations was his

weekly game of taroc [sic], a popular card game based on Kaballa. It was there that he first presented his ideas on dream interpretation.[7]

Imagine, for the moment, that Freud was an adept Tarot reader and wished to incorporate this tool into psychoanalysis. In place of free association and dream analysis, fantasy content is stimulated and analyzed through the projective properties of the cards, with the analyst perhaps taking copious notes from behind the card table next to the couch. Of course, Tarot's manifest content would not seem unduly disguised to Freud; Swords and wands would be easy marks for phallic symbols, The Lovers thinly disguising "oedipal wishes," The Devil a symbol of "oedipal guilt," The Hanged Man, naturally, signaling "oedipal failure," along with the Queen of Swords an obvious example of 'castration anxiety' and the Queen of Wands, "penis envy."

Freudian interpretation has tended to degrade symbols by confusing them with signs, and then reducing them to presupposed basic drives. In the unlikely scenario above, the 'here/now' transference reactions are directed away from the analyst, at least for the moment, and displaced onto the cards themselves which serve as solicitous receptacles of projection. Interpretation, in this context, relates Tarot associations and reactions to long-standing conflicts in the individual, or so it might unfold in the waning days of classical analysis. The absurdity of this vision, however technically feasible, suggests the anachronistic decline of classical Freudian analysis today, though it hardly describes the current vitality of contemporary Post-Freudian psychoanalysis in general.

Perhaps more than any other, Fairbairn's revisioning epigram, "libido is object seeking, not pleasure seeking," captures the shifting currents of contemporary psychoanalytic theory and practice.[8] The dictum strongly suggests that human beings are fundamentally relational creatures, that our interest in 'objects' is not a secondary derivative of some presumably more basic drive. A significant body of contemporary psychoanalytic theory deals with 'internalized' object relations. This dimension of psychological complexity is well adapted and reflected by the Tarot method as well. Tarot cards can be seen to both stimulate and mirror the internal affect-imagery that guides and disturbs one's capacity to form and maintain adult relationships. As projective 'presses' of internalized object imagery, the relational dynamics emerging from a reading can be seen to reveal early representations of self and others, which may in fact emerge in the subject's interaction with virtually any card in the deck. Certain spread positions ('ego/object') are particularly designed to confront this psychological dimension. While a fair accounting of the rich resurgence of Post-Freudian psychoanalysis is well beyond the scope and concern of this study, several general observations can be made that relate to potential opportunities for the Tarot method.

An important trend over the past four decades has been the steady shift away from Freud's emphasis on instinctual wishes including the conflicts and defenses connected to those wishes, towards the increasing importance placed on the development of self and object representations (images), particularly at the pre-ego developmental stages between 18 to 36 months of age ("on the road to object constancy"). Later in this book we will observe how a Tarot reading can be used to elucidate such representations through spread cluster interpretation, as we have already suggested in the previous chapter. Tarot applied in this framework can function as an adjunctive tool, a focusing technique of sorts, whose usefulness will depend on the phase of treatment and the therapist's specific intent.

As psychoanalysis itself unfolds through its own developmental stages, the traditional significance once accorded instinctual gratification and conflict, particularly oedipal conflict, has been replaced with concern over the successful achievement of separation-individuation (Mahler), self-cohesiveness (Kohut), and supportive object relations (Kernberg). However, even current psychoanalytic trends continue to uphold Freud's tendencies towards pathological reductionism, symbol degradation, and emphasis on the primacy of the past. Such distinctions and their alternatives will be taken up in Chapters V and VIII. But now we will turn to the other major school of 20th-century depth psychology, Jungian analytical psychology.

The Wise Doctor from Zurich

Carl Gustav Jung's psychoanalytic roots and early association with Freud, the founder and father of psychoanalysis, are well known. Their saga includes an early exchange of groundbreaking ideas between 1903 and 1906 regarding arcane theories of the unconscious, their energetic correspondences during that period, their shared invitation to lecture in America in 1909 that culminated in Jung's appointment as President of the First Psychoanalytic Congress. At this early stage in their unrivaled friendship, the Swiss psychiatrist was so esteemed by the father of Psychoanalysis as to be regarded his eldest son and future Crown Prince to the psychoanalytic throne.

Curiously and perhaps inevitably, it is the subject matter over which occurred the eventual breakup of these two giants, officially in 1913, that is directly relevant to our study of Tarot. Years later Jung was to recount this parting of the ways (as told by Joseph Campbell in *The Portable Jung)*:

> "My dear Jung," [Freud] urged on this occasion, "promise me never to abandon the sexual theory. That is the most essential thing of all. You see, we must make a dogma of it, an unshakable bulwark...." In some astonishment Jung asked him, "A bulwark—against what?" To which [Freud] replied, "Against the black tide of mud...of occultism."

Taken aback, Jung countered that this was the very thing that struck him most profoundly:

> I knew that I would never be able to accept such an attitude. What Freud seemed to mean by 'occultism' was virtually everything that philosophy and religion, including the rising contemporary science of parapsychology, had learned about the psyche. To me the sexual theory was just as occult, that is to say, just as unproven a hypothesis, as many other speculative views. As I saw it, a scientific truth was a hypothesis that might be adequate for the moment but was not to be preserved as an article of faith for all time.[9]

It is said that Carl Jung, among his extraordinary contributions throughout his long career, was first to provide a strong foundation for the serious study of occult traditions by establishing a rational position from which to take the irrational seriously. This remains a controversial subject to this day, however, and provides an opening in this book for us to set the record straight regarding that unvanishing and most troublesome of terms to the modern sensibility, 'occultism'. Let it be known for our purposes here that Jung's description (even as he impugned it to Freud) is most apt for a working definition of 'occultism,' that being "virtually everything that philosophy and religion, including the rising contemporary science of parapsychology [has] learned about the psyche." Of course, the adjective 'occult' as in 'the occult sciences' means nothing more or less than "beyond the range of ordinary knowledge; mysterious; secret; or hidden" (*Random House College Dictionary*).

Hopefully those of my audience who are generally unacquainted with such things will refer back to these working definitions throughout the course of this book and not be otherwise distracted by the deviancy and occasional weirdness which strangely has been known to masquerade beneath the banner of occult(ism). Genuine occult traditions and practices are not explored in this volume due to our psychological emphasis and the author's limited knowledge. However, part of the mission of this work is to extricate a valid Tarot method from its collective misperceptions, which in all fairness have been enhanced by certain self-serving purveyors of Tarot's own storied past. All talk of cults, witchery, and other such aberrations has no real place in this method's psychological development and application unless such things are well grounded in sound psychological and ethical principles. From here on this point will be assumed. The author is well aware that such concerns must be addressed, but hopefully we may now return to the incomparable Professor Jung, founder of analytical psychology.

While Jung was an accomplished scholar and enthusiast of a great range of esoteric and metaphysical topics (alchemy, astrology, Eastern religion, gnosticism, *I Ching*, comparative mythology, parapsychology, quantum physics), and though he claimed throughout his career that interest in these matters, above all else, was essentially of an empirical and phenomenological nature, it is quite surprising then that Jung himself by all indications was never adequately schooled in Tarot. In fact, throughout his voluminous writings addressing so many related topics, only one mention of Tarot is ever made, to wit (in *The Archetypes and the Collective Unconscious,* paragraph 81) Jung remarks:

> It also seems as if the set of pictures in the Tarot cards were distantly descended from the archetypes of transformation, a view that has been confirmed for me in a very enlightening lecture by Professor Bernoulli.[10]

Serious Tarot study would fall more to his later adherents, though indirectly, as Jungian ideas were to filter more generally through ever-widening circles of psychological and spiritual exploration of which Tarot is but one manifestation.

Analytical Psychology

Why Jung was unlearned in this method is unclear, but easily pardonable given the great breadth of his researches. But it seems quite conceivable, at least to this author, that had he chosen to explore deeper, Jung would have quickly found in Tarot a natural ally of analytical psychology, as it so naturally fits within his own theoretical framework. A number of key parallels between Tarot and analytical psychology can be cited. First, post-Jungians today find obvious parallels between the Tarot's Major Arcana and the archetypal images of Jung's "collective unconscious" (as will be explored in Chapters VII and VIII). Such obvious examples of correspondence between The Empress and the archetype of The Great Mother, The Lovers and the archetype of anima/animus, The Hermit and the archetype of The Wise Old Man, and so on can be followed throughout the Major Arcana, which as Jung himself suggests, may comprise a full compendium of the "archetypes of transformation." Still, other significant parallels are found as well.

Tarot's Minor Arcana divisions into four suits naturally correspond to the four elements of Hermeticism and the four personality functions of Jungian typology: thinking (Swords), feeling (Cups), intuition (Wands) and sensation (Pentacles). Several Tarot researchers have begun to explore striking parallels between the

16 court cards and the 16 personality types described in the Jungian-based Myers-Briggs Type Indicator (MBTI).

The laws of opposition (enantiodromia) can be seen to operate clearly through the structure and application of the Tarot pack, a notion central to Jungian thought (and also explored later in this book). Also, mandala symbolism, that is, circular religious imagery that suggests psychic wholeness, a key theme in archetypal psychology, appears widely in Tarot, most notably in such trumps as The Chariot, The Wheel of Fortune, The Moon, The Sun, and The World, corresponding with Jung's theory of 'the archetypal self.' As was suggested in the first chapter, Tarot may be conceptualized as a psychological wheel; some in fact have speculated that the word 'Tarot' itself is derivative of the Latin 'rota' or wheel. These themes will be developed later when we explore themes of polarity, circularity and universality implicit in the Major Arcana.

The history and symbolism of Tarot forms a syncretic blend of Classical, Medieval, and Renaissance esoteric traditions, with certain philosophical borrowings from the East as well—unquestionably all subjects close to Jung's heart and theory. Of course, the relationship between Jung and Tarot has grown quite reciprocal over recent decades as well; tarotists have in turn relied heavily on certain analytical ideas such as compensation and opposition, shadow projection, the collective unconscious, introversion/extroversion, number and dream symbolism, etc., themes which have taken a central place in the intuitive arts in general, if only through osmosis.

Yet it is ultimately Tarot's methodology itself that most interlinks it with Jungian theory. Tarot divination, based as it is on 'empowered' random selection, brings to the clinical format an efficient, direct, Western application of one of Jung's least understood but, nevertheless, most compelling psychological contributions, namely, the theory of 'synchronicity.' This notion of "acausal connection through meaning" or "meaningful coincidence" was first presented in Jung's now celebrated foreword to the Richard Wilhelm translation of the *I Ching*, the Chinese "book of changes." In his autobiography, Jung describes his fascination with this Chinese oracle of divination, the catalyst and cultural breeding ground of his theory of synchronicity:

> During the whole of those summer holidays I was preoccupied with the question:
>
> Are the I Ching answers meaningful or not? If they are, how does the connection between the psychic and physical sequence of events come about? Time and again I encountered amazing coincidences which seemed to suggest the idea of an acausal parallelism (synchronicity, as I later called it).[11]

I Ching

Synchronicity is a concept that has drawn keen interest from a diverse ensemble of depth psychologists, parapsychologists, quantum physicists and others. While a closer look at the synchronicity hypothesis will be taken up in detail in Chapter IX, Tarot's relation to the *I Ching* deserves some further comment here. Cross-cultural anthropologist and Tarot scholar Angeles Arrien notes that whereas the Eastern *I Ching* translates from the Chinese to mean the "Book of Changes," the Tarot should be thought of as the *Western* Book of Changes. Both Tarot and *I Ching* are synchronistic techniques that operate by reframing a presenting question or problem into an image language like that of dreams. Both subtly capture the rhythm and pulse of psychological change and inter-relationship.[12]

But while the *I Ching* communicates oracular content through a "word net" of poetic allusion and sagacious aphorism, Tarot's vehicle of communication is primarily through immediate visual imagery. Owing to its symbolic richness and unmediated numinosity, Tarot's visual imagery is arguably more directly and spontaneously perceived by a subject than the rather cryptic and culturally-dependent wordgrams of the *I Ching*. Indeed, throughout Jung's writings in various contexts, the psychological primacy of imagery is emphasized, which is seen to contain or amplify the symbol and contain the context within which the symbol is embedded. According to Jung, "the image is endowed with a generative power; its function is to arouse; it is psychically compelling."[13]

As with other therapeutic uses of image and symbol, notably dreamwork, (Kalffian) sandplay, art therapy, and active imagination, Tarot operates primarily on the nonverbal level first; the unique placement of images, symbols, and numbers in the preset positions of a Tarot spread presents a powerful, visual-affective 'hold' over the psyche of the subject. A certain "glance access" is provided to what now becomes a wholistic, symbolic map of dynamic interrelationship. The numinous agency of the cards, like mantic inkblots, quietly stimulates a procession of associations, emotions, possibilities. The net effect is to 'relativize' an observing ego whose defenses are more geared for rational reloading than intuitive scanning. A more cohesive picture of a situation emerges, or else, a compelling new possibility is offered that is "in synch" with the questioner's experience. Only its mysterious method of access and its direct linkage to ancient wisdom fundamentally distinguish Tarot from other depth-oriented techniques.

Dreamwork and Sandplay

Dream analysis, arguably the deepest and purest glimpse into the inner maze of the psychic underworld, unfortunately suffers in the time-limited constraints of present-day treatment for several practical and theoretical reasons. As any analyst would likely agree, a dream 'report' is a sketchy, ego-mediated tale, that often metamorphosizes away from the actual dream event like the original communiqué passed along by children in the game of telegraph. Much gets lost in the translation. Dream recall itself is a talent not universally shared, and for interpretation to be effective and properly absorbed, generally a cogent series of dream events with sufficient time for analysis and integration is required.

If the dream can be described as an endogenous arising of numinous psychic contents from the unconscious, then perhaps Tarot can be thought of as an exogenous arising of those same contents, though bound by different laws due to its external source of origination and its formal ties to esoteric traditions. Certainly Tarot's inherent formalism, its large but undoubtedly finite collection of themes and subject matter can be seen as a limiting force when compared to the unbridled plethora of expression that is the dream.

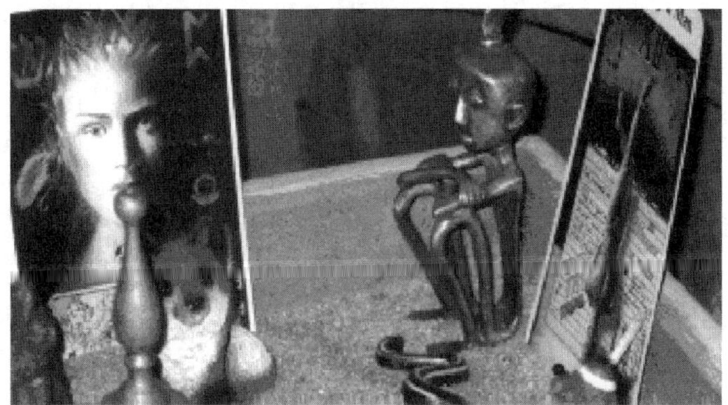

Tarot cards combined with sandtray objects
Rosengarten, 1999

In that regard, perhaps the three-dimensional objects and figurines of (Kalffian) sandplay therapy more closely recapture the amorphous imaginal landscapes of dream analysis, as sandplay pieces can vary dramatically by scale and combination, and are far freer to openly defy the conscious (consensual) rules of logic, physics, correspondence, and rational order. Developed by Dora Kalff in concert with Jung, sandplay is a commixture of miniature objects selected from a vast collection of things, people, animals, symbols, and the like, and then spontaneously placed by a client into a small sandbox wherein the subject is instructed simply to "make a scene." Interpretation or amplification is offered sparingly, while the therapist's prime duty is to offer a "safe and protected" space for the symbolic process to take hold.[14] Unquestionably, sandplay therapists and Tarotists have much to share and learn from each other.

Given that all three methods share an express interest in the access and interpretation of psychic imagery, certain practical advantages can be found with Tarot either in lieu of (or else in concert with) both dream analysis and sandplay therapy. Although dream decoding varies by the theoretical and constitutional orientation of the decoder (true for Tarot as well), in dreamwork one rarely has the luxury of framing a direct query to the unconscious (e.g., "what hidden factors are currently operating in my marital situation?") for which the dream purportedly becomes the answer, short of those rare events of lucidity or so-called "intentional dreams." Not so with Tarot, which as an oracular tool comes from a long and prosperous line of direct 'prognostication' (literally, the act of "foreseeing, prophecy, prediction"); the Tarot method, cultivated to a subtle art, has built into its very design and purpose a mandate to process such direct inquiries.

Besides its capacity for prognostication, the Tarot method is 'deep' and efficient, a point that we will repeat throughout this chapter. The efficiency of dream analysis is somewhat haphazard by comparison. While the advantages of tracking the natural recall, rhythm and pace of the dreamer's psyche may be a veritable edict in Jungian or Freudian practice, such orthodoxy must unfortunately be offset today by limitations that are artificially but nonetheless pragmatically placed onto the appointment hour due to non-clinical concerns over cost containment and delivery exigencies that plague the changing economics of psychotherapy, effecting what has been called the "rape of psychotherapy."[15] Time, we might say, in a Managed Care world, waits for no dream.

By contrast, the Tarot method in many ways provides a far more direct and economical route to unconscious contents. It requires no vast collection of objects and shelves to store them on as with sandplay, but simply a deck of cards. While it may not be as psychically unadulterated and pristine as the raw dream experience, it has the added advantage of a methodology that can be targeted to specific ends like decision-making, brainstorming, sorting, shadow work, strategizing, conflict resolution, etc. Unlike the dream, Tarot operates during waking hours, inside a therapist's office, and often in no longer than a 50-minute hour.

I have found that a blending of dreamwork and Tarot can be a particularly effective combination when the cards are used as symbolic markers of significant dream images. The dream ego's falling from a cliff, for instance, is marked by The Fool, or perhaps The Tower reversed. After all, both dream and Tarot images emanate presumably from the same profound imaginal wells of the deep human unconscious. One method is to place the full deck of cards face up before the client, and encourage him or her to select cards that capture ("feel like") each image that is reported in the dream. Afterward, the dream is "laid out" or mapped through the corresponding Tarot cards selected by the client. Amplification is thus given added richness of association, and the once amorphous dream is now made accessible to easy recollection and conscious incorporation. I have rarely found a dream image that did not correspond to a Tarot card.

When sandplay is blended with Tarot, the cards are (randomly) added to the vast menagerie of shelved three-dimensional objects out of which a small set of items are spontaneously selected by the client and placed into the sandbox (52x72x7cm) where a 'scene' is constructed. Tarot cards supply another dimension of representation to this marvelous imaginal art; they are commonly selected and fit naturally with the form and process. In many ways indeed, Tarot is a natural extension and enrichment of analytical techniques—a rich and untapped resource easily adapted to the analyst's technique.

The Changing Tides of the "Talking Cure"

For all its undisputed good works and substantial results, today in the traditional format of psychotherapy, 'talk' has proved neither cheap nor necessarily curative in and of itself. Other methods have developed to quicken and enhance psychological change. As a "map of consciousness," Tarot may become another new tool that aids the therapeutic process. Tarot is not strictly limited to esoteric tradition or the Jungian approach, nor should it be considered the exclusive domain of any single system. Quite to the contrary, the symbols and themes depicted in Tarot are universal and multifaceted, and they can be adapted into the professional argot and allocation of virtually any system of psychotherapy or spirituality. As primarily a visual language, Tarot is free to communicate complex symbolic ideas through compacted 'spectrums' of meaning. Obviously, it will appeal less to those belief systems which are inherently uncomfortable with self-exploration and identify their goals along the lines of prediction, control, and change of behavior.

Behaviorism

Traditional behaviorism with its emphasis on the rational mind and objectivity, linear thinking, quantification, control, and mastery will initially clash with the Tarot method much as it has traditionally clashed with psychoanalysis. Questions regarding reliability and validity will no doubt linger as laboratory demonstration and replication of this highly subjective method are fraught with experimental obstacles, although interestingly enough, initial experimental research has shown some encouraging signs.[16]

Nevertheless, the map of Tarot can be seen to illustrate behavioral constructs that may be quite educational and therapeutic to a client. Conventional cause-and-effect and stimulus/response (S-R) patterns of behavior are easily observed in Tarot, primarily through a card's directionality and the linear sequence of spread positions. Past causes are displayed adjacent to future effects, even if they have been established through nonlinear avenues. If the responses stimulated by Tarot cards are 'real', as we believe, then behavioral psychologists should not be deterred by metaphysical explanations or a scarcity of laboratory trials to make practical use of their efficacy. Tarot's advantages, as we have suggested, are in its unique powers of communication and visual demonstration.

In recent developments, however, in keeping with the changing tides which are affecting all models of therapy, behavioral therapists themselves have begun to stray from their Watsonian roots that once categorically rejected the relevance of subjective inner states, intentionality, and the importance of social and cultural context in favor of the classic belief that people's behavior is determined solely by focused S-R relationships. According to Fishman and Franks, behavior theorists today have rediscovered "personality" from the trait worldview, rediscovered "the family as a system" from the organismic worldview, and rediscovered "psychotherapy process" from the transactional worldview.[17]

Cognitive-behavioral therapy, a popular and relatively recent theoretical submovement of behaviorism, derives its main impetus from the so-called cognitive revolution in general psychology. Cognitive-behavioral therapists emphasize that personal thinking styles are intimately connected with affect and behavior. As Kendall and Bemis have summarized:

> The task of the cognitive-behavioral therapist is to act as diagnostician, educator, and technical consultant, assessing maladaptive cognitive processes and working with the client to design learning experiences that may ameliorate these dysfunctional cognitions and the behavioral and affective patterns with which they correlate.[18]

The cognitive-behaviorist spotlights an extremely important topographical area on the relief map of human suffering, and his contribution should never be underestimated. His basic tenet is thus:

> The thought manifests as word
> The word manifests as deed
> The deed develops into habit
> The habit hardens into character.

This equation of course predates American cognitive-behaviorists like Aaron Beck, Martin Seligman et. al., as this precise formulation of cognitive causality was first spoken some 2500 years earlier and is attributed to The Buddha (c. 563-c.483 B.C.E.). In Gautama's version, however, the refrain is completed with one further crucial admonition:

> So watch your thinking mind with care
> And let it spring from love
> Born out of concern for all beings.

In Tarot too, the act of cognition is dramatically depicted through the cards; the act of thinking itself is shown to be a contextual unit of affect-imagery, coded by image, color, number, and suit symbolism. Thoughts (i.e., Swords) and their attendant affects are reified in the composition of the card, and placed dynamically into the card's storyline to suggest more intuitively (and true to life) the inseparability of thought and emotion, and thought and behavior. Negative thinking styles, the crux of 'cognitive dysfunction,' including distortion, polarization, catastrophizing, self-fulfilling prophecy, etc., are illustrated in Tarot visually by poignant and sometimes anguished scenes in the cards themselves, particularly in the mental/intellectual suit of Swords (see next page). Core beliefs about self, when set out in the dynamic, pictorial language of Tarot, will carry the greater range of subtlety and nuance (that entwines a belief) than the rather studious word charting and diagramming that normally is practiced in cognitive-behavioral techniques.

Due to Tarot's intrinsic polarities (see Chapter VI), each card will always suggest both the cognitive problem and solution under examination. Tarot's more human and intriguing artistic renderings of these important constructs convey to the depressed or anxious client a certain 'lived' texture and realism that may be otherwise lacking in the cerebral exercises cognitive-behaviorists assign for restructuring and reframing. By placing problematic cards into their larger developmental and functional perspectives within the same suit, or even beside other perceptual possibilities reflected in the deck as a whole, the client is given visual representations which conjure desirable alternatives.

In the examples that follow, for instance, the dysfunctional thinking styles reflected in the 8, 9, and 10 of Swords might be contrasted with better adapted cognitive models as reflected in the Knight, Queen, and King of Swords. Meanings are broken down into Tarot 'spectrums', which will be explained in detail in Chapter VI. But even here one can see impressionistically that cognition is now given visual markers that symbolically represent embodiments of both healthy and unhealthy thinking styles (see diagrams on the next page). Those who scan the word columns beneath each card may be surprised to find certain descriptors that seem contrary to the others. For instance 'rebirth' under the 10 of Swords or 'self-righteous' under the Queen of Swords. This is because Tarot is built around the laws of opposition, and every card will contain a suggested energic polarity. As we shall learn, because Tarot is a multi-level, vision-based, image language, the laws of opposition are expressed implicitly in various contexts.

Dysfunctional Cognitive Styles

8 of Swords

spectrum of:
Interference
oppression
paralysis
guilt
powerlessness
helplessness

9 of Swords

spectrum of:
Distortion
hopelessness
agony
doom
shadow
demons

10 of Swords

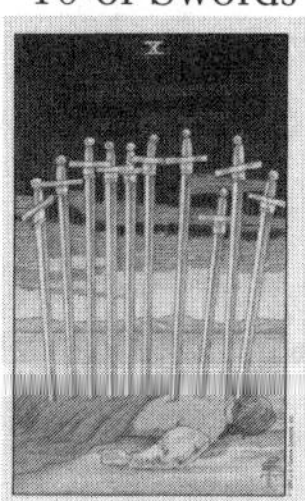

spectrum of:
Surrender
ruin
rebirth
repression
reversal
release

Healthy Cognitive Styles

Knight of Swords

spectrum of:
Insight
focus
discrimination
rationalization
obsession
evaluation
reduction

Queen of Swords

spectrum of:
Accuracy
penetration
honesty
vindication
self-righteousness
congruence
consistency

King of Swords

spectrum of:
Clarity
precision
judgment
intellectualize
judgemental
crystalize
awareness

Brevity and Depth

Mainstream American psychology over the past 50 years, in its efforts to emulate the more standardized, prescriptive, and categorical model of allopathic medicine, has progressively eclipsed an otherwise long line of fascination and concern with the nature of experience and the depths of the human soul. Earlier conventions of psychotherapy which had once couched emotional difficulties in terms of morality, character, and values issues have gradually evolved (or degenerated) into what today has become a psychotherapy that is nearly entirely assimilated into a medical, "health-sickness" framework. It is theorized that the medical model has come into favor not simply because medicine is seen as more 'modern' and 'scientific', but also because medicine largely partakes of the "healer" tradition, evoking age-old attitudes and experiences of "faith and participation in wellness" as much as it relies on physiology or biochemistry. In this regard, Tarot usage tends to resonate more with problems related to former traditional healing concerns, such as moral, character, and values issues rather than the utilitarian alleviation of symptoms, such as anxiety, stress, and trauma.

But as Watchel and Messer note in their scholarly examination of contemporary psychotherapy, in terms of actual therapy hours today, much of the true focus in daily practice remains significantly more oriented towards values questions than medical ones.[19] The 'medicalization' of psychotherapy is inappropriately emphasized. London suggests that the reframing of people's moral and values conflicts into the rhetoric of 'symptoms' of 'disease' or 'disorder' brings to psychotherapy the prestige (and hence curative potential) accruing to medicine and technology in our society.[20] Of course, the implementation of either Tarot or traditional psychotherapy in this antiseptic, labcoated milieu of medical professionalism coupled with actuarial charts, sanctimonious 'gatekeepers', and computer-generated treatment plans, would seem a significantly less suitable healing atmosphere or "holding environment" than the personalized private setting traditionally established for intimate exploration of identity, values, character, pain, and growth issues.

Modern psychotherapy, to withstand the scrutiny (and envy) of the medical model and its confused relationship to it, has itself appeared rather 'schizophrenic' in terms of what it sanctions as 'legitimate' practice. Research and development, study and professional training have been dominated by an aggressive resurgence of academic and institutional interest in objective, scientific empiricism and emphasis on standardized tests and measurements, the brain and psychopharmacolgy, cognition and behavior. Therapists are now trained not simply in the care of the human soul but also as scientific technicians, corporate diplomats, statisticians, medication dispensers, and market-savvy entrepreneurs. In the wake of this long pendulum swing, psychoanalytic and depth approaches have since come under fire for their lack of precision, theoretical top-heaviness, and lengthy requirements for training and treatment, as well as their questionable efficiency, clinical effectiveness and cost effectiveness. In a summary article Hornstein describes the bitterness between these two approaches:

> To the [psycho]analysts, science had nothing to do with method, with controlling variables or counting things.... Constructing a science of the mind could mean only one thing—finding some way to peer through the watery murk of consciousness to the subaquean reality that lay beyond. The efforts of the psychologists, with their bulky equipment and piles of charts and graphs, seemed superficial and largely irrelevant.[21]

Today, political and economic factors as well continue to wage marked effects on which modes of psychotherapy theory or practice will predominate, be funded, studied, marketed, and sought. Newer therapeutic approaches hover over this teetering pivot point, attempting to acknowledge the "subaquean reality that lay beyond" but equally recognizing the merits of empirical study and practical delivery. Adjusting to this field in transition has left many practitioners seeking to retain the art and depth of traditional psychotherapy but tailored within the 'brevity' and 'targeted objectives' models of the medicalization and corporatization of today's changing mental health systems. Walking this narrow tightrope, a natural ally and good friend will be found in Tarot. Less time-consuming and relationship-dependent than traditional analytic and client-centered approaches, Tarot can be directed efficiently as we have discussed, either to reflect unconscious process, to explore and enhance conscious possibilities of self and other, to predict likely future outcomes, and perhaps to create special maps for their achievement as well.

Integrative Approaches

Watchel and Messer, as noted earlier, emphasize that despite strong commitments which a large number of therapists hold for a particular approach, two main contradictions in this century-old field exist today: (a) that there is little evidence that any of the over 400 different schools of psychotherapy is more effective than another, and (b) despite the abundance of societies, institutes, centers, and journals devoted to particular therapy approaches, the majority of practicing therapists today do not identify themselves as adhering to one particular approach, but instead refer to themselves as 'eclectic' or 'integrative'.[22] So-called psychotherapy integration attempts to look beyond the confines of single-school approaches in order to see what can be learned from other perspectives. It is characterized by an openness to various ways of integrating diverse theories and techniques. Here perhaps marks Tarot's clarion call. Notes psychologist Hal Arkowitz:

> Some who hear about psychotherapy integration are puzzled to find out that there is no single overarching theory that is emerging and that neither is there a single well-defined integrative therapy that characterizes the field.... Psychotherapy integration is a way of thinking about and doing psychotherapy that reflects an openness to points of view other than those with which one is most familiar.[23]

Humanism

For instance, the eclectic but humanistically-oriented therapist, less focused on thought processes than is the cognitive-behaviorist, or on assessment of pathological patterns than is the psychodynamic therapist, will find in the Tarot cards striking visual metaphors which reflect the uniqueness and 'wholeness' of the individual, especially aided by a client's direct participation in the process. With his new quest for brevity, the humanistic practitioner is given a virtual roadmap of client possibilities and choices to prioritize. Tarot helps organize dimensions of human experience into discernible categories. Tarot's inherent neutrality furthers the dissipation of expectations and projections of authority placed onto the therapist as redeemer, and returns responsibility and a sense of equality to the client.

In accordance with the humanistic perspective, Tarot is most effective at mirroring the multidimensionality of personhood. Cards that correspond to subpersonalities, roles, underdeveloped potentials, unique talents, or split-off and conflicting parts, when laid out like a symbolic patchwork quilt, present a marvelous collage of personality parts that captures the simultaneous richness and diversity of the individual. Normal pluralism or "multiplicity of self" now becomes articulated through discernible card names, symbols, numbers, and faces for visual identification and differentiation. The "therapeutic method" of interpretation, as we saw in the last chapter, implements a person-centered, non-directive approach to consultation. The client is encouraged to explore his or her own myths, narrations, and spontaneous experiences of each card whether selected randomly or consciously chosen (from face-up cards); prescribed interpretations are curtailed, the reader as 'expert' is culled, and support for the self-discovery process is highly encouraged.

Role-play and dialogue exercises become natural extensions of the symbolic procedure, and the creativity of clinician and client alike is fostered in this context. Gestalt therapists, for instance, might encourage dialogue between parts of a card's composition, or between specific cards in a spread, while emphasizing the here/now awareness of the experience. Tarot is a natural 'hook', its preponderance of human faces and motifs instantly elicit visceral correspondences to personal, interpersonal and family issues. The numinosity of its imagery is evocative of the subtle affects and memories for which language is typically inadequate, and invariably, like some disarming invisible sage, Tarot commands respect and sincerity from those who participate in it (despite the occasional baffled injunction or critical eye brought on by the incredulous rational mind that sits in scrutiny away from the experience).

Each Tarot spread will always carry a unique combination of themes and relationships intelligible to the particular language and life experience of the recipient, varied and distinct from one another as the infinite variance of patterning in snowflakes, or for that matter, the indelible uniqueness of each human drama. The set of possibilities from which these unique card combinations crystallize is indeed large and diverse, but ultimately, it is finite. In a typical ten-card spread, the chances of reproducing an exact duplication are simply staggering when one calculates the probability from a deck of 78 highly differentiated cards. But with Tarot, a transpersonal commonality is equally brought to bear upon human individuality and difference. This perhaps is why Tarot's light shines through all quadrants of the psychological universe and may be applicable in varying degrees to diverse theoretical persuasions.

The symbolic language of Tarot compacts multiple levels of meaning into each card illustration, and synchronistically one soon learns that there are no accidents in Tarot (or life), or to put it differently, accidents themselves are inherently meaningful. Universal themes of human experience unfold within original permutations of the Tarot matrix, reflecting countless variations on common myths, such as the perennial stages of human suffering and attainment, the psychological tasks and demands of human development, and the mysteries and potentials of the human spirit.

Dynamic Therapies

Whereas the cognitive-behaviorist and the eclectic humanist may utilize the cards to specific ends in accordance with their respective approaches, so too will the short-term psychoanalytically-based therapist find her own purposes in Tarot. As mentioned earlier, ancient divination methods share with modern psychodynamic approaches an essential insight into the workings of the human psyche, namely, that beneath each presenting symptom or problem lies an unconscious intelligence trying to communicate something crucial to us about ourselves. In longer term treatment wherein a larger container is provided for the psyche to heal at its natural pace, Tarot may be used sparingly. In such cases, the method is carefully introduced as an adjunctive technique, perhaps in the middle phase of treatment as an insight-engendering tool (when the timeliness of interpretation becomes more appropriate), or at later stages as an integrating agent facilitating eventual closure and termination. But as noted by current changing trends, many practitioners will be left to forego the traditional rhythms and phases of longer term treatment. That unconscious 'intelligence' lying beneath presenting symptoms may now require a gentle push for quicker availability.

Short-term dynamic therapists will find in Tarot an excellent tool for mirroring and illustrating psychological complexity, dualism, defense, and process, particularly as reversed cards in a reading suggest not only conflictual or compromised states of the theme represented but also the symbolic interior (introversive) dimension of the subject's experience (while cards facing upright indicate an 'outward' or extroversive direction). A King of Cups (Minor Arcanum), for example, is seen to correlate with an outer person of authority, be it father or therapist, while the fatherly attributes of the "archetypal Father" embodied by The Emperor card (Major Arcanum), or perhaps The Hierophant, are understood by contrast to reside as 'imagos' innately within the subject himself. Object is clearly differentiated from image. More of this will be said later.

The distinction between object and image undoubtedly aids in the resolution of transference confusion, and when visually portrayed in Tarot, a client may find such distinctions more clearly drawn. From its oracular and independent standpoint, the Tarot often presents transference and countertransference themes through a neutral "third party" (the agency of the cards), thus defusing transferential roadblocks which these emotionally-laden issues often carry. In effect, no one is analyzing the other in the usual timbre; at least temporarily such co-transferences are suspended, presenting a welcome opening and indeed respite from the otherwise intense crucible of scrutiny. At other appropriate interludes, Tarot can be used skillfully to facilitate dialogue pertaining to the therapist/client relationship. Resistance is lessened owing not only to the impersonality of the source, but to the leveling effect which emerges from a shared perception of Tarot's uncanny magic, if we may call it that. When a reading is particularly meaningful, the therapeutic process itself is elevated, at least for the moment, to a level of transcendence that can only be described as an almost mystical reverence shared by client and therapist alike for some unseen intelligence at work.

Newer Methods

With the rapidly shifting postmodernist trends that examine how reality is fundamentally constructed and narrated in the mind of the subject, along with the related sciences of consciousness that seek to integrate quantum physics, cognitive science, phenomenology, the philosophy of mind, shamanic states, artificial intelligence, and transpersonal psychology, the exotica of Tarot when utilized as a tool of psychotherapy should be greeted as no more strange or experimental than other such pioneering techniques which themselves have no discernible precedent in psychotherapy.

Two of many examples of exciting new therapeutic tools and techniques of the 1990s are the MARI Card Test[24] and Thought Field Therapy[25] which we will very briefly introduce in this section. The MARI Card Test is an assessment tool consisting of symbolic shape and color cards that are constructed by the subject into circular designs. It often accompanies a picture drawn by the subject from selected crayons and pastels on an empty sheet of paper that bears the outline of a large circle or mandala. MARI as a projective test taps into the symbol-generating nature of the psyche, likening the contents that emerge to a "blood sample" taken to reflect treatment process and changes at specific intervals. Psychological process and physical illness have indeed been shown by this technique to unfold through "archetypal stages of the great round of mandala."[26] MARI, however, unlike Tarot, is not a therapeutic technique so much as an adjunctive psychological test.

Symbolic interpretation is primarily reductive, and the subject's cards and colors are selected by preference (not randomly as in the Tarot method). Interpretation is based on prescribed meanings for particular symbol/color patterns as developed by Joan Kellog through her careful studies. Complex psychodynamic profiles are thus formulated using MARI both for psychopathological and developmental assessment and, refreshingly, human potentials and spirituality as well. By comparison, however, MARI lacks much of Tarot's multidimensionality, present-centeredness, and versatility. Though it is certainly diagnostic, the MARI process is not numinous, oracular or synchronistic. Tarot is generally more open-ended in interpretation, phenomenological, emotionally captivating, and durable (with its 600 year tradition and evolution). Nevertheless, MARI's controlled experimental studies over repeated trials, its research with special populations, its psychological sophistication, its applicability in assessment, and its careful marketing to professionals are impressive examples for Tarot.

Thought Field Therapy, one of the new "power therapies" of the 90s, uses (of all things arcane) simple gentle finger-tapping on specific meridian points in the body (similar to what an acupuncturist does with a needle) to rapidly alleviate chronic and acute psychological symptoms of distress. In so doing, TFT™ attempts to bypass much of the therapeutic process itself and cut straight to the 'cure'. Based on the body's system of electromagnetic energy, therapists using simple meridian 'algorithms' can in a matter of minutes remarkably reduce if not entirely eliminate a client's subjective units of distress (SUDS) associated with phobias, trauma, anger, and addiction, claiming an unheard of 80-90 percent rate of success.

In their purposes, applications and methods, undoubtedly TFT™ and Tarot are worlds apart, yet they do share certain commonalties relevant to our discussion. As Thought Field Therapy is an adjunctive technique intended for the rapid and enduring alleviation of psychological distress, Tarot, we might say, is an adjunctive technique intended for rapid self-reflection and the creation of enduring meaningful possibilities. Neither is meant to replace the larger therapeutic process which carries other functions as well. One further note: in TFT™ what is termed the "apex problem" alludes to the common tendency for recipients of the treatment, incredulous of the dramatic effects won in a matter of minutes, to ascribe credit for their uncanny success to more familiar factors other than the treatment itself. In Chapter IX we will describe a similar phenomenon that occurs when randomly selected Tarot cards rather mysteriously and incredulously seem to accurately portray a client's subjective experience. Tarot, as we shall see, must deal with an "apex problem" of its own. Finally, in a paper delivered at the annual APA meeting in 1995, TFT's founder Dr. Roger Callahan reminded the audience of a particular section of the preamble to the Ethical Principles of the American Psychological Association which bears repeating here:

> Psychologists are open to new procedures and changes in expectations and values over time.[26]

Notes

[1]Hillman, James and Ventura, Michael, *We've Had a Hundred Years of Psychotherapy and the World's Getting Worse*; San Francisco: Harper, 1992, p. 31.

[2]*The Mystical Core of Organized Religion*; 1989.

[3]Karasu, T.B. (1986). The Specificity Versus Nonspecificity Dilemma: Toward Identifying Therapeutic Change Agents. *American Journal of Psychiatry*, 143, 687-695.

[4]Frank, J.D. (1973, 2nd edition), *Healing and Persuasion*; Baltimore: Johns Hopkins University Press.

[5]Personal correspondence, 1998.

[6]Freud, S. (1964), *New Introductory Lectures*. Standard Edition (vol. 232, pp. 3-182); London: Hogarth. (Original work published 1933).

[7]Bakan, David (1958), *Sigmund Freud and the Jewish Mystical Tradition*; Princeton, NJ: D. Van Norstrand, p. 48.

[8]Fairbairn, W. R. D. (1952), *Psychoanalytic Studies of the Personality*; London: Tavistock Publications and Kegtan Paul, Trench, & Trubner.

[9]Jung, C. G., *The Portable Jung* (edited by Joseph Campbell); New York, Viking Penguin, 1976.

[10]Jung, C. G., *Collected Works*, Vol. 9 Part 1: *The Archetypes and the Collective Unconscious*; Bollingen Series, Princeton University Press, 1969, paragraph 81.

[11]Jung, C. G., *Memories, Dreams, Reflections;* Vintage Books, Random House, 1961, p. 373.

[12]Arrien, Angeles, *The Tarot Handbook: Practical Applications of Ancient Visual Symbols*; Arcus Publishing Company, 1987, p. 18.

[13]Samuels, Andrew, Sorter, Bani, Plant, Fred, A *Critical Dictionary of Jun-*

gian Analysis; Routledge & Kegan Paul, London, 1996, p. 73.

[14]Kalff, Dora, M., *Sandplay: A Psychotherapeutic Approach to the Psyche*; Sigo Press, Boston. 1980.

[15]Fox, Matthew, 1995.

[16]Rosengarten, Arthur, E., *Accessing the Unconscious, A Comparative Study of Dreams, The T.A.T. and Tarot* [doctoral dissertation]; University Microfilms International, Ann Arbor, Michigan, 1985.

[17]Fishman, D. B., & Franks, C. M., *Evolution and Differentiation within Behavior Therapy: A Theoretical and Epistemological Review*. In D. K. Freedheim (Ed.), *History of Psychotherapy: A Century of Change* (pp. 159-196); Washington, DC: American Psychological Association, 1992.

[18]Kendall, P. C., & Bemis, K. M., *Thought and Action in Psychotherapy: The Cognitive Behavioral Approaches*. In M. Hersen, A. E. Kazdin, & A. S. Bellak (Eds.), *The Clinical Psychology Handbook* (pp. 565-592); Elmsford, NY: Pergamon Press, 1983.

[19]Wachtel, Paul L. and Messer, Stanley B., *Theories of Psychotherapy: Origins and Evolution*; American Psychological Association, 1997, pp. 6-11.

[20]London, P., *The Modes and Morals of Psychotherapy* (second edition); Washington D.C., Hemisphere, 1986.

[21]Horstein, 1992.

[22]Wachtel, Paul L. and Messer, Stanley B., *Theories of Psychotherapy: Origins and Evolution*; American Psychological Association, 1997, p. 272.

[23]Kellog, Joan, *Mandala: Path of Beauty; ATMA, Inc., Belleair, Florida, 1978.*

[24]Kellog, 1991.

[25]Callahan, Roger J., and Callahan, Joanne, *Thought Field Therapy* [TM;] Indian Wells, Ca., 1996.

[26]Ibid.

PART TWO

THE PSYCHOLOGY OF TAROT

Chapter V

SYMBOLIC DIMENSIONS

> What is important to remember is that symbols are a universal language that bridge invisible and visible worlds. Within symbolic structures, there are mythic figures that reveal inherent psychological processes of a universal nature.[1]
>
> —Angeles Arrien

> What to the causal view is fact, to the final view is symbol.
>
> —C. G. Jung

Intuitions of Possibility

It should be noted as we begin to delve more deeply into the psychic substance of the deck, that we as travelers to the unknown land of Tarot must be wary of our own assumptions and presuppositions that come from, in a pedestrian sense, where we ourselves come from. The symbols of Tarot are wayshowers, they direct us past the gates (and limitations) of conscious knowledge. They are expressions of everyman, and they are reflections of ourselves as well, beyond what we may be normally aware of. Tarot cards conjure living realms quite distinct from ordinary experience. In this respect, Jung forever expounded on the true function of psychological symbols, that being to point their perceiver towards an unknown reality, in contradistinction to the sign:

> Those conscious contents which give us a clue to the unconscious background are incorrectly called *symbols* by Freud. They are not true symbols, however, since according to his theory they have merely the role of *signs*

> or *symptoms* of the subliminal processes. The true symbol differs essentially from this, and should be understood as *an intuitive idea that cannot yet be formulated in any other or better way*.[1] (Italics mine)

Signs, sometimes mistaken for symbols, are designed to simplify and concretize the known world. In clinical practice, it is the sign which often points to well known and understood syndromes and mental conditions. If I draw a small circle, add short spikes that extend outwards around the circumference, give it a happyface or paint it yellow, we might all recognize a sign of the sun. But if instead, I draw a naked child joyously smiling from the back of an unsaddled white horse, who carries in her left hand a long red banner that waves before a walled garden with ripened sunflowers, and above her sits a serenely smiling orb in all its glory gazing confidently outwards into our eyes, while atop its crown is the Roman numeral XIX—this would more likely qualify as a symbol. In fact, it describes the classic Waite/Smith (Universal) version of Arcanum 19, The Sun. Its meaning includes but is far greater than the celestial body we call sol or sun. Symbols are images whose meaning vastly transcends their content. They are immensely more than they appear to be.

Trump XIX The Sun
Waite/Universal

Tarot symbols, in effect, are not collections of human knowledge so much as intuitions of human possibility. They offer captivating and enigmatic portrayals of psychic life which cannot be simply stated otherwise. In this sense, they play a crucial mediatory role between the known and the unknown and are not to be taken literally or allegorically, for then they would be about something already familiar. Signs, on the other hand, certainly serve a necessary function of their own, and heaven help the road carnage that would ensue if bright red stop signs suddenly became "stop symbols." Tarot symbols, we might say, serve as psychic vehicles that transport their unknown contents to a surfacing consciousness. Creating and expanding consciousness, in fact, may well be the very purpose of life. Notes Edward Edinger:

> The key word is "consciousness." Unfortunately, the experiential meaning of this term is almost impossible to convey abstractly. As with all fundamental aspects of the psyche it transcends the grasp of the intellect. An oblique, symbolic approach is therefore required.[2]

Each of the 78 cards of the full Tarot pack carries a specific, differentiated, discrete, and oblique symbolic meaning emanating, as Buddhist teachers are fond of saying, "from its own side." The vehicle through which such meaning is conveyed has traditionally been called 'divination', admittedly a term quite foreign if not disconcerting to conventional professional parlance and practice. Divination, in its modern psychological context, can be thought of as conscious blind selection, or as I prefer 'empowered randomness'. As we shall see, this fascinating procedure operates within the philosophical parameters of Jungian synchronicity and is inferred in the ancient Buddhist doctrine of dependent co-origination (mutual co-arising). Empowered randomness assumes with great confidence that personal meaning will be accessed from an intelligent nonpersonal source. The medium of that intelligence is the symbol.

A debate in the emerging science of consciousness centers around the co-occurrence of phenomenal and psychological properties of experience. As philosopher David Chalmers laments:

> We have no independent language for describing phenomenal qualities. Although greenness is a distinct sort of sensation with a rich intrinsic character, there is very little that one can say about it other than that it is green. In talking about phenomenal qualities, we generally have to specify the qualities in question in terms of associated external properties, or in terms of associated causal roles. Our language for phenomenal qualities is derivative on our nonphenomenal language.[3]

It seems to me that what is often overlooked in this debate are the unique properties of symbols. J.E. Cirlot, author of the classic *A Dictionary of Symbols* notes the essence of a true symbol "is its ability to express simultaneously the various aspects of the idea it represents."[4] Symbolic expression may include affinity and correspondence to related entities (as the moon corresponds to love), but never reduction to a single conclusion (the moon means love). The latter is considered the "degradation of the symbol." Symbols whose integrity is upheld tend to generate and catalyze great psychic energy. Out of this super-charged bundle of possibility, each Tarot card is a condensed collage of image, number, and color symbolism expressing simultaneously and energically the various aspects of the mystery it represents. In Jung's words, each card is "an intuitive idea which cannot yet be formulated in any other or better way."

Depending on the artist's execution, individual cards may themselves include their own internal symbolism, much say as the fish inside the Ace of Cups is associated with the zodiacal sign of Pisces and the cup itself to the transcendental Chalice of the Holy Grail, or The Empress's red roses serve as a symbol of passion ("dyed from the blood of Aphrodite"). While mastery of each individual symbol is not necessary to grasp a particular card's gestalt meaning, a reading's true interpretive elegance, much as the signature of a "big dream" or the selectivity of a successful poem, is often carried in the detail. Appreciation of symbolic particulars will enhance a reading's richness, but practitioners can still be quite effective without thorough comprehension of a card's every feature. Like less analytical-reductive approaches to dream interpretation or even the Rorschach, Tarot symbols can also be read impressionistically as well.

Beyond Projective Receptacles

Psychologists are mistaken if they believe Tarot symbols are no more than projective receptacles like the provocative Rorschach inkblots or TAT (Thematic Apperception Test) photographs which unconsciously stimulate a subject to project whatever s/he wishes (or wishes not) to see in them. Although the cards surely can and will stimulate unconscious projection, their greater value, like all things of taxing beauty, is in their own inherent 'meaningfulness' emanating from their own side. As Samuels notes, "the symbol is an unconscious invention in answer to a conscious problematic."[3] The meaningfulness, in such cases, is not so much a mental solution as a "feeling experience" which touches the recipient profoundly and intelligently, and which adds greater self-awareness and cohesion, while remaining ultimately mysterious and inexhaustible. While interpretation of a dream will never be entirely complete, the same holds true for Tarot.

Rorschach and TAT illustrations, on the other hand, are meaningless from their own side until the correlation analysis demonstrates a connection—to the clinician—although to the patient himself that connection remains largely unknown and unacknowledged. As meaning is *extrinsic* to the pictured illustrations of such methods, one hardly leaves a Rorschach session feeling emotionally or spiritually touched (in the positive sense of the word). In modern test construction, projective patterns are typically chronicled and categorized from exhaustive data collection and analysis, after which clinical inferences, i.e., their meanings, are then mechanically fashioned from response correlations to pathologic behavioral tendencies.

This perhaps points to the inevitable limitation of the scientific method when applied to the human soul: quanta over qualia. As psychological instruments, there are no agreed upon "correct answers" or established meanings in Rorschach and TAT projective images but rather structural tendencies that reflect either intact, patterned, or grossly disturbed psychological perceptions based on quantitative norms. As Bertrand Russell remarked, "Science is what you know, philosophy is what you don't know." If it walks and talks like large numbers of ducks do, it's likely to be duckish. That much is known. The mystery and meaning of *duckness*, aside from its frequency of appearance under particular circumstances, is left to philosophers, theologians, theoreticians, and perhaps, children to decide. The Tarot cards, by contrast, are themselves *intrinsically* meaningful and offer through such meaning a route to the unconscious in which the patient (querent, subject, etc.) himself chooses, participates in and benefits from. When taken as a whole, the full Tarot deck represents a symbolic compendium of human possibility. And of course, *that which is possible suggests what is naturally able or even likely to occur,* while "most of the things worth doing in the world had been declared impossible before they were done."

Unlike projectives, card illustrations in Tarot often vary from deck to deck owing to the particular emphasis of the artist; however, their essential meanings are consistent (though never exhausted) between decks. This inexhaustibility is due to their archetypal nature, which on a formal level allows for infinite variation dependent upon individual imaginal and artistic expression. For example, in Tarot, a Devil is a Devil no matter where his furtive horns are hung or his entrapping chains are cuffed. Traditional meanings which have been passed down through the ages vary in depth of viewpoint and particular cultural shading or emphasis given by their commentator and era. For instance, in the example of The Devil we find: "destiny, fatality, the Dragon of the Threshold (Papus)"; "ravage, violence, vehemence (Waite)"; "black magic, illness, improper use of force (Gray, Eden)"; etc.

When compared to the modern insights of psychology and psychiatry, however, such tradition often suffers from a naiveté regarding more recent observations of the structural and dynamic aspects of the human psyche. A modern therapist, for example, might see The Devil card as representing in its 'pathologizing aspect' various degrees of self-deception, splitting, projected guilt, manipulation, sociopathy, object attachment, acting-out, sexualizing, perversion, addiction, dissociation ("the devil made me do it"), or obsession. Of course, with the explosion of 20th century psychological science and theory, and its ubiquitous bible—the

DSM—an ample body of research and discussion is now readily available for any one of these pathological behaviors, presenting a tremendous challenge and opportunity for enrichment of Tarot traditions.

The modern therapist will find in the more adaptive aspects of The Devil card, themes pertaining to risk-taking, experimentation, sexual exploration, shadow awareness, paradox, playfulness, disinhibition, and even humor (or "mirth" as Arrien calls it). By employing this pre-modern tool, interpretation using such modern and postmodern constructs has the added value of connecting contemporary themes to historic traditions and universal experiences, satisfying, perhaps, an innate need for inclusion and continuity with a linking mythic heritage and imagery that energizes much of religious and cultural expression. The timelessness of these images makes them universally recognizable, language-independent, and perennially contemporary.

Unfortunately, for those not suffering a particular mental malady, the heritage of Western psychology has been generally lacking in its concern for the non-pathological expressions of human possibility, marking positive human achievements with such dampening accolades as 'normalcy', 'adaptivity', and of course today's grandest psychological compliment—'functionality'—which have become the implied endpoints or objectives of mental life. Consequently, a map of "healthy functioning" is notably lacking in the contemporary psychological archives (though it should be remarked that the differentiation of "higher states" has been the great genius of Eastern, i.e., Buddhist, Taoist, and Yoga psychologies, which will be discussed later on as well). Here again, the Tarot offers Westerners a crucial missing piece of the psychological puzzle: a tradition, a language, and an imagery which reflect human potentials in their proper nuance, dimension, and level of psychological development. Arrien echoes this sentiment:

> ...the inherent value of Tarot, if it were used within a therapeutic context, could be as a counterpart to the DSM-III Manual , which is a psychopathological diagnostic manual defining categories of dysfunctional behaviors, whereas the Tarot could be used as a psycho-mythological manual. It supports and serves as a diagnostic mechanism enabling persons

to recognize their inherent wisdom, which is logos, their love nature, which is eros.[5]

The Minor Arcana of Tarot (the 40 pips and 16 courts) offers rich, dynamic, and humane reflections of personality development in an imagery that resonates with the Western psyche, capturing both its predicaments and its curiosity. The Major Arcana (Magician to World, with a touch of The Fool) portrays Tarot's archetypal and esoteric levels, pointing to universal psychological motifs and transformational potentials. In our Devil example, transpersonally (or spiritually), we might say, the card is an expression of humanity's errant or dark side in need of light, reflecting the individual or collective shadow, though now gaining an acknowledged visibility from its pictorial power. The Devil card as such is not unlike the provocative 'wrathful deities' portrayed in mandala thankas of Tantric Buddhism or the startling monstrosities beautified in modern art.

Such symbolic iconographies carry exaggerated personifications of false identification with power, aggression, perversion and control (egotism). With a deliberate and conscious courtship of such symbolism, through meditation, insight, artistic expression, contemplation, active imagination or simply by their perceptual presence alone, these large but splitoff reserves of psychic energy embedded in this (or any card's) symbolism can be elevated to conscious awareness, observed and studied. Eventually, one hopes, they can be transformed and integrated into the whole self, thus enlarging and further differentiating individual identity. In a Tarot reading, a window of self-study is thereby opened to safely consider such shadow themes, teaching and empowering one to become master and maker of one's fate, in all its facets, rather than its victim and/or victimizer. Surely it is in the latter where the causes of man's suffering reside and recycle.

Levels of Meaning

Cirlot notes that for most psychologists the indelible meanings (or archetypes) carried in each card reside wholly in the mind and are then projected outwards upon Nature, while orientalists and esoteric thinkers, on the other hand, base symbolism upon the incontrovertible metaphysical equation: macrocosm=microcosm. In the latter view, the psyche is considered to be as much a function of the world as the converse, with mind and matter understood as two aspects of one unified field much as quantum physicists have demonstrated. Curiously, these two camps split along the same fault lines as those between dualistic cognitive scientists on the one hand, and holistic theorists and idealistic philosophers on the other.

Most recently, the debate has stimulated an emerging cross-fertilization of psychologists and, surprisingly enough, environmentalists, who have banded together to form a movement appropriately called 'ecopsychology'. Their rallying cry is expressed in James Hillman's observation: "an individual's harmony with his or her 'own deep self' requires not merely a journey to the interior but a harmonizing with the environmental world."[6] Tarot's purient world of psychical ideals interacting with an outside intervention of random selection may be seen to recreate nothing less natural than the undisturbed perfection of a virgin forest's ecosystem. Curiously, the occult dictum, "As above, so below" (later to be reframed by Goethe "as without, so within"), thus finds today a postmodern ally in deep ecology and "green" psychology. As without, so within.

In *Psychology and Religion* Jung notes: "The symbol always ranks below the level of the mystery it seeks to describe."[7] If the iridescent diamond holds the great mystery we seek, then its sparkling shape and color are merely means to this end. Its physical placement within the earth now takes on spatial metaphorical significance. As a symbol, it can be approached from either a horizontal or vertical vantage point of meaning. From a depth perspective, one can imagine a sort of subterranean elevator shaft which travels up and down the many levels of psyche and cosmos. Only from the ground floor can one move directly outwards to apprehend the objective universe at large. This is what is meant by *horizontal* movement. Find the lobby and exit to the countless material realms of existence on the horizon, as in this case, the sparkling gem itself.

Horizontally, that is, *exoterically*, Tarot symbols capture multiple aspects of the people, places, projects, pleasures, predicaments, and problems that fill our outer public lives. Imbuing these outer forms with numinous, mysterious symbols adds dimension and context to everyday experience. Life as we formerly knew it, we could say, has now become animated through certain hints of meaning and mystery. In one case, a marriage is viewed within the laws of a particular water element ("fluid, mercurial, deep"), or in another case, a job position is seen to stimulate an unacknowledged conflict between opposing Major Arcana (archetypal) and Minor Arcana (egoic) energies competing within the subject. In this way a client is given a meaningful symbolic context to the themes that fill his or her life.

For the rest, one either descends down the many levels of the subjective psyche or ascends up to the etheric heights of the gods. This is what is meant by *vertical* movement and points to regions of the interior psyche. Find the lower and upper floors and exit to the realms of essential or etheric reality, i.e., the depth dimensions. With our diamond symbol, we might imagine "the impenetrable brilliance of the mystic center" or with less psychopomp, "the diamond-like hardness" of a particular ego defense mechanism.

Residing in these subjective spheres are the soul and spirit of humankind, its conscience and memory, its imagination and emotions. Spatial dimensions of 'upper' and 'lower' are merely metaphors of psychological space and should not be taken literally. The water element alluded to in the previous example of marriage may now vertically come to signify a 'process dimension' of separation/individuation, or perhaps some symbolic flow of change within the individual. The Queen of Cups, perhaps, recommends forgiveness and self-nurturing, while Temperance (with its "one foot on land, one foot in water") counsels blending and perseverance. In all, interpretative 'scope' is counterbalanced with depth and height, horizontal objectivity is counterbalanced with vertical subjectivity. An illustrated case may be in order here. Take The World card for example.

XXI The World
Tarot de Marseilles (1761)

In Trump 21, The World card (Marseilles), the eagle appearing above right symbolizes horizontally (i.e., objectively) worldly 'ascent', perhaps representing an outer career or relational aspiration involving flight and journey. Vertically, however, the eagle is a metaphor for one's spiritual ascent towards the higher reaches of subjective reality, that is, psychological wholeness or spiritual enlightenment. On this same card, the lion appearing below represents horizontally the earthly opponent of the eagle in the sky, a champion of great physical strength, self-assertion, and regal dignity. Vertically, however, the lion may be seen as a metaphorical index of latent passions or ferocious instinct. Moreover, the eagle and the lion are merely two of six symbols that appear in The World card, and they are by no means the most prominent. Esoterically, a select region within the interior operating throughout Tarot, the eagle is associated with the astrological sign of Scorpio and points to elemental water, signifying the Maternal, the Great Mother, as well as the unfathomable and mysterious well of Wisdom contained within the subconscious mind. The lion carries traditional associations with the element of fire, the Sun (and the astrological symbol of Leo) and corresponds principally to alchemical gold or "the subterranean sun," alluding to divine intelligence.

Each of these levels captures a certain band within the card's spectrum of possibility, and some will be more conscious than others.

In most introductory Tarot texts, color and number symbolism (numerology) are discussed and included in the general description of each card. In The World card, the number 21 implies a root connection to the 3 (21=2+1=3) and thus is tied in significance to Trump 3, The Empress (Earth Goddess archetype). Such numerological connections are never lost in Tarot, and with greater study these more subtle correspondences become meaningful as they illustrate one card's archetypal affinities and hidden ties with another.

Color symbolism, notes Cirlot, usually derives from one of the following sources: (1) the inherent characteristic of each color, perceived intuitively as objective fact; (2) the relationship between a color and the planetary symbol traditionally linked with it; or (3) the relationship which elementary, primitive logic perceives. Modern psychology and psychoanalysis seem to place more weight upon the third of these formulas than even the first.

Should the card's position be inverted (i.e., reversed), the significance is altered again to emphasize either the conflictual nature of the card's meaning and/or its internalized, hidden, or subjective aspect. Therapists using Tarot will do well to utilize reversals, as they often carry disturbed content of maladaptation, but nevertheless illustrate in graphic terms the psychological truism that it is never so much the 'content' of one's situation that breeds experience, whether negative or positive, as one's cognitive and emotional relationship to that content. As our discussion develops, more will be said of reversals.

The Numinosum

When a Tarot card is taken as a whole, with its many symbolic levels, it carries an integrated 'resonance' or rhythm which operates 'magically' to instill an emotional connection to its meaning. A certain unusual and captivating energy is then released. By magical, in contrast to 'magical thinking' ("the moon is made of green cheese"), we are speaking not so much of the "magical arts" such as natural, hermetic, ceremonial, or even stage magic, but more the magical *experience* of "mysterious enchantment" *(Random House College Dictionary)* that tingles the spine and inspires the spirit. Even the most secular of therapists (who as a group typically abhor magic) certainly are familiar with the related exhilarations and elations that accompany an unusually powerful session. It is the excitement and awe one feels in the living presence of mystery, discovery, change, and wisdom. This descriptive, phenomenological connotation for magic is akin to what Jung calls the 'numinosum':

> A dynamic agency or effect not caused by an arbitrary act of will.... The numinosum is either a quality belonging to a visible object or the influence of an invisible presence that causes a peculiar alteration of consciousness....[7]

Jung borrowed the term 'numinous' from theologian Rudolf Otto to describe the essence of religious experience outside of ordinary experience which remains inexpressible and "eludes apprehension in terms of concepts."[8] For Otto, the numinosum stirs the soul with a peculiar affective state:

> ...it may at times come sweeping like a gentle tide, pervading the mind with a tranquil mood of deepest worship...[or] it may burst in sudden eruption up from the depths of the soul with spasms and convulsions.[9]

Yet talk of such metaphysically-shaded states and religious openings might seem better suited for Merlin types or mystical crusaders, not quite the standard fare in the worldly province of the hard-toiling therapist's office. Of course there are notable exceptions in this regard, given that the humanistic therapist describes certain transcendent states as "peak experiences," the hypnotherapist suspends the ego through trance, the behaviorist reinforces progressive relaxation, pastoral counselors treat "spiritual emergency" and the transpersonal psychologist speaks of "altered states." Corbett makes a partial list of how the experience of numinosity is likely to appear relative to psychological practice: as a numinous dream, a waking vision, an experience in the body, within a relationship (including transferences), in the wilderness, by aesthetic or creative means, as a synchronistic event.[10] Tarot, naturally, falls into the final category.

Corbett further notes that the nature of this realm of experience opens the subject to the risk of being seen as either inflated, hysterical or frankly psychotic. In more everyday practice terms, it is likely that the majority of therapists who have dealt with 'the numinosum' firsthand have indeed done so through its pathological side, whether in hospitalizing the floridly psychotic patient for his disturbed ramblings of a pseudo-religious nature, attempting to subdue the love-crazed recklessness brought on by Cupid's shenanigans, or even when having to confront the expansive fantasies of the wired adolescent 'fried' on psychedelics, or for that matter, "dungeons and dragons," "Myst" or whatever. Samuels (1987) notes: "an experience of the numinosum is more than an experience of a tremendous and compelling force; it is a confrontation with a force that implies a not-yet-disclosed, attractive and fateful meaning."[11]

But here, paradoxically, is suggested an explanation for why Tarot consultation may actually soften the intensity of the numinosum, reducing it, as it were, to a quiet expectation and a containable urge. For such magical properties to emerge, Jung felt that a prior readiness, conscious or otherwise, to trust a transcendent power was a necessary prerequisite. With Tarot that prerequisite is immediately attained. Whether explicitly stated or simply implied, divination is itself a prescribed method (all the more so when administered by a trusted professional) whose very purpose is to access undisclosed, attractive, and fateful symbols of considerable psychic force.

From the outset, due to its odd manner of random selection, a mysterious and exotic mechanism is assumed to operate and is accepted simply as part and parcel of Tarot's normal workings; 'magical' effects from the cards are more or less greeted as predictably as rainbows after rain. Unlike the numinous emotions precipitated by rare events (the birth of a child, the view from a mountain peak, the dream of flying) which tend to erupt with great force (and evaporate nearly as fast), the numinosum stimulated in Tarot, by comparison, is received in a relatively calm and matter-of-fact manner. The Tarot method itself seems the natural midwife of such birthings. Perhaps even more unbelievable than the uncanny and statistically improbable 'accuracy' of divined cards in a reading is the relative ease and comfort with which these strange happenings are experienced and accepted by a subject.

With Tarot, however, it is not the natural spectacle of a setting sun that casts a haunting purple aura, but The Hanged Man card imploring our disengagement from momentary struggle, or perhaps the 5 of Cups echoing our need to soulfully grieve. It is not the aerial maneuvers of a superb bald hoopster that inspire our awe, but the synchronicity of The Wheel of Fortune card that falls in our future, with all its multileveled symbolic implications. These things really matter. After all, this is not television, this is our life.

But here we may be getting a little ahead of ourselves. Before we can fairly present and evaluate the accuracy of a Tarot reading, and indeed its numinosity, we must first learn more of the underlying structure of Tarot itself. In the following chapters we take a closer look at some of the essential spectrums operating throughout the deck of human possibility.

Notes

[1]Jung, C. G., *The Collected Works* (Bollingen Series XV); Trans. R.F.C. Hull; Princeton University Press, paragraph 105.

[2]Edinger, Edward F., *The Creation of Consciousness: Jung's Myth for Modern Man*; Inner City Books, 1984.

[3]Chalmers, David J., *The Conscious Mind: In Search of a Fundamental Theory*; Oxford University Press, 1996, p.22.

[4]Cirlot, J. E., *A Dictionary of Symbols* (Second Edition); Routledge & Kegan Paul Ltd., London, 1962, p. xxxi.

[5]Arrien, Angeles, *The Tarot Handbook: Practical Applications of Ancient Visual Symbols;* Arcus Publishing Company, 1987, p. 19.

[6] Hillman, James, "A Psyche the Size of the Earth," in Roszak, Theodore, Gomes, Mary E., Kanner, Allen D., *Ecopsychology: Restoring the Earth/Healing the Mind*; Sierra Club Books, San Francisco, 1995, p. xvii).

[7] Jung, C. G., *Psychology and Religion* [Based on the Terry Lectures]; Yale University Press, New Haven, 1938.

[8]Jung, C. G., *The Collected Works* (Bollingen Series XI); Trans. R.F.C. Hull. Princeton University Press, paragraph 6.

[9] Otto, Rudolf (1917), *The Idea of the Holy*; Oxford Press, 1923, p.12.

[10] Corbett, Lionel, *The Religious Function of the Psyche*; Routledge, 1996, p. 15.

[11] Samuels, Andrew, Shorter, Bani, and Plant, Fred, A *Critical Dictionary of Jungian Analysis*; Routledge & Kegan Paul Ltd, New York, 1987, p. 100.

Chapter VI

THE LAWS OF OPPOSITION

> The opposite of a correct statement is a false statement. The opposite of a profound truth may well be another profound truth.
>
> —Niels Bohr

Principles of Opposition

Since Aristotle's pioneering treatises in *Categories of Interpretation* and *Metaphysics* the concept of opposition has been shown in Western philosophical traditions to express a natural propensity of human thought. Opposition appears to be a universal concept suggesting the quality of being "over against" or "being so far apart as to be or seem irreconcilable" [Webster's New Collegiate Dictionary, 1974]. Word equivalents are found throughout the Indo-European family of languages including Greek, Latin, and Sanskrit, as well as related designations in Egyptian hieroglyphs, Chinese, Hebrew, Austronesian languages, and one suspects, all human languages. The inherency of opposition as a concept is thought to begin with the human capacity to make spatial differentiations of location, relative direction, and distance the prerequisites for coping with the material environment, including, of course, other human bodies.[1]

The psychological implications of opposition extend back considerably further to the mystical writings of the Chinese Taoist sages like Lao Tsu and Chuang Tsu, and to the great Pre-Socratic Greek mystic, Heraclitus. Notes Jung:

> Old Heraclitus, who was indeed a very great sage, discovered the most marvelous of all psychological laws: the regulative function of opposites. He called it *enantiodromia*, a running contrariwise, by which he meant that sooner or later everything runs into its opposite.[2]

Through the laws of enantiodromia, sooner or later, even our postmodern obsessions with technology and information shall in time, one may hope, run into their own opposites, simplicity and being. Friends one day shall become enemies, enemies friends; and cock-sure cognitive scientists, behavioral psychologists, and med-dispensing psychiatrists will at last turn to Tarot, the deck of human possibility. For it is in Tarot that the laws of opposition, "the most marvelous of all psychological laws," are most eloquently expressed and communicated.

Due to Tarot's essential non-verbal, visual, and symbolic nature, opposition arrives economically through multiple routes. Ordinary linguistic conventions expressed through alphabetic 'sound-based' languages (i.e., all Indo-European derivatives) tend to force whole, multi-faceted constructs into one-sided divisions that obscure intrinsic opposition and polarity (e.g., "Today I am happy"). When one side of any coin is posited, however, quite naturally the other side instantly co-arises (either consciously or unconsciously) vying like a dismissed sibling for reentry into the whole equation. In English, for example, there is typically a scarcity of single words that combine oppositions and are multivalent. Referred to as 'antagonyms' or 'contronyms' (Lederer, Richard, 1989), they tend to be appreciated more as linguistic novelties than psycholinguistic maps bearing the laws of opposites. For example, the antagonym 'awful' can at once mean either "extremely unpleasant," or quite to the contrary, "awe-inspiring." 'Last' can connote, paradoxically, 'just prior' or else 'final' as in "My last book will be my last publication." 'Anxious' connotes both "mental distress due to apprehension of danger" ("We were anxious about the nearby gunshots") or else the very opposite—eager or looking forward to, as in "I was anxious for the reading to begin."

Though awkward to our ears, even forced word blends such as "Today I am *happy/sad*" reflect actual experience *as it is lived* within its innate oppositional matrix (as in response to the above question, "How do you feel today on your 50th birthday?") Answer: "Happy/sad." Opposition, as such, is perhaps most evident in experiences that are rich in emotion. However, descriptors that retain their intrinsic polarities are best captured not through words, but through visual symbols or pictures. As a picture is worth a thousand words, assures Confucius, it is well known that Chinese writing is unique in that it does not employ an alphabet, but rather characters or ideograms that were originally pictures (symbols) or conventional signs. Notes Alan Watts:

> The ear cannot detect as many variables at the same time as the eye, for sound is a slower vibration than light. Alphabetic writing is a representation of sound, whereas the ideogram represents vision and, furthermore, represents the world directly, not being a sign for a sound which is the name of a thing.[3]

What is lacking in verbal constructions is symbolic depth, that is, the ability to express simultaneously the various aspects of the idea (or emotion) represented. As the great wordsmith Dan Quayle characteristically notes: "verbosity leads to unclear, inarticulate things." However in Tarot, a vision-based image language, ideas including the laws of opposition are expressed pictorially and can be perceived and interpreted at simultaneous levels of reality; for our purposes, we may describe these as *the structural, numerological, dimensional, and directional* levels of meaning. *Structurally*, for instance, the presence of opposition is found in at least three areas: (1) in the dueling interactions between the Majors and Minors; (2) in the elemental oppositions between suits; and (3) in the synchronistic conjoining of card with spread position. Let's first examine the case of Major/Minor opposition.

As tarotists are well aware, a pip or court card's significance will be greatly diminished when clustered around the more archetypally-charged trump card, or in the least, its impact will be eclipsed by the Major's superior psychic energy and scope of meaning.

Imagine, if you will, the 5 of Wands when 'crossed' by the Major Arcana Star card (Trump XVII), or for that matter, imagine a minor spat with your husband over morning coffee when 'crossed' by the triumphal newspaper headlines: "AIRFORCE CONFIRMS FIRST CONTACT WITH EXTRATERRESTIAL CRAFT." The relationship is equivalent dynamically to the juxtaposition of minutia and miracle, ego and archetype, the mundane and the sacred, or perhaps, the individual and the cosmos. In each case the more universal and transpersonal energies invariably oppose and typically outshine the lesser will of the individual ego. Existential awareness itself is generated through such tensions and accounts for much of life's animation, struggle, and moral philosophizing. According to Jung:

> Every energic phenomenon (and there is no phenomenon that is not energic) consists of pairs of opposites: beginning and end, above and below, hot and cold, earlier and later, cause and effect, etc.[4]

A related phenomenon pertains to elemental values (water, air, fire, earth) that may also polarize the energy of a reading. Any pattern, preponderance, or notable absence of a particular element/suit will activate (constellate) 'elemental' oppositions in the subject's unconscious, much as the compensatory framework found in Jungian typological categories that posit "superior/inferior" personality proclivities and polarizations. A strong "thinking type" like the Knight of Swords, for instance, often dreams in richly evocative colors or else effusively sentimental feeling tones; such is regarded analytically as compensation between opposites, namely, between conscious thinking and unconscious feeling. In Tarot as in Jungian typology, Swords (air/thinking) are considered opposed to Cups (water/feeling), and Pentacles (earth/sensation) opposed to Wands (fire/intuition).

Besides these implicit and subtle unconscious compensations, structural oppositions are often explicit and obvious as well. Witness a reading that has inquired about a new love interest, for instance, where the preponderance of cards drawn are found in either Swords or Cups, and one soon discovers an explicit opposition between "head and heart." A certain transparency is now brought in large precise brushstrokes to what has been otherwise left semi-conscious or unacknowledged (to put it charitably) in the subject's awareness. Another reading focuses on solving a work problem—the marketing strategy of a specific widgit—and reveals patterned oppositions between various Wands and Pentacles, suggesting a tension between intuitive and practical approaches to the problem. Often such oppositions provide the needed "whack on the head" that leads to creative brainstorms and alternative solutions. Elemental affinities, neutralities, and antagonisms also fall within this structural category of opposition, such as the natural antagonism between fire and water, the neutrality between fire and earth, or even the affinity between fire and air. Gender oppositions might be added to this category as well, with Swords and Wands associated with the masculine (the yang), Cups and Pentacles with the feminine (the yin). Encountering such oppositions guards against the imbalances of one-sided thinking and is helpful in rounding out one's vision of the whole.

A third case of structural opposition (see illustration on the next page) involves card to spread position, wherein opposition is set in motion by the structural pairing of randomly selected card to fixed constant position, instigating an interaction between sheer randomness and intentional design. For example, imagine the dynamic tension between the randomly selected 'Death card' when appearing in the predesigned 'past' position—leaving the querent to consider the spectrums of Death in the context of her past history. "I felt reborn after the death of my marriage," one might associate, or "when I left the church it was kind of a death of my childhood beliefs." But note how the tension of this synchronicity strikingly shifts when the same randomly selected 'Death card' appears instead in the prefigured 'future' position. Associations will now take a decidedly different track, gravitating towards something as yet unmanifest, potentially dangerous, perhaps anxiety-ridden, impermanent and changing. No doubt quite a different tinge of meaning is stimulated.

In either case, however, we mark the built-in opposition between variability and constancy, randomness and fixity. Such opposition mirrors the structure of everyday life where 'the known' invariably rubs up against 'the unknown', the expected interfaces with the unexpected. In a real sense, Tarot's deliberate structuring of randomness and chaos with fixity and order brings

Structural Opposition

Opposition between Card and Position

Corresponds to: variability to constancy
randomness to fixity
unknown to known

4. Past Influence

XIII DEATH

10. Future Outcome

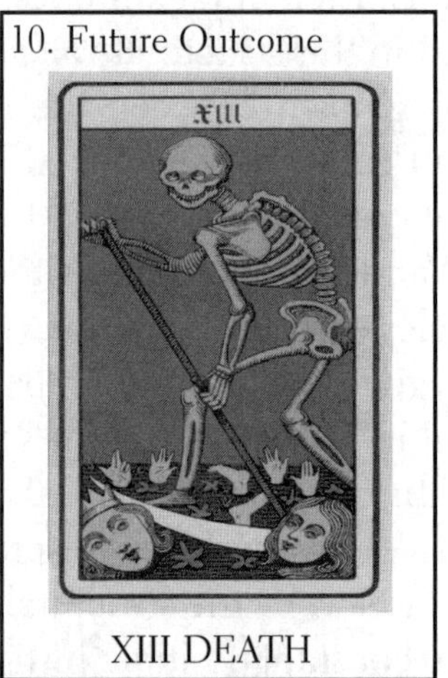

XIII DEATH

psychological reflection closer to the lived natural world. Divination, we might say, returns the unpredictable to its proper lofty status in the scheme of things. In each of the areas noted above, Tarot's inherent *structure* engages the subject's psyche to encounter the realm of opposites.

Number Opposition

Numerology, of course, assumes that numbers are appreciated *qualitatively* for their symbolic implications rather than quantitatively for their mathematic values (although the latter may be seen as a subset of the former). The number two, the first real number of relationship and opposition, is naturally of the most primary and metaphysically essential "number archetypes" of all human experience. Twos are differentiated in each of the four Tarot suits but also in various partitioned examples within a single card where they have been 'split-off' from other number aggregates as for instance, the 7 of Swords (Waite/Universal) where the illustration shows five swords grasped by a human figure while two have been discarded to the ground.

The card suggests the figure has abandoned a former allegiance represented by the two fallen swords; moreover, the five that are 'grasped' are themselves divided in sets of two and three swords. In keeping with the psychological belief that we perceive and construct our worlds primarily through relational contexts, we find implicit themes of twoness and opposition throughout the numerology of Tarot.

Split-Off Two's in the Seven of Swords

In the Majors, opposition is primarily rooted in Trump II, The High Priestess, who connotes "initiation into the law of opposites." The Priestess, however, is well connected to a fine lineage of "number cousins" that likewise represent themes of opposition in the Major Arcana, including: The Emperor (IV)—representing "forming the opposites," The Lovers (VI)—"combining the opposites," Strength (VIII)—"embodying the opposites," Justice (XI)—"balancing the opposites,"—Temperance (XIV)—"blending the opposites," The Devil (XV)—"separating the opposites," Judgment (XX)—"proclaiming the opposites," and finally The World (XXI)—"integrating the opposites." Of course, two 2s, so to speak, form the number insignia of the full family of '22' trump cards. The Fool, which carries no number at all (zero), is perhaps best understand as the condition that both precedes and supersedes formal existence itself, suggesting "absence of or the extinguishing of opposites."

Dimensional Opposition

Dimensional opposition is expressed by vertical and horizontal (exterior/interior) levels of interpretation. A passing stranger's innocuous glance may go unnoticed on a busy street, unregistered amidst the undifferentiated waves of extraneous stimuli. Or else it can trigger tidepools of forgotten memory and emotion and precipitate hours of private fantasy and pages of personal diary in an acutely sensitive observer, while objectively speaking, this momentary passing would seem to be most inconsequential. Dimensional opposition points to the polarity existing between exterior and interior dimensions of subjective experience, the horizontal and vertical levels described in the previous chapter.

Depending on the subject's point of reference, a selected Tarot card may say little about her outer life but volumes about her inner world and its blindspots, or vice versa. Much will depend on the dimension she chooses to address. This often is witnessed when a questioner asks about 'work' and gets answers about 'self' (perhaps to her initial disappointment), or else inquires about her happiness and is barraged with symbols of misery. Tarot, in such cases, has certainly done its job—only it has interpreted the question from a different angle than was consciously expected by the questioner. I recall once consulting the cards to gain more insight into my financial planning and family budgeting and was struck by a pattern of cards that carried strong qualities of a dreamy, sentimental and feeling nature. Hardly things I would address with my accountant. The response quite unexpectedly opened my eyes, however, to include certain emotionally-tinged preferences which technically made little financial sense, but were nonetheless important factors in my personal relationship to money.

This is often the way of the psyche and the way of Tarot. Whether things indeed "happen for a reason" is debatable, but that we seem unconsciously to attract what is most needed (though not necessarily wanted) underscores the undeniable intelligence of the natural order. Themes of opposition often operate simultaneously on multiple dimensions of meaning for every subject, many of which are otherwise short-shrifted in conventional language usage or in conventional psychological treatment. The Tarot reader does not so much obsessively seek to exhaust each and every dimension of opposition as skillfully discover which dimension(s) are presently meaningful (and emotionally charged) to the client.

Directional Opposition

Finally, a fourth level of opposition—*directionality*—is signaled by the upright or upside-down direction of the cards. It is here that we learn rather quickly a card's energic path, whether extroversive or introversive, expansive or contractive, prospective or regressive, positive or negative. The Chariot's upright direction, for instance, may signal outer expansion, interaction, challenge, and industry. Its energic disposition is definitely extroverted and travels outwards towards greater participation with the world. But were that Chariot reversed, quite a different spectrum of possibility is suggested, e.g., inner expansion, or in some cases, neurotic expansion, or perhaps neurotic contraction. Now that the card's energy is introjected back onto the self, the Charioteer's natural surge outwards is either thwarted in purpose, or else intentionally redirected towards some inner mission. But again, it is the tension between such oppositions, like The Chariot's polarity of expansion/contraction, that animates a card's dynamic impact and supplies its depth and life force; without it, a card grows anemic in purpose and empty of substance. Notes the ancient Chinese sage Lao Tsu in the classic *Tao Te Ching* (6th century B.C.E.):

> That which shrinks
> Must first expand.
> That which fails
> Must first be strong.
> That which is cast down
> Must first be raised.
> Before receiving
> There must be giving.
>
> This is called perception of the nature of things. [5]

Imitating the poetics of the great sage, if I may be so impudent, I have created two updated versions which attempt to convey similar sentiments for the practice of Tarot and Psychology:

(Lao Tsu)	(Rosengarten)	
Tao	**Psychology**	**Tarot**
That which shrinks	He who shrinks	That which is possible
Must first expand.	Must first amplify.	Must first be imagined.
That which fails	That which ails	That which pales
Must first be strong.	Must first be healthy.	Must first be limitless.
That which is cast down	That which is repressed	So below
Must first be raised.	Must first be conscious.	As above.
Before receiving	Before insight	Before serendipity
There must be giving.	There must be disclosure.	There must be divination.

This is called perception of the nature of things.

Opposition, Harmony, and Change

To illustrate the above distinctions we might begin with one example from the deck, perhaps the 2 of Pentacles chosen for its numerology, reversed for its directionality, and placed in the second position, 'the obstacle,' for its structure. In terms of its dimensionality, let us begin with the objective, horizontal level of interpretation that reflects upon the exterior world outside of us. Edinger writes:

> The experience of consciousness is made up of two factors, 'knowing' and 'with-ness' i.e. knowing in the presence of an 'other' in a setting of twoness. Symbolically the number two refers to the opposites. We thus reach the conclusion that consciousness is somehow born out of the experience of opposites.[6]

In each of the suits, 'twos' express this birth of consciousness within the dynamic tension between opposites. In our example of the 2 of Pentacles (Disks), the element is earth, so we are concerned primarily with the realm of physical things, embodiments, and material reality; the dynamic tensions portrayed in the 2 of Pentacles would thus involve solid objects of some kind. In therapy situations, or equally in non-clinical contexts as well, Pentacles apply not simply to physical, somatic or financial concerns, but more generally to the psychological operations of construction, concretization, and objectification of experience. Pentacles reflect spirit in matter and point us to our most basic level of organization, the physical. To explore the 2 of Pentacles in greater depth, I have included three examples to better calibrate the archetypal threads running through artistic executions:

Marseilles **Universal/Waite** **Crowley/Thoth**

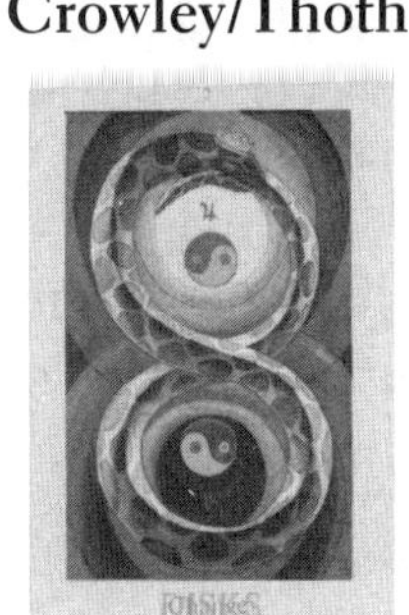

In all three classic versions of the 2 of Pentacles the symbolic connotation of the card is "harmonious change." The imagery suggests these graceful transitions are a product of a careful balancing of the essential polarities or opposites within things. In the original Marseilles version published in 1761 by Nicolas Conver, the two pentacles (coins or disks) are joined by a flowering symbol of infinity, the lemniscate. The card illustrates an elegant cyclical flow of twoness in dynamic balance. In the two modern 20th century decks, this central theme is carried over, but embellished with supporting symbols to expand the card's character and meaning.

In the Waite version, a juggler is seen dancing near the sea, symbol of unconscious depths. The pentacles are again connected through a lemniscate (symbol of infinity), though here the act of juggling is strongly suggested, particularly as the art of juggling carries the equilibrium and rhythm necessary to foster the skillful maintenance and balance of dual realities. In the Thoth deck (on the right), the lemniscate is incorporated into the archetypal 'uroborus,' the coiled serpent biting its own tail. The uroborus symbolizes a primal state of awareness involving darkness and self-destruction but also fecundity and potential creativity, a state which is believed to exist before primal opposites are first differentiated. Situated within the lemniscate of the serpent's coils are displayed two pentacles now bearing the Chinese symbol of Tao, universal principle of polarity (yang/yin). In its esoteric meaning, the yin/yang principle is not what we ordinarily call a dualism, but rather, to quote Alan Watts:

> an explicit duality expressing an implicit unity.... Opposites are like the different, but inseparable, sides of a coin, the poles of a magnet, or pulse and interval in any vibration. There is never the ultimate possibility that either one will win over the other, for they are more like lovers wrestling than enemies fighting.[7]

Lexicographer Adrian Room in her introduction to *Dictionary of Contrasting Pairs* makes the following related observation:

> When contrasting words are combined ('good and evil', 'for better for worse') as distinct from being opposed ('Many are called but few are chosen'), the result is a totality of concept, so that 'male and female' implies *all* humans, regardless of sex, but 'male or female' points to the difference between the two sexes.[8]

In each of our three Tarot illustrations above we see that themes of change are intimately tied to themes of polarity. Linguistically-speaking a là Room, a balancing of opposites, the geist of the 2 of Pentacles, is synonymous with a *combining* of the contrasting pairs (such as "life *and* death" or simply, "life/death"), whereas imbalance between opposites implies the *opposing* of contrasted pairs ("life *or* death"). Either operation falls within the realm of opposition. Still, beyond the curiosity of so-called 'antagonyms', the special act of combining (opposites) bears the synthetic fruits of consciousness, i.e., inclusion, integration, balance, and expansion, whereas the act of opposing (opposites) brings exclusion, fragmentation, and stagnation. In Psychology, the distinction is reflected in the prefix 'counter' which, according to Reber in *The Dictionary of Psychology* (1985):

> generally means opposed but with two different connotations (a) *against*, as in countersuggestion or counteract; (b) *complementary or reciprocal*, as in counterpart.

Both operations, regardless, relate to the framework in which psychological explanation is structured. To follow our example a bit further, the (opposed) contrasting pair "life or death"—when put in *combination*—expresses an implicit unity between opposite poles of a spectrum, that is, "life *and* death" are now seen as constituents of the larger spectrum 'existence'. On the other hand, the opposed construction "life *or* death" more narrowly suggests struggle and competition between two existential adversaries.

Suppose the 2 of Pentacles were reversed, or else situated in the 'obstacle' position. We might then infer from these directional and structural coordinates not only that "harmonious change" is impeded in this placement, but that contrasting pairs are currently opposed (rather than combined). We thus assume that adversarial relationships pertaining to earthly embodiments (Pentacles) have become the rule. Additionally, by employing dimensionality to this equation, with its elevator ride up and down multiple levels of reality as previously discussed, we can further assume that the 2 of Pentacles reversed points simultaneously to interior as well as exterior levels of the problem or mystery supplied. But for our example, it is enough to begin on the horizontal level of interpretation, that is, to reflect possibilities pertaining to the first order of business: objective, external, tangible physical and material reality from which to address our themes of polarity and change.

The following table contains such contrasting pairs associated to the 2 of Pentacles reversed as are likely to appear in the quiet healing chambers of the therapist's consulting room. A hypothetical querent will be used to bring this discussion into clearer focus: William T., 42 years old, separated, non-custodial father of two adolescent girls is a recovering alcoholic with several years of sobriety. William works 60 plus hours per week as an editor for a small press in Philadelphia. He presents with symptoms of mild depression, isolation, burnout, insomnia, and fear of relapse. Now at his third therapy session, at the therapist's suggestion William has randomly selected the 2 of Pentacles reversed in the obstacle position of a ten-card (Celtic Cross) Tarot spread.

The elaborations that follow are intended to instruct a greater Tarot paradigm, and are not meant to suggest the usual operating procedure for would-be therapist/Tarot readers. Based solely on William's associations to this card, and in their own order of importance based on his priorities, I have broken down relevant contrasting pairs into columns that first show their current 'opposed' state, reflective of normal linguistic constructions in English, followed by the preferred 'combined' state (in potentia) which synthesizes word pairs into their oppositional wholeness such as our earlier example, "happy/sad." Additionally, I've added the "totality of concept" or what I will refer to as the "whole spectrum" of the issue represented which I will define more precisely afterwards.

CONTRASTING PAIRS

2 of Pentacles (reversed) in the 'obstacle' position

William's associations:

Opposed	Combined	Spectrum of Concept
work or family	work/family	highest priorities
reconcile or divorce	reconcile/divorce	marital resolution
confront or submit	confront/submit	communication
use or abstain	use/abstain	recovery
date or remain celibate	date/remain celibate	singlehood
Prozac or self-reliance	Prozac/self-reliance	symptom relief
buy condo or rent	buy condo/ rent	new housing
roommate or solo	roommate/solo	habitation
attorney or mediator	attorney/mediator	divorce negotiation
custody or visitation	custody/visitation	single parent status
zoo or soccer	zoo/soccer	Saturdays w/ the girls

From the third column we see that combined pairs may not necessarily exhaust the "totality of concept," but rather co-exist as polar opposites that include other contrasted pairs within the whole spectrum. For instance, on the above "communication spectrum" combined pairs "confront/submit" hardly exhaust the full range of possibilities available, which might additionally include intermediate stations such as: assert, negotiate, listen, "pull for sex," etc. In keeping with Aristotelian 'categories', four sub-classes of opposition may be further differentiated (relatives, contraries, contrarities, privation and possession, affirmation and negation). Without venturing too far afield with these often over-lapping technicalities (see Ogden, C.K.,[9] and Needham[10]) it is enough to know for our purposes that some types of oppositions offer intermediate stations, while others do not. Some have mutually exclusive poles while others may coexist in a complementary fashion. Opposition can vary in kind and degree while still maintaining their essential nature of one part being "over against" its opposite, presenting a seemingly irreconcilable gulf.

We may now leave our Philadelphia editor, as his brief appearance is meant only for demonstration. On page 127 I have compiled a sturdy but hardly exhaustive list of contrasting pairs applicable not simply to one individual like William, but more globally to the clinical practice of psychology in general. Following William's example, a small glossary of psychotherapy "contrasting pairs" will be categorized by each dyad's 'opposed' and 'combined' relation to its opposite. My purpose is to demonstrate the divisive tendency of sound-based alphabetic languages to split experience into unnecessary opposing pairs, thereby obscuring the wholeness otherwise laden in all experience. As Jung said:

> A psychological theory, if it is to be more than a technical makeshift, must base itself on the principle of opposition; for without this it could only re-establish a neurotically unbalanced psyche. There is no balance, no system of self-regulation, without opposition. The psyche is just such a self-regulating system.[11]

As with our Philadelphia editor, in the lists that follow I have given each dyad a third column representing the "totality of concept" or *spectrum* of meaning (for reasons that will become clearer when we then move over to Tarot). *Spectrum,* by definition, *is a range of components separated and arranged along some special dimension.* Our initial example of "happy or sad" when operating in the more ambivalent and subtle tones of lived experience combines as "happy/sad" (with perhaps an emphasis on one pole or its opposite depending on circumstance). The "totality of concept" or spectrum measured in this example might be called "response to turning 50." Obviously, many other degrees of feeling are additionally included between these designated poles of happiness and sadness.

In the chart that follows (p. 127), I have listed 50 general psychotherapy constructs and have separated and arranged them along lines of opposition. Afterwards when we turn to Tarot, the concept of "spectrums of possibility" will be made clearer.

The Language of Psychotherapy

While the arcane world of technical terms and lingo applicable to modern psychotherapy largely exceeds the small sample to follow, as indeed Reber's most recent *Dictionary of Psychology* includes over 17,000 such items, I have elected to stop at a mere 50 entries. My criterion for selection is fairly arbitrary, though I have tried to pick terms of greatest recognizability and practical value to those participating in this linguistic exercise. Though we are setting some of the groundwork here to carry over to Tarot, in no way are we suggesting that psychotherapy constructs and Tarot card meanings are systematically analogous to each other.

Clearly, these two traditions are quite distinct as disciplines and language systems, though at times the two seem clearly complementary, while at other times they appear more irreconcilable. Nevertheless, it is the premise of this book that the language and methods of Psychology and those of Tarot may be mutually edifying and challenging, particularly as each helps to contextualize and deepen the other. Noted linguist C. K. Ogden once wrote: "an analysis of the nature of opposition is fundamental for all work on a universal language [see endnote 9]." And certainly from the perspective of this study, Tarot must be considered to possess certain special attributes which qualify it as an emerging new kind of universal language.

Upon examination of the following terms, the careful reader may object to certain pairings or spectrum labels on either theoretical grounds or technical imprecisions, to which I respectfully request his or her forebearance. Others may have hoped for certain crucial opposites in keeping with their own theories, but I suspect such objections will soon be seen as secondary to the discussion at hand. In my own investigations, I have found it rather curious that many standard terms are not so clearly delineated after all, and that certain basic conceptions in Psychology carry significantly altered connotative meanings

CONTRASTING PAIRS

PSYCHOTHERAPY CONSTRUCTS

No.	Opposed	Combined	Spectrum
1.	abuse or dependence	abuse/dependence	addiction
2.	aggressive or passive	aggressive/passive	communication
3.	anima or animus	anima/animus	(uncs) contrasexuality
4.	anorexia or bulimia	anorexia/bulimia	eating disorder
5.	attack or defend	attack/ defend	autonomic response
6.	auditory or visual	auditory/visual	hallucination
7.	bipolar or unipolar	bipolar/unipolar	major depression
8.	body or mind	body/mind	etiology of illness
9.	broad or narrow	broad/narrow	range of affect
10.	cognitive or affective	cognitive/affective	perception
11.	conscious or unconscious	conscious/unconscious	personality
12.	content or process	content/process	therapeutic focus
13.	dementia or depression	dementia/depression	senility
14.	denial or acceptance	denial/acceptance	relation to death
15.	dependence or autonomy	dependence/ autonomy	separation
16.	dominant or submissive	dominant/submissive	control
17.	elevation or despair	elevation/despair	bipolarity
18.	endogenous or exogenous	endogenous/exogenous	depression
19.	euphoria or dystonia	euphoria/dystonia	wellbeing
20.	explosion or implosion	explosion/implosion	emotional response
21.	fragmented or integrated	fragmented/integrated	ego cohesion
22.	gay or straight	gay/straight	sexual orientation
23.	guilt or shame	guilt/shame	neurotic source
24.	idealize or devalue	idealize/devalue	object distortion
25.	inflation or deflation	inflation/deflation	compensation
26.	insight or oblivion	insight/oblivion	awareness
27.	introvert or extrovert	introvert/extrovert	constitution
28.	latent or manifest	latent/manifest	dream content
29.	learned or inherited	learned/inherited	trait origin
30.	left or right hemisphere	left/right hemisphere	brain processing
31.	masculine or feminine	masculine/feminine	gender traits
32.	narcissist or borderline	narcissist/borderline	character pathology
33.	obsessive or compulsive	obsessive/compulsive	repetition behavior
34.	pain or pleasure	pain/pleasure	sensation
35.	pace or lead	pace/lead	induction
36.	potency or impotence	potency/impotence	sexual performance
37.	precocious or delayed	precocious/delayed	intellectual development
38.	psychosis or neurosis	psychosis/neurosis	psychopathology
39.	REM or NREM	REM/NREM	sleep
40.	reveal or conceal	reveal/conceal	function of dream
41.	self or object	self/object	object relations
42.	sign or symbol	sign/symbol	imagery
43.	supportive or reconstructive	supportive/reconstructive	psychotherapy objective
45.	sympathy or empathy	sympathy/empathy	compassion
46.	thinking or feeling	thinking/feeling	personality type
47.	toxic or nurturing	toxic/nurturing	family interaction
48.	transference or countertrans.	transference/countertrans.	therapist/client relationship
49.	victim or victimizer	victim/victimizer	abuse
50.	willpower or surrender	willpower/surrender	recovery

depending on theoretical source and historical juncture of usage. Also, some terms have multiple levels of meaning depending on their therapeutic context. Others remain rather loose and nonspecific, but this I suppose is the nature of psychological ideas especially when put forth in sound-based alphabetic language.

For instance, in defining so central a term as 'self' Reber notes: "The diversity of uses, not surprisingly, is extremely broad and rather unsystematic and the meaning intended is often confounded by the fact that the terms may be used in ways which interact subtly with grammatical forms."[12] Crucial psychological constructs often seem to evaporate into nothingness when poured into the linguistic test tube. Chalmers makes the same point with the word 'consciousness' as it is defined in *The International Dictionary of Psychology:*

> The term is impossible to define except in terms that are unintelligible without a grasp of what consciousness means.... Consciousness is a fascinating but elusive phenomenon: it is impossible to specify what it is, what it does, or why it evolved (Sutherland, Keith, 1989).[13]

Opposition in the Minor Arcana

Our somewhat "useless exercise" of the previous page has shown first the inherency of opposition in Psychology (as indeed, in all fields of human knowledge), and then has pointed us to the desirability of a more balanced and systematic lexicon of Tarot. It is my belief that each Tarot card carries multi-leveled oppositions in meaning, often subsumed under two or more psychotherapy terms. Accordingly, each card contains not merely positive/negative aspects within its innate dualism, but also interior/exterior (that is, esoteric/exoteric) oppositions as well. Consequently each card should be appreciated both for its full combined spectrum of meaning and for the specific vantage point of the subject, which should be placed within this larger non-dual spectrum. Support for this idea is found in no less a work than Butler's classic *Dictionary of the Tarot* wherein the author affirms that: "each of the suits, each of the Minor Arcana, is a two-edged weapon; it can cut or cure."[14]

As with the language of Psychology, certain vagaries of connotation will be evident in Tarot as well, depending likewise on theoretical source and historical juncture of usage.

Some cards' meanings will also vary by context (spread position, symbolic level, etc.) and still others will be seen as somewhat loose and nonspecific, as was the case with certain therapy constructs. But when contextualized within the range of opposition outlined in the beginning of this chapter, i.e., the structural, numerological, dimensional, and directional levels, an extraordinary coherency and compactness is brought into the Tarot system. It is not the author's contention, however, that the deck of possibility is some perfectly formulated, all-inclusive, well-oiled, and complete dream machine of psychospiritual omniscience. It too has evolved and will need to evolve further. Rather, I believe Tarot is indeed one finely-tuned, intricately engineered, new class of psychological vehicle with a surplus of horsepower and great versatility for traveling far and wide through the cosmos of the human psyche. For those not yet initiated, I would simply ask them in for a test drive.

One final note is necessary before a presentation of opposition in Tarot can be promptly made. As specialty schools and technical designations were strictly avoided in our list of general psychotherapy terms, the same rule will apply to Tarot definitions. Not only am I simply unqualified to represent the great many esoteric variegations and permutations that have mushroomed in recent decades over the Tarot noosphere, but quite equally, my intentions here are more narrowly gaged, to wit, the forwarding and systematization of a balanced, integrated, and universal Tarot lexicon that properly appreciates the law of opposition and other core, well-founded, psychological principles.

What follows then is a classification of the entire Minor Arcana. Associated Majors, of course, equally constituted within the laws of opposition, are referenced by number at the end of each row and will be taken up in greater depth in our next two chapters. To convey this lexicon concisely and compactly we will borrow a bit from our list of contrasting pairs of psychotherapy, at least in procedure, though the format here has evolved to include meaning dimensions unique to Tarot. Accordingly, each of the four suits is first structurally laid out by elemental affinity (Air, Water, Fire, Earth) and then numerologically through the sequential convention of Pips (Ace to Ten) and Courts (Page, Knight, Queen, King).

Card meanings are then approached through modern interpretations based on the twentieth century so-called 'Golden Dawn' conventions of Waite, MacGregor Mathers, Crowley, Paul Foster Case, and others (see Butler's *Dictionary of the Tarot*)[15] along with the modern symbolist tradition (see Cirlot's A *Dictionary of Symbols*)[16] and an eye to Jungian constructs (see Samuels, A *Critical Dictionary of Jungian Analysis*).[17] Single word renderings (and their opposites) have additionally been revised and upgraded through a synthesis of more contemporary commentators like Greer, Arrien, Pollack, DuQuette, et al., (see Riley's *Tarot Dictionary and Compendium)*[18] as well as my own interpretative bents, experience, and psychological proclivities.[19] Each "card pair" is further subdivided into *exterior, reversed, interior*, and *full spectrum* levels.

In the column headings, *exterior* lays out the more general and external dimension of meaning; *reversed* accounts for the negative poles or compromised direction of meaning, i.e., the shadow side; *interior* expresses the inner psychological or experiential dimension; and finally, *spectrum* is meant to capture the totality of the concept described. I should also note that 'interior' meanings, for the purposes of this discussion, will tend to emphasize more of the psychological nuance than particular metaphysical or magical formulations. As for notation, each single word pair is indicated by a solidus (/)—the oblique stroke used to denote alternatives such as: either/or. Following each whole spectrum on the chart is a final column noting the suggested corresponding trump card (by number).

Finally, the lexicon that follows is notably absent of phraseology, a key aspect of live readings, including proverbs from around the world. In Appendix A, however, I have included a list of key phrases and proverbs I use for each card. This appendix is a full banquet for effective face-to-face readings. Phrases such as "night journey of the soul (8 of Cups)" or "turns things out like hotcakes

(8 of Pentacles)" in practice are important vehicles for the effective communication of Tarot symbols. Proverbs also make excellent handles for interpretation as they are thought to contain the essence of wisdom. It is said that wisdom comes from experience and experience comes from making mistakes. Proverbs, therefore, are a record of someone's mistakes, turned into an example for posterity.

But my intent with the lexicon on the following page is precisely and comprehensively to elucidate each card's spectrum(s) of meaning through single word constructs and leave the phraseology and proverbial embellishment to individual styles of interpretation. Afterwards, a condensed table summary entitled "Psychological Spectrums of the Minor Arcana" is added at the close of this chapter to more concisely organize the Minor Arcana simply around its respective full spectrums of meaning without the dimensional/directional particulars. Readers who wish to learn the Tarot deck will do well to integrate this lexicon into their studies. In the chapters that follow, the laws of opposition will be further developed in our exploration of Tarot's higher deck, the Major Arcana.

TAROT LEXICON

MINOR ARCANA
AIR

Suit of *SWORDS*

	Exterior	Reversed	Interior	Spectrum	Trump*
	Thought/Penetration	Separation/Mentalism	Thinking/Knowing	Mind	
Pips					
Ace	Idea/Intellect	Illusion/Confusion	Discovery/Lucidity	Intelligence	1
2	Friendship/Loyalty	Doubt/Betrayal	Affinity/Respect	Trust	2
3	Melancholy/Heartbreak	Shame/Blame	Suffering/Introspection	Sorrow	13
4	Rest/Withdrawal	Stress/Isolation	Mental Cleansing/Refueling	Retreat	9
5	Strife/Defeat	Pessimism/Disdain	Division/Dissonance	Despair	15
6	Passage/Flight	Escape/Paralysis	Journey/Change	Transition	10
7	Futility/Resignation	Evasion/Avoidance	Stealth/Deceit	Defense	16
8	Oppression/Paralysis	Guilt/Entrapment	Powerlessness/Helplessness	Interference	15
9	Shadow/Demons	Depression/Doom	Hopelessness/Agony	Distortion	18
10	Ruin/Rebirth	Denial/Repression	Turning It Over/Release	Surrender	13
Courts					
Page	Detachment/Cunning	Suspicion/Paranoia	Calculation/Caution	Observation	12
Knight	Focus/Discrimination	Rationalization/Obsession	Evaluation/Reduction	Insight	5
Queen	Penetration/Honesty	Vindictive/Self-Righteous	Congruence/Consistency	Accuracy	2
King	Precision/Judgment	Intellectualize/Judgmental	Crystallize/Awareness	Clarity	20

MINOR ARCANA
WATER

Suit of *CUPS*

	Exterior	Reversed	Interior	Spectrum	Trump*
	Love/Healing	Dissolution/Stagnation	Flow/Feeling	Soul	
Pips					
Ace	Receptivity/Fluidity	Despair/Numbness	Desire/Ecstasy	Emotion	17
2	Union/Intercourse	Fusion/Abandonment	Attraction/Appreciation	Relation	6
3	Celebration/Joy	Protest/Bitterness	Affection/Sharing	Expression	14
4	Comfort/Discomfort	Apathy/Lethargy	Promise/Probability	Expectation	4
5	Loss/Grief	Devastation/Shock	Clinging/Letting Go	Separation	13
6	Sentiment/Nostalgia	Regret/Fixation	Tenderness/Yearning	Memory	2
7	Fantasy/Possibility	Fragment/Projection	Choice/Profusion	Multiplicity	18
8	Journey/Withdrawal	Decompensate/Stagnate	Descend/Divest	Retreat	9
9	Pleasure/Enjoyment	Indulgence/Addiction	Sustenance/Satisfaction	Fulfillment	21
10	Affirmation/Gratitude	Inflation/Deflation	Excitement/Infatuation	Inspiration	17
Courts					
Page	Innocence/Openness	Moodiness/Lability	Affection/Dependency	Vulnerability	8
Knight	Romance/Quest	Narcissism/Infidelity	Passion/Idealization	Heart	6
Queen	Care/Healing	Smothering/Punishing	Giving/Sending	Nurturance	3
King	Wisdom/Support	Manipulate/Betray	Empathy/Sympathy	Compassion	5

**Correspondence to Major Arcana* (see the following chapter)

1 Magician	2 Priestess	3 Empress	4 Emperor	5 Hierophant	6 Lovers
7 Chariot	8 Strength	9 Hermit	10 Wheel of Fortune	11 Justice	12 Hanged Man
13 Death	14 Temperance	15 The Devil	16 The Tower	17 The Star	18 The Moon
19 The Sun	20 Judgment	21 The World			

MINOR ARCANA
FIRE
Suit of *WANDS*

	Exterior	Reversed	Interior	Spectrum	Trump*
	Imagination/Will	Conflagration/Aggression	Creativity/Intuition	Spirit	
Pips					
Ace	Initiation/Creation	Darkness/Frenzy	Individuation/Adventure	Aspiration	1
2	Synthesis/Convergence	Confusion/Anxiety	Possibility/Resonance	Choice	2
3	Effort/Action	Ambivalence/Impotence	Visualization/Direction	Intention	7
4	Freedom/Passage	Status-quo/Inactivity	Appreciation/Integration	Creativity	14
5	Competition/Struggle	Passive-Aggression/Combat	Division/Multiplicity	Conflict	16
6	Achievement/Victory	Arrogance/Defeatism	Confidence/Anticipation	Optimism	7
7	Tests/Obstructions	Stubbornness/Inflexibility	Loyalty/Positionality	Persistence	9
8	Assertion/Movement	Aimless/Dispersed	Focus/Direction	Goal	7
9	Power/Dominion	Domination/Bullying	Potency/Alertness	Force	8
10	Burden/Overextention	Entrapment/Abuse	Depletion/Exhaustion	Oppression	16
Courts					
Page	Message/Information	Disguise/Obfuscation	Sharing/Showing	Communication	5
Knight	Pursuit/Tenacity	Impetuous/Explosiveness	Charisma/Warrior	Determination	7
Queen	Conduit/Catalyst	Repellent/Retardant	Pacing/Channeling	Energy	19
King	Empowerment/Control	Dictatorial/Megalomaniac	Manifesting/Envisioning	Vision	17

MINOR ARCANA
EARTH
Suit of *PENTACLES*

	Exterior	Reversed	Interior	Spectrum	Trump*
	Solidity/Materialism	Density/Nihilism	Sensation/Connection	Body	
Pips					
Ace	Conception/Seed	Inertia/Chaos	Ground/Core	Manifestation	1
2	Balance/Change	Splitting/Onesidedness	Grace/Health	Polarity	6
3	Working/Crafting	Impeding/Defiling	Concretizing/Building	Construction	3
4	Power/Gain	Attachment/Avarice	Structure/Shape	Form	4
5	Want/Need	Covet/Envy	Humility/Adjustment	Loss	13
6	Give/Take	Obsess/Compulse	Measure/Compare	Compromise	11
7	Delay/Ripen	Failure/Frustration	Incubate/Vegetate	Patience	14
8	Study/Practice	Expediate/Rebel	Differentiate/Repeat	Discipline	9
9	Abundance/Simplicity	Nature/Instinct	Nurture/Refine	Cultivation	3
10	Prosperity/Security	Conformity/Dissipation	Commitment/Investment	Embodiment	8
Courts					
Page	Dissection/Analysis	Reify/Compartmentalize	Separate/Reduce	Objectivity	1
Knight	Economy/Utility	Density/Compulsivity	Account/Contain	Practicality	14
Queen	Home/Happiness	Phobic/Careless	Sensitivity/Aesthetics	Ordinary Magic	3
King	Achievement/Enterprise	Corruption/Failure	Integrity/Increase	Responsibility	4

**Correspondence to Major Arcana* (see the following chapter)

1 Magician	2 Priestess	3 Empress	4 Emperor	5 Hierophant	6 Lovers
7 Chariot	8 Strength	9 Hermit	10 Wheel of Fortune	11 Justice	12 Hanged Man
13 Death	14 Temperance	15 The Devil	16 The Tower	17 The Star	18 The Moon
19 The Sun	20 Judgment	21 The World			

To further summarize, I have added the following chart which lists by suit and number only the "totality of concept" or "full spectrum" for each card of the Minor Arcana.

This list is simply taken from the spectrum columns of the previous pages and can be seen to contain the overall key teachings of the Lesser Arcana.

Psychological Spectrums of the Minor Arcana

(Taken from the preceding lexicon)

Suit	*SWORDS*	*CUPS*	*WANDS*	*PENTACLES*
Element	Air	Water	Fire	Earth
Function	Thinking	Feeling	Intuition	Sensation
Realm	Mind	Soul	Spirit	Physicality
Pips				
Ace	Intelligence	Emotion	Aspiration	Manifestation
Two	Trust	Relation	Choice	Polarity
Three	Sorrow	Expression	Intention	Construction
Four	Retreat	Expectation	Creation	Form
Five	Despair	Separation	Conflict	Loss
Six	Transition	Memory	Optimism	Compromise
Seven	Defense	Multiplicity	Persistence	Patience
Eight	Interference	Retreat	Goal	Discipline
Nine	Distortion	Fulfillment	Force	Cultivation
Ten	Surrender	Imagination	Oppression	Embodiment
Courts				
Page	Observation	Vulnerability	Communication	Objectivity
Knight	Insight	Heart	Determination	Practicality
Queen	Accuracy	Nurturance	Energy	Ordinary Magic
King	Clarity	Compassion	Vision	Responsibility

Notes

[1]Needham, Rodney, *Counterpoints;* University of California Press, London, 1987, p. 29.

[2]Jung, C. G., *Collected Works,* Vol. 7 Part 1: *Two Essays on Analytical Psychology;* Bollingen Series, Princeton University Press, 1953, p. 71.

[3]Watts, Allan, (with collaboration of Al Chung-liang Huang) *Tao: The Watercourse Way;* Pantheon Books, New York, 1975, p. 23.

[4]Jung, C. G., *Collected Works,* Vol. 6: *Psychological Types;* Bollingen Series, Princeton University Press, 1921, par. 337.

[5]Feng, Gia-Fu, and English, Jane, *Lao Tsu: Tao Te Ching;* Vintage Books, 1972.

[6]Edinger, Edward F., *The Creation of Consciousness: Jung's Myth for Modern Man;* Inner City Books, 1984.

[7]Watts, Allan, (with collaboration of Al Chung-liang Huang) *Tao: The Watercourse Way;* Pantheon Books, New York, 1975, p. 14.

[8]Room, Adrian, *Dictionary of Contrasting Pairs;* Routledge, London, 1988, p.ix.

[9]Ogden, C.K., *Opposition: A Linguistic and Psychological Analysis;* Indiana University Press, 1967.

[10]Needham, Rodney, *Counterpoints;* University of California Press, London, 1987.

[11]Jung, C. G., *The Collected Works* (Bollingen Series VII); Trans. R.F.C. Hull. Princeton University Press, p. 60.

[12]Reber, Arthur, S., *Dictionary of Psychology;* Penguin Books, London, 1985.

[13]Chalmers, David J., *The Conscious Mind: In Search of a Fundamental Theory;* Oxford University Press, 1996.

[14]Butler, Bill, *Dictionary of the Tarot;* Schoken Books, New York, 1975, p. 85.

[15]Ibid.

[16]Cirlot, J. E., A *Dictionary of Symbols* (Second Edition); Routledge & Kegan Paul Ltd., London, 1962.

[17]Samuels, Andrew, Shorter, Bani, and Plant, Fred, A *Critical Dictionary of Jungian Analysis;* Routledge & Kegan Paul Ltd, 1986.

[18]Riley, Jana, *Tarot Dictionary and Compendium;* Samuel Weiser Inc., York Beach, ME, 1995.

[19]Rosengarten, Arthur, *Tarot as a Psychotherapeutic Tool;* self-published manual, Encinitas, Ca., 1994. (54 pages).

Chapter VII

UNIVERSALITY

> When you see the Earth from space, you don't see any divisions of nation-states there. This may be the symbol of the new mythology to come; this is the country we will celebrate, and these are the people we are one with.
>
> —Joseph Campbell

> Call on God, but row away from the rocks.
>
> —Indian Proverb

Difference

Common sense would seem to dictate that a cosmos of human complexity and diversity far exceeds any singular formulation and categorization. "Universalism" at first blush sounds soothing and inspiring but grows increasingly elusive under closer scrutiny. In Chapter IV we noted the remarkable fact that little evidence is found for any one of the estimated 400 different schools of psychotherapy to be significantly more effective than another. If so much difference exists among therapists, one can only imagine the multitudinous forms of clientele. Of necessity therefore, it should not be surprising that the majority of practitioners today consider themselves 'eclectic' or 'integrative'. So much for the one universal cure.

Healers and mental health professionals of every stripe and color will obviously add practical benefit to their eclecticism when having at their disposal an effective assortment of therapeutic tools, techniques, and interventions within their so-called "bag of tricks."

By the same token, any single intervention claiming universal applicability and efficacy would seem inappropriately overextended, conflated or inflated, fraudulent, or destined for disappointment. Simply put, modern man, woman, and child, therapist, patient, and psychology itself are mixed bundles of sweet unabiding human difference resistant to simple generalization.

Yet, on the practical side (as it always comes down to it eventually) few would argue that a necessary function is served by the systematic categorization of any set of complex factors otherwise felt to be cumbersomely large and unwieldy. Though the libertarian might recant, a certain utilitarian necessity is served through generalized common denominators. Whether we speak of the comprehensive structure and operations of human personality in its entirety or the numbering of the solar days of the year, whether we seek to know the diverse course and treatment of human suffering or the progressive brackets of income taxation across all socioeconomic sectors, whether to exhaust type and trait distinctions of the human individual or systematize the hodge-podge of so-called 'sub-genres' of a Hollywood music awards ceremony ("The Best Vampire Rock/Alternative Polka Written for Hawaiian Documentary Category"), such classifications, however imperfect, prove extremely useful for the access and organization of the constituency described therein.

This point is certainly not lost on that Emerald Tablet of all contemporary clinical practice, the omniscient *Diagnostic and Statistical Manual of Mental Disorders* (DSM) itself. Noting the limitations of the categorical approach, its own authors caution:

> DSM-IV is a categorical classification that divides mental disorders into types based on criteria sets with defining features. This naming of categories is the traditional method of organizing and transmitting information in everyday life and has been the fundamental approach used in all systems of medical diagnosis. A categorical approach to classification works best when all members of a diagnostic class are homogenous, when there are clear boundaries between classes, and when the different classes are mutually exclusive. Nonetheless, the limitations of the categorical classification system must be recognized.
>
> In DSM-IV, there is no assumption that each category of mental disorder is a completely discrete entity with absolute boundaries dividing

> it from other mental disorders or from no mental disorder. There is also no assumption that all individuals described as having the same mental disorder are alike in all important ways. The clinician using DSM-IV should therefore consider that *individuals sharing a diagnosis are likely to be heterogeneous even in regard to the defining features of the diagnosis.*[1] [Italics mine].

The facts of human heterogeneity in personality extend well beyond the diagnosis of clinical syndromes and mental disorders into nearly every aspect of human affairs. In psychotherapy, inherent dissimilarity and irregularity are equally present on the therapist side of the equation, not only in terms of therapeutic style and theoretical orientation between schools or the heterogeneity in personal attributes and training of practitioners, but even with differences in adherence that one practitioner brings to a single style and orientation. Even when such factors appear reasonably uniform, much will depend simply on the subjective context of the moment.

No two Gestalt therapists, for example, will conceptualize or intervene in precisely the same manner, not simply due to their personal differences, but also due to the unique interactive field that springs forth with each client. For the same reasons, no two Jungians will analyze a dream with precisely the same emphasis, or self psychologists draw the same band of transferences and countertransferences. The fact of human difference cannot be denied or overlooked in Psychology. Homogeneity, the presence of a uniform or identical structure throughout, as noted in the DSM-IV, is perhaps better served in non-psychological realms such as medicine where clear-cut boundaries exist between classes and the different classes are mutually exclusive.

Sameness

Yet given the heterogeneity of Psychology, given the non-uniformity and vast differentiation both within patients, therapists, and psychological methods, is it not extraordinary that human beings remain for the most part homogeneous, that is, remarkably similar in body and soul? Beyond the genetic spectrum of determinants in physiology and biochemistry, one easily observes a discrete level of conformity, uniformity and equality throughout human behavior and custom, throughout human need, want, motivation and vulnerability, throughout human expression, daily concern and ultimate aspiration. Though mixed bundles of sweet human difference surely abound, there is also quite another layer of essential singularity and predictable sameness as well. The seeming contradiction between these two facts mirrors the relationship between Minor and Major Arcanas.

I recall a casual conversation at a party years ago with a professor of psychiatry whose task it was to prepare first-year medical residents for their initial rather intimidating encounters with acute regressed schizophrenic patients. Understandably, some of these greenhorns felt not a little trepidation before their first day of rounds on the locked back wards of state mental hospitals. "What I tell my psychiatric residents the first day," he said, "is to remember that schizophrenics are *more like you than different from you.*" At the time, I was struck by the truth of his comment. Given how apparently dissimilar the human species seems in general, let alone the bizarre deviancies of the significantly mentally ill, one certainly might suspect otherwise. It would be not hard to envision, for instance, a human community fragmenting like a collective madhouse of chaos, with personality differences progressing each day along increasingly disparate, idiosyncratic fault lines, until eventually, individual and cultural dissimilarities on a grand scale would become so pronounced that all connecting links and sympathies would simply dissolve into utter futility and anarchy. Science fiction films like *Blade Runner* and *Waterworld* capture some of this disturbing vision.

But why has this, in fact, not happened and is likely never to happen? Why have not trends towards individual difference ruled the course of human development and produced increasingly anomalous individualists who have grown as dissimilar to one another as frogs to bicycles? I believe the answer is easily surmised, as the premise itself is but half true. Beyond certain constitutional and genetic differences of body-type, IQ, personality type, and race, the realm of human difference in reality is no more than a surface phenomenon, involving mainly stylistic and character tendencies, personal preferences and cultural proclivities, along with a small suitcase of acquired talents and trademarks that help adorn the individual with small vestiges of 'personality'. Such things, though they are considerable, reside mostly within the outer spectrums of conscious knowledge: persona, habit, choice, story, and artifact.

Carrying our argument a bit further, if indeed unabiding human difference were truly the rule, would it not follow that the greatest dissimilarities in the human species would be most clearly evident in individuals at the zenith of difference, those human beings who would perceive and construct their realities from the most radically dissimilar vantage points imaginable? For example, consider (metaphorically) the agnostic and urbane graduate professor and Chief of Neuropsychology at the 70-bed Stanford University Center for Head Trauma in Menlo Park, California. He is affluent, well-educated, politically correct, a man of some stature in the academic and professional circles of American psychiatry. Let's say for argument's sake we compare him to his apparent opposite, the dentally-challenged, semi-literate white Baptist earthworm harvester from Hueytown, Alabama who runs a roadside "worms and jerky" stand out past Little Lick Creek. He is marginal, fifth-grade educated, a baseball fan, a racist and bigot. Quite a reasonable comparison of opposites one might think.

Yet beyond the obvious initial incongruities, we hardly encounter here individuals of any profound degree of dissimilarity, but to the contrary, two men who possess merely a moderate smattering of surface difference (though, quite true, this twosome won't be swapping sitters or exchanging e-mail anytime soon). But the fact that they share an historical era, a spoken and written language (loosely), a Newtonian explanation of time and a Cartesian duality of mind/body, a nation, constitution and vote, an economic, monetary, and taxation system, a stint in the United States Army, a professed love for pepperoni pizza and the ritual of turkey on Thanksgiving—connect these two apparent strangers, relatively-speaking, like virtual twins separated at birth. In the broadest strokes of human possibility these two gentlemen are nearly interchangeable.

No, for a comparison that truly bears deep structural dissimilarity and unquestioned mutual otherness, unexplainable by cultural diffusion, we would do far better to compare professor or worm harvester with, perhaps, the 14th-century aboriginal Inupiat seal hunter from Arctic Alaska. Here one moves closer to the height of heterogeneity. The chasm of difference separating this isolate 600-year-old aborigine and our 50-year-old Stanford professor (and his lowbrow counterpart) can be measured in their fundamentally disparate and alien perceptions of the world around them, including the diverse frameworks from which meaning is given to experience, their unrelated cognitive and linguistic constructions of subjects, objects and events, and the very different culture myths (ethos) from which they were raised, function, and which they continue to shape. Time is perceived in radically different units, the Inupiat perceiving change in seasonal cycles, weather patterns, caribou herds and lunar days, the Californian and Alabaman in linear solar minutes marked off by either a digital desk chronometer or Chevy pick-up dashboard clock, as the case may be. Respective languages operate through syntactic patterns of unconnected and unrelated semantic origin, and vocabulary often refers to objects for which the other has no appreciable concept. External environments, physical structures, technology, terrain, climate, etc., offer little in the way of shared experience.

Yet, curiously, 14th-century aboriginal Inupiat and modern American are each internally and socially guided to become husbands and fathers, to marry within their own group, and to observe the strict taboo of incest; both Inupiat and American covet approval from their elders and seek out spirit doctors in times of self-doubt or conflict; both are energized by challenge and accord leadership (begrudgingly) to those of superior personal attributes in trading, hunting, human relations skills, energy and wisdom; both devise and apply tools to enhance their skills; both invent games, dance, gamble, make music for recreation, and tell stories and make jokes for their amusement; both seek union with their gods and magic to restore their faith; both crave solitude for refueling, and grow at once troubled and incited before the great mysteries of existence.[2] The fact that both share these things (which we ourselves take for granted) can hardly be explained by some interconnecting conscious knowledge, custom, belief, or ratiocination. The fact is, our seal hunter and psychologist/worm harvester share little if any outward points of reference, and we may assume their paths have never crossed.

Archetype

Instead, it is far more plausible to consider that such parallel motivations, feelings, and behaviors shared by this odd twosome are likely to be universal experiences innate to homo sapiens regardless of culture or consciousness. This conclusion grows in credibility as we find similar examples of homogeneity in other radically differing pools of human culture, as one suspects will be found equally in the native Bonpo goatherders of ancient Tibet when compared with the Cuban cab drivers circling the dusty city streets of downtown Havana. We may assume such likenesses in personality are products of inherent, underlying, core structures of the human psyche which operate uniformly in individuals of even the most radically discrepant intellectual, historical, geographic, and cultural contexts. How such tendencies are passed to individuals and cultures remains a mystery to date—whether due to certain vital factors, morphogenic fields, genetic programs, or metaphysical properties is still open to speculation. But that such behaviors are instinctively sourced and driven, are uniform and universal, suggests their existence has little to do with independent conscious thinking. Notes Jung:

> In addition to our immediate consciousness, which is of a thoroughly personal nature and which we believe to be the only empirical psyche (even if we tack on the personal unconscious as an appendix), there exists a second psychic system of a collective, universal and impersonal nature which is identical in all individuals. This collective unconscious does not develop individually, but is inherited. It consists of pre-existent forms, the archetypes.[3]

Though Jung believed archetypes *per se* were not accessible to human perception, he contended that archetypal expressions emanating from deep psychic quarters (the collective unconscious) were recognizable in visual images and could be empirically observed in dreams, fantasies, culture myths, fairytales, and creative productions. So-called archetypal images are equally observable in outer behaviors as well, as in our above examples of seal hunter and psychologist, and particularly in those behaviors that cluster around universal experiences of humanness, such as birth, initiation, marriage, parenthood, play, transcendence, one's relation to the cosmos, separation, and death.

Jung's critics, notes Corbett, have tended to over-mystify the notion of archetypes (as even today Jung's ideas remain largely banished from mainstream academic and scientific circles), but, in fact, conceptionally archetypes merely represent the operation of natural law as it expresses itself in the psyche, analogous to the laws of matter and biological instinct.[4] As Jung repeatedly states, archetypes are empirical facts. Yet in fairness to his critics, Jung's expositions through dense and arcane historical descriptions of archetypal imagery as found for instance in Renaissance alchemy (see *Mysterium Coniunctionis*) have left many non-Jungians (and Jungians alike) gasping for air. Perhaps even the master himself had something of the problem of getting the correct message out to those who might appreciate it most. But Cirlot observes correctly:

> Jung uses the word 'archetype' to designate those universal symbols which possess the greatest constancy and efficiency, the greatest potentiality for psychic evolution, and which point away from the inferior towards the superior.[5]

Demystifying the archetypes and embodying them in natural, observable and creative forms, without degrading them, is surely a worthy goal for any psychological researcher wishing to systematize the universal blueprints of human possibility and make Jung's rich vision more accessible. But we should keep in mind that the notion of the archetype is not a new idea. It endures from the tradition of Platonic Ideas, the Forms which were once presumed to reside in the minds of the gods and serve as the models of all entities in the human realm. In former times, notes Jung, despite some dissenting opinion and the influence of Aristotle, it was not too difficult to understand Plato's conception of the Idea as supraordinate and pre-existent to all phenomena.

The notion of pre-existent forms laden in man's psyche which function instinctively as universal blueprints of psychological development is found in Kant's *a priori* categories of perception and Schopenhauer's prototypes. Theories of innate psychological structures are implicit in the work of Piaget with regard to cognitive development, in Noam Chomsky's linguistic "deep structures," and in Levi Strauss's structural anthropology, not to mention the psychoanalytical works of Freud, Klein, Isaacs, Bion, and Money-Kyrle. Samuels,[6] as well as Young-Eisendrath and Hall[7] have compared the theory of archetypes to structural thought as well.

But given Jung's assertion that the archetype's pure form is unknowable and can be only inferred in a special class of psychic imagery, and given a desire to organize and classify a whole body of such archetypal themes, we are then left to pursue (if we dare) the daunting task of assembling a comprehensive pantheon of archetypal imagery that would, in principle, reduce this "second system of the psyche" to its most universal, discrete, and cohesive elements. Like Odysseus turned psychological chronicler, we would face either the immense challenge of collecting and classifying an insurmountable personal and collective storehouse of subjective dream images, fantasies, mythic and visionary content, or else we would have to whittle away at a virtual mountain of cultural artifact and idea which, in theory, might contain those quintessential clues to human development and possibility. Which few items will prove the most primary, universal, cross-cultural, non-reducible, timeless, enduring?

For such high intellectual stakes, unfortunately, navigational maps are not readily available. When breakthroughs towards this end have indeed occurred in the past, such as cracking the hieroglyphic code of the Rosetta Stone or the genetic code of the DNA molecule, the new maps that emerge have opened wide and exciting vistas to a small coterie of adherents and professionals; but they have also tended to fall narrowly within the linguistic bounds and limitations of specialized disciplines and paradigms, or else suffered the general obscurity of mathematical formalae, scientific specialty, or esoteric abstraction.

Herein lies a great advantage for any map that would take the symbolic approach, seeking to express simultaneously the multiple aspects of the idea represented through engaging, immediately recognizable pictorial images, a map of symbolic representations, each transcending singular description but suggesting instead the manifold inexhaustibility of the universal possibilities portrayed. Ralph Metzner, writes in *Maps of Consciousness*:

> ...it is not surprising that an attempt should have been made to express the archetypes of psychic transformation in direct, visual form; a form that would resonate in the mind and feelings of the perceiver without the intermediary of language or code. To show in images the steps that must be taken, the many phases of the inner work, and thus to ensure the teachings a universality that transcends cultural and linguistic conventions. This is the Tarot.[8]

Structuring the Universal

When exploring the multiplicity of forms generated by any single archetype, one soon discovers an inexhaustible well of possibility both in form and substance, yet one that is sufficiently coherent and continuous within its own boundaries as to produce a definite and discrete spectrum of meaning; a spectrum that is structurally different from all others. Of course, the same can be said of any of the 22 trumps of the Major Arcana. For instance, Socrates, Albert Einstein, Obe-wan Kenobe, George Burns, Sri Aurobindo, Santa Claus and my late Uncle Harry, who had mastered the art of blowing perfect smoke rings by imported cigar, may each be construed as images of the archetype of the Wise Old Man. Though heterogeneous in form and content, they are continuous and discrete in function. They are avuncular agents of determination in the service of the soul. In Tarot, we associate this archetype with trump 9, The Hermit card.

Compare this principle to another class of masculine luminary, organized around what we might call the archetype of The Hero, that may include the images of Michael Jordan, Hercules, John F. Kennedy, Rocky, Joan of Arc, (early) Bob Dylan, and Luke Skywalker. The corresponding Tarot card in this spectrum is trump 7, The Chariot. In Tarot, The Chariot symbolizes qualities associated with attainment, action, pursuit, tenacity, and challenge, often against all odds. Nichols notes:

> The Chariot pictures a state of ego inflation which the ancients called hubris. In psychological terms this represents a condition in which the ego, or center of individual consciousness, identifies with (imagines itself to have become) an archetypal figure transcending human limitations.[9]

The Wise Old Man

The Hero

In reality, of course, all individuals are composites of many archetypal energies, with stronger and weaker personality proclivities appearing and disappearing during crucial stages of lifespan development. The examples given above are not of the actual people themselves, who are unknowable in their true wholeness, but more their personas and public image. In fact, we all are driven by The Chariot and perhaps counseled by The Hermit at various times and circumstances of our lives.

Still, a spectrum of possibility exists within the boundaries of both concepts. By what criteria do these two differing principles draw their special membership? As symbols of universal possibility, within precisely what internal spectrum of meaning is each given entry? Is there a "differential diagnosis" which might separate the "men from the boys"? And of course the crucial question, would these two distinct casts of characters (as opposed to their outer cultural "faces") be equally recognizable to our 14th-century Inupiat seal hunter, our 20th-century neuropsychologist and our worm stand operator from Little Lick Creek?

The Invariants of Archetypal Reality

Polly Young-Eisendrath and James A. Hall in presenting a constructivist perspective to Jung's self psychology have isolated four "invariant principles" which they believe are present in all psychic contents, whether (in Jungian terms) "complex or archetype." Drawing from the philosophical works of Jung, R. Harre, Piaget, and many developmental, psychoanalytic, and constructivist theorists, the authors list the following four necessary and sufficient conditions which structure every archetype:

Invariants of Archetypal Reality

1. ***Agency:*** the experience of personal causation, authorship of action, intentionality. [If they could speak to us, they might say: "I am an agent of________. My intention is ________."]

2. ***Coherence:*** the experience of unity or "core being"; the collusion of body/psyche; the location of oneself as a point of view with an immediate knowledge of psychical boundaries and discrete bodily organization. ["I am organized around_____."]

3. ***Continuity:*** the experience of "going on being" over time that provides the functional connections that eventually result in foresight and nonverbal and verbal memory as the bases of self narratives that permit us to connect to the present with past and future. ["I am in the process of______. I am becoming________."]

4. ***Emotional arousal:*** the instinctual patterns of arousal, expression, and motivational readiness that are relatively fixed systems of subjective relating between persons, and with organisms and things, throughout the lifespan. ["I am aroused and motivated by_______."][10]

Working with these principles, let us now return to our abovementioned examples, the archetypes of The Wise Old Man and The Hero, or in Tarot terms, The Hermit and The Chariot, and apply this "acid test" to their construction.

In the model stated above, The Hermit can be seen as an

agent of wisdom and self-knowing (agency). He coheres (or is organized) around the path of withdrawal or retreat (coherence). He is in the process of introspection and self-actualization (continuity), that is, the intentionality around which he left off yesterday, he begins anew today, and heads towards tomorrow. And finally, The Hermit is aroused and motivated by spiritual fulfillment (emotional arousal). Cirlot details the archetype of The Hermit:

> ...an old man carrying in his right hand a lantern partially covered by one of the folds of his cloak, which is dark outside (signifying withdrawal and austerity) but with a blue lining (representing aerial nature). If he finds the serpent of the instincts in his path, he does not destroy it but simply charms it into twining itself round his staff, as Aesculapius did. He is a master of the invisible.[11]

In contrast, trump 7, The Charioteer, is an agent of worldly attainment; he is organized around action, in the process of self-assertion and communication, and aroused (motivated) by challenge. Whereas by nature The Hermit is introverted, The Chariot is an outer-directed dynamic extrovert. Whereas The Hermit embodies age, differentiation, and experience, The Charioteer embodies youth, valor, and intensity. Though quite different personalities, what they indeed share is fierce tenacity and determination. Notes Cirlot of The Chariot:

> The cuirass of the charioteer represents his defence against the baser forces of life; it is secured with five gold studs, denoting the four elements and the quintessence. On his shoulder are two crescent moons representing the world of forms. The chariot is drawn by what at first seems to be a pair of sphinxes but which is in fact a two-headed amphisbaena, symbolizing the hostile forces which one must subjugate in order to go forward.[12]

Young-Eisendrath and Hall believe the reduction into universal invariants (agency, coherence, continuity, and emotional arousal) "provide the conditions in which a person is predisposed to create an emotionally infused image of subjective individuality." With inclusion of the laws of opposition and polarity to this formulation, we can more precisely see that The Hermit is an agent of "wisdom/ignorance," who coheres around the polarities of "withdrawal/approach," unfolds through the process of "detachment/attachment," and is aroused by "soul/ego." Such oppositions are implied in the forthcoming lexicon, though not listed as such. Additionally, because we engage in purely archetypal forces in the trump cards, we can further assume the interior dimension is primary, the exterior dimension secondary. By comparison, the cards of the Lesser Arcana should be taken as "degrees of conscious activity" each associated with a particular corresponding Major Arcanum.

On the pages that follow, I have attempted to chart a concise lexicon of the Greater Arcana synthesized from the same multiple sources noted at the end of the last chapter. This lexicon, however, is organized primarily around the four invariant principles of archetypal reality discussed above. Single-word referents are assumed to include the full spectrum of each construct, although certain competing theoretical constructions, as well as individual preferences, emphases, and personal associations, perhaps leave this global classification open for revision and adjustment. Where better offerings are found, I gladly stand corrected.

My intent, as with the Minors, is to simplify and crystallize a glossary of Tarot that is more readily accessible to practitioners of therapy and is constructed upon well-founded psychological principles. As mentioned earlier, key phrases and proverbs used for each card are presented in Appendix A. It should be noted, however, that the "invariants of self" model above suggests an underlying reality of individual existence; this presupposition of 'selfhood' is a premise not empirically demonstrated as such or universally shared. In the chapter that immediately follows the lexicon, we will explore several alternative philosophical frameworks from which the Major Arcana can be approached. But now we shall examine this new lexicon of the Major Arcana, and then work psychologically in the chapters that follow with these defined constructs.

TAROT LEXICON

MAJOR ARCANA

No.	Arcanum	Agency (intention)	Coherence (organization)	Continuity (process)	Emotional Arousal (motivation)
1	**MAGICIAN**	Will	Power	Transformation	Mastery
2	**PRIESTESS**	Insight	Penetration	Intuition	Mystery
3	**EMPRESS**	Nurturance	Love	Healing	Creation
4	**EMPEROR**	Order	Structure	Construction	Authority
5	**HIEROPHANT**	Guidance	Ethics	Learning	Understanding
6	**LOVERS**	Relationship	Harmony	Accommodation	Union
7	**CHARIOT**	Attainment	Action	Pursuit	Challenge
8	**STRENGTH**	Confidence	Endurance	Acceptance	Self-esteem
9	**HERMIT**	Wisdom	Retreat	Introspection	Soul
10	**WHEEL OF FORTUNE**	Change	Timing	Flow	Opportunity
11	**JUSTICE**	Equanimity	Balance	Adjustment	Equality
12	**HANGED MAN**	Awareness	Suspension	Surrender	Transcendence
13	**DEATH**	Metamorphosis	Dissolution	Dying	Life
14	**TEMPERANCE**	Transmutation	Integration	Blending	Refinement
15	**DEVIL**	Separation	Opposition	Deception	Domination
16	**TOWER**	Destruction	Resistance	Evacuation	Liberation
17	**STAR**	Luminosity	Inspiration	Emergence	Hope
18	**MOON**	Psyche	Imagination	Fluctuation	Emotion
19	**SUN**	Consciousness	Energy	Activity	Awareness
20	**JUDGMENT**	Resolution	Completion	Awakening	Accountability
21	**WORLD**	Wholeness	Universality	Participation	Celebration
0	**FOOL**	Possibility	Openness	Discovery	Play

Notes

[1]*Diagnostic and Statistical Manual of Mental Disorders* (Fourth Edition); American Psychiatric Association, Washington, DC, p. xxii.

[2]*Ethnographic Portraits: The Inupiat Eskimo of Arctic Alaska;* Internet: http:www.lib.uconn.edu/Arctic Circle/Cultural Viability/Inupiat/1800s.html.

[3]Jung, C. G., *Collected Works,* Vol. 9 Part 1: *The Archetypes and the Collective Unconscious;* Bollingen Series, Princeton University Press, 1969, paragraph 90.

[4]Corbett, Lionel, *The Religious Function of the Psyche;* Routledge, London, 1996.

[5]Cirlot, J. E., *A Dictionary of Symbols* (Second Edition); Routledge & Kegan Paul Ltd., London, 1962.

[6]Samuels, Andrew, Shorter, Bani, and Plant, Fred, *A Critical Dictionary of Jungian Analysis;* Routledge & Kegan Paul Ltd, 1986, p. 27.

[7]Young-Eisendrath, Polly, and Hall, James A., *Jung's Self Psychology: A Constructivist Perspective;* The Guilford Press, New York, 1991.

[8]Metzner, Ralph, *Maps Of Consciousness;* Collier Books, New York, 1971, p. 55

[9]Nichols, Sallie, *Jung and Tarot: An Archetypal Journey;* Samuel Weiser Inc, York Berach, Maine, 1980, p. 145.

[10]Young-Eisendrath, Polly, and Hall, James A., *Jung's Self Psychology: A Constructivist Perspective;* The Guilford Press, New York, 1991, p.5.

[11]Cirlot, J. E., *A Dictionary of Symbols* (Second Edition); Routledge & Kegan Paul Ltd., London, 1962. p. 147.

[12]Ibid., p.44.

Chapter VIII

THE FOOL'S JOURNEY

> If the place I want to arrive at could only be reached by a ladder, I would give up trying to arrive at it. For the place I really have to reach is where I must already be. What is reachable by a ladder doesn't interest me.
>
> —Ludwig Wittgenstein (1889-1951)

Imaginal Doors

For centuries Tarot scholars have approached the 22 Major Arcana through their esoteric roots and properties, which unfortunately appeals less to psychological practitioners who would otherwise incorporate these symbols into conventional psychotherapy. Robert V. O'Neill (1986) for instance, in his landmark study of the Major Arcana's historical and esoteric foundations, has detailed Tarot's likely emergence in the Italian Renaissance, along with its philosophical and metaphysical underpinnings to the ancient teachings of Plato and Neoplatonism, gnosticism and mystery religions, hermeticism, Christian mysticism, Jewish Kabbalah, Eastern religion, alchemy, medieval memory arts, numerology, and astrology.[1] But what we seek in this study, with our practical feet to the ground, are contemporary psychological symbols and steps that are meaningful to a large and eclectic range of modern and postmodernist psychotherapists and clients alike, images which require no special understanding of complex esoteric systems, however profound.

Other authors like Greer[2] and Giles[3] have written thorough accountings of Tarot's fascinating evolution up to the present, including Tarot's early 20th-century developments largely influenced by the British *Order of the Golden Dawn*, under the tutelage of Waite, Crowley, MacGregor Mathers, William Butler Yeats, Israel Regardie, Paul Foster Case, et al., who have shown Tarot's intimate relationship to the hermetic Kabbalah. Additionally, Giles has described Tarot's more recent American ascendancy towards archetypal psychology and New Age spirituality, and its relevance even to quantum physics and the creative arts. Nevertheless, Giles notes:

> Tarot begins in the realm of the imagination. Imagination is the faculty that allows us to experience the immaterial. Ordinary perception operates through the senses, and so is confined entirely to experience of the material world, but imagination is not bound by the rules of space and time which govern materiality. Through the mode of imagination, it is possible to travel instantaneously into the past or future, to other lands, beyond the earth, and even to realms that don't exist in the material dimension.[4]

It is within the imaginal doors of mind, apart from specialized esoteric training and initiation, that we now traverse the Major Arcana. As we proceed through the Greater Arcana we must guard against a tendency to confine or reduce the meaning of a symbol to its most narrow limit, as for instance Freudians have done with sexuality, a practice we have described as "degrading the symbol." "Penis envy," for instance, degrades the multiple forces vying for discovery. The symbol's influence must be free to pervade all levels of reality, for only then can its primal intensity, spiritual grandeur and psychological depth fully flower.

The Fool's Journey

Many scholars have imagined the Tarot trumps to chronicle The Fool's movement of psychospiritual initiation through the essential 21 'doors' of personality development and transformation that comprise the Major Arcana. The Fool, alone of no real number, the great unmanifest zero, is thought to embody everyman (woman, and child) in all his or her innocence, potentiality, and absence of fear. The Fool is the blank slate of infinite possibility (or as Rupert Sheldrake suggests, the ready and waiting fully-loaded

automatic camera) who now is possessed to make his way through the rigors of experience and the phenomenal world. Each numbered key (or trump) opens for The Fool one essential door on a sequential procession through psychological initiation, growth, maturity, and integration. As one step is trodden and assimilated, a natural progression is made ready for the incorporation of each next developmental step of the great journey.

On this so-called "Fool's Journey" through the Major Arcana, linear assumptions first mark the commencement at the earliest stage of development, namely at trump 1, The Magician. As we saw in the lexicon of the previous chapter, The Magician, as prime mover, is an agent of human will, organized around personal power, in the process of self transformation, and he is aroused and motivated by mastery of the world. As The Fool enters The Magician's chamber, these lessons will be studied at many individual points within the querent and The Magician's spectrums of possibility, for as Emerson correctly observed, "Life is a succession of lessons, which must be lived to be understood."

A client in therapy perhaps finds this first door relates to her pattern of victimization, and is given to consider The Magician's unique talents for self-creation, responsibility through choice, resourcefulness and personal empowerment. Another client is taught to visualize desired outcomes or perhaps the use of positive affirmation. Through countless cycles of the journey, The Fool will repeat this and every other door's challenge until the time when, hypothetically, the lesson has become sufficiently absorbed and integrated.

Developmental progress is then tracked through The Fool's forward movement progressively and numerically, one door at a time, from door "number 2" to door "number 20," up until the final door is entered, that being The World card (trump 21), agent of wholeness, organized around universality, in the process of participation, and aroused by transcendental celebration ("the dance of life"). The journey presumably ends there, where in principle, this final state is now fully opened, apprehended, realized, and complete.

Yet despite this final attainment on The Journey, the primacy of importance is still awarded to the earliest trumps of the procession, the archetypal mothers and fathers, the magicians, priests and priestesses of the primary trumps—the so-called 'root' cards—if only by their initiatory agency as first causes. The World, for instance, as number 21, reduces numerologically downward (2+1) to its earliest value, The Empress (trump 3). Judgment (trump 20) reduces to The Priestess (2+ 0) or trump 2, and The Majestic Sun (1+9=10=1+0=1) reducing first to The Wheel of Fortune (trump 10) but more profoundly to its root in The Magician (trump 1). In a manner of speaking, one must first achieve "root card success" much as the Freudian implores "Oedipal success" (or the Post-Freudian demands "object constancy") before The Fool is sufficiently prepared to take on the greater demands of psychological maturity.

Number symbolism thus becomes crucial to the linear unfoldment of the process, as development conceptualized through a "past, present, and future" now adds a progressive arithmetical dimension to Tarot's numerology. The Fool's Journey is predestined from the beginning, out of which a hierarchy of sorts is predetermined. For example, trump 3, The Empress is seen as 'higher' (or at least, likely to occur 'later') on the evolutionary spiral than trump 2, The Priestess—but by what guiding principle exactly? In all cases, does the insight and penetration of The Priestess always precede the nurturance and love of The Empress?

Some tarotists have ventured into thicker linear woods still. Addition and subtraction become attractive operations once the symbolic magic of numbers reaches our calculating minds. Through a simple arithmetic operation, trump 2 may then be added to trump 3 to create trump 5, the priestly Hierophant. Elaborate metaphysical formulae and Kabbalistic rationales are then applied to justify such calculations. I believe, however, that such seductive meanderings will soon lead The Fool to his early retirement. Numerological entities have become "trumped up" to take on additional mathematical properties, in effect, mixing in one steaming cauldron both number quality and quantity. Add a Priestess to an Empress and voila! Out comes a Pope. But does this truly make good sense?

The linear formulation of The Fool's Journey through progressive doors of growth and initiation is similar to contemporary Western theories of personality development; ironically, both are formulated within scientific (mechanistic) constructions of causation and evolution that were popular at the turn of the last century when much of the groundwork for Psychology was laid. *The view assumes a linear path of change and growth.* Even when framed within esoteric doctrine, Tarot paradigms have often carried structural presuppositions parallel to mainstream cultural and scientific perspectives. Linear time, an essential feature of this worldview, is in fact a metaphysical assumption all its own. No matter how matter-of-fact it appears to us today, linear time assumes that change flows like a line, independently of the events it supposedly contains. It assumes The Fool passes through the successive doors of the Major Arcana with a predetermined script, following a developmental yellow brick road of sorts, independent of his own subjective inclinations to veer off onto various sidestreets or poppyfields. But as we know, for all the hoopla surrounding his wizardly eminence, the great Oz of Emerald City was something of an embarrassment.

Rather surprisingly, notes Brent Slife, the extraordinary success of this relatively recent paradigm of linear time owes its greatest debt to nothing more temporal than the Industrial Revolution's introduction and marketing of mass produced, affordable wristwatches. Imagine—our brave new world invented by the precursors of the Timex! Now all citizens could confidently point to their timepieces as proof that their hours, and indeed their lives, were speedily ticking away. What we have since taken for granted as 'time' in many ways is no more than a modern invention manufactured in the 19th-century. The full ramifications of this point are obviously larger than our brief mention here. But Slife makes a clear and, I think, critical differentiation:

> Time is distinguishable from linear time: Time is a concept having to do with change. Linear time is a concept having to do with the organization or interpretation of that change.[6]

The fact is, linear time remains today so confounded with Time (the overall concept) that the two are virtually indistinguishable for most people in Western culture. The progressive stages of The Fool's Journey mirrors this Newtonian paradigm of "Time's arrow": an absolute measurement of change that moves progressively forward towards a future, but is independent of the events that are contained. While subjective accounts are variable, the path itself is predetermined. Effects are linked more to the influence of previous causes than to parallel events, or future possibilities. Inferred in this premise is the placement of primacy to the past. Ontologically, the past is thus considered the "mother of experience" as the linear premise attributes greatest weight to the earliest events; the 'first' in a sequence is the temporal entity that supposedly starts the process. Slife notes:

> The metaphor of the line means that the present and future must remain consonant with the past. The past is thought to be the temporal entity with the most utility. The present is less useful because it is just a stopover on the line of time, and the future is even less useful because it is not yet known with any certainty. Only information from the past is viewed as substantive and certain enough to be truly known and understood.[7]

Most 20th-century models of psychological development accord primacy to the past as well. Freud, without rival, was to make Psychology's dependence upon the past an established fact. Childhood experiences are still today viewed as crucial to present emotional problems, biographical history continues to dominate assessment, and "how we were raised" is still the preferred self explanation (or justification) for present behavior. The same linear inclination can be seen transferred to the myth of The Fool's Journey in Tarot.

Even theorists that are diametrically opposed to Freud on most issues, both within Psychology and Tarot, seem to agree with him on the significance of the past. Cognitive-behavioral therapists, for instance, attend to past inputs and memory encodings; humanists refer to long lost opportunities for growth and are champions of therapeutic 'process'; behaviorists consider reinforcement history, progressive relaxation, and immediately *preceding* stimuli. Tarotists, likewise, construct elaborate progressive explanations for each card's developmental link on the timeline of universal truth, some of which seem reasonable, while others seem more of a stretch [as for example, the strange developmental logic that explains why Temperance (14) is developmentally sandwiched between Death (13) and The Devil (15)]. While the influence of the past can never be denied, and linear laws must be accorded their rightful station in the scheme of things, in all of the cases above some form of the linear past is granted special "causal status" and presumed to have primacy in importance over simultaneous and interconnected behaviors in the present, to say nothing of the influence of the future.

The Fool's Itinerary

Often this so-called journey through the Majors is further subdivided into three parallel lines of seven trumps, corresponding to the three-fold Hegelian dialectic of change (thesis/antithesis/synthesis), the laws of becoming, or psychological process. Such subgroupings give the Fool's itinerary a new set of hierarchies. Depending on the theorist, the first row of seven may signify the stages attending the development of consciousness [Magician (1) through Chariot (7)], the second those attending the features of the unconscious [Strength (8) through Temperance (14)], and the third, those attending the collective unconscious or transpersonal realms [Devil (15) through World (21)]. Presumably, this procession through grade levels of psychospiritual education guides the soul's initiation into higher consciousness.

Variations on the theme are sometimes suggested to conform to related philosophical/metaphysical theories. Roberts, for instance, contends that the Major Arcana makes more sense when divided into two rows of nine [Magician to Hermit] [Wheel of Fortune to Moon] (with the remainder of four), owing to the hermetic properties of the 'Magic Number 9' which show "the ability to preserve the original archetypal meaning of the number to which it is added, and yet transforms that number as well."[8]

Still other Tarot commentators have suggested splitting the Major Arcana into two parts, separated at the midpoint of The Wheel of Fortune and Justice. In this division by halves, The Fool's Journey is marked off by central oppositional cycles in the lifespan, such as the ascent/descent of spirit and matter, the first half/second half of life, the structuring and deconstructing of reality, or even the personal/transpersonal stages of individuation. However, implicit in each of these models remains the presupposition of linear development and change, one which I believe ultimately places unnecessary limitations on experience and possibility.

As a curious reminder of the inherent problematics that can spin away from an over-reliance on linear laws, Tarot historian O'Neill to the chagrin of many tarotists, has discovered early evidence of significant variance in the numbering system of the Major Arcana. For example, a 16th-century variation of the deck inverts trumps 7 and 8 and furthermore reverses the sequence of trumps 9,10, 11. Purists beware! Noting up to eight variations of the traditional Tarot de Marseilles (circa 1567) not including Waite's well-known modern inversion of trump 8 (traditionally Justice) with trump 11 (Strength), followed almost religiously by contemporary designers, O'Neill notes:

> But even if we argue successfully for the ordering of the Tarot de Marseilles…we still have problems with numbering. The sequencing of the cards causes little problem for the interpretations developed throughout our studies. But variations still cause problems for our study of Numerology.[9]

By Kaballistic (Hermetic) tradition, the 22 letters of the Hebrew alphabet describe in their sequence the entire cycle of existence, and in combination, the infinite units of creation. The 22 images of the Major Arcana appear to be an attempt to convey symbolically the essence of each letter. The Fool's Journey (from Aleph to Tav—Fool to World) can certainly be viewed as 22 episodes in the life of the universe, or of a man or woman, or of an enterprise, or perhaps even of a course of analysis. Sequences can be divided into groups such that they reveal a myriad of operating formulae fixed within this universal structure. However, in the final analysis, as Lon Milo DuQuette, author *of The Tarot of Ceremonial Magick,* distinguishes:

> It is not the Fool's Journey but the Fool's *Story* (illustrated by the infinite *combination* of letters to form words) that affords us a mind-boggling peek at the workings of the divine mind—a creative consciousness in which patterns and formulae play a secondary role in a cauldron churning with the potentiality of all possible possibilities. This would explain the desirability to transfer the concept of each letter to cards that can easily be shuffled and grouped in nearly infinite combinations.

Non-linear Avenues: Love Minus Zero

Einstein once remarked, "not everything that can be counted counts, and not everything that counts can be counted." As it is quite certain this Zen koan-like observation attributed to the father of modern physics was not referring to the differentiation of number and numerology in Tarot, it nevertheless applies to our discussion here as well. Thus far we have tracked, however cursorily, a numeric succession of linear steps unfolding through the medium of 'time'. But as time is simply a concept pertaining to change, it need not be interpreted exclusively from a Newtonian standpoint which postulates an absolute and continuous sequence of changes like that of real numbers. In the Newtonian construction, the rate of change is believed to exist independently of the events taking place within it.

Given this paradigm, the spontaneous *subjective* direction of life's "adventure" is given little validity or play. Newton might well argue that if unfolding through time were indeed a subjective experience, distinctions between sacrosanct temporal dimensions—the past, present, and future—would be (heaven forbid) left up to the perceiver himself, leaving an objective science to falter along fissures of the self. The mechanistic hypothesis would soon be in great danger along with its impeccable aura of stainless steel certainty. Experientially, past and future occur in the present only. Newton, I daresay, would grow quite glum presenting his causal paradigm to the impeccable Zen master of San Francisco, circa 1975, the honorable Bishop Syaku, whose kindly retort to all well-conceived and articulated ideas was a predictable belly laugh and the friendly injunction: "Ah yes! Big concept of your mind!" in reference to virtually any variety of 'childish' supposition sent forth, especially those jucier ones like reality, time, cause and effect, or even Buddha. "There is no 'reality'. (Laughter). Only concepts of your mind!"

Yet in Psychology, dependence upon linear causality even today has been taken for granted as the accepted explanation for change. Psychological *becoming* in Western psychology takes great precedence over psychological *being*. Adolescence, for example, is studied more as a transitional task between childhood and adulthood to be suffered, managed, and mastered, than appreciated as a whole experience unto itself (which if you recall, was truly a whole experience unto itself!). 'Being' a teenager, unquestionably, is given less serious attention than 'becoming' an adult.

But a 15-year-old today trying to explain his own salacious urge for body-part piercing or "gothic rock" as "fulfilling my core developmental need for peer identification in preparation for adulthood" simply isn't believed. Linearity, unavoidably, imposes such structural guidelines and absurd explanations onto direct phenomenology. The subjective experience of meaning, that which gives life its 'lived' quality, is excluded from the operation. Most psychological subject matters are similarly approached in this way. They emphasize 'why' questions to explicate cause and effect answers. Indeed, key presuppositions based on a linear framework have become second nature to contemporary psychological explanation, including the notions of objectivity, continuity, process, and reductivity. But as Lao Tsu observed some 2500 years ago:

> A good traveler has no fixed plans, and is not intent on arriving.

Quantum Paradigms

Ironically, modern scientific criticism of linear time has come foremost in physics, the place it was born. Einstein's conceptual forerunner, Ernest Mach, believed a linear conception of time was incapable of embracing the multiplicity of relations in nature. Instead events are more properly understood as functionally interdependent, with no particular event taking precedence simply because it occurred before the other in time. Quite to the contrary, Einstein's theory of relativity was largely based on his examination and rejection of the Newtonian linear view of time. Einstein believed that time is not absolute, but relative. As the special theory of relativity shows, time measurements depend upon the state of motion of the observer (or the state of awareness of the subject). Noting that time, in truth, is not a substance that "flows equably without relation to anything external" (as Newton believed), Einstein wrote:

> Concepts which have proved useful for ordering things easily assume so great an authority over us that we forget their terrestrial origins and accept them as unalterable facts. (As cited in Slife, p. 16)

Although the Newtonian view remains today dominant in Western culture and psychological explanation, modern quantum physicists have not only disputed the reductivity, linearity, and objectivity of time; they have also challenged the continuity of events across time. For instance, electrons move from one orbit to another instantaneously (without time lapse). Electrons simply disappear from one quandrant and reappear in another, demonstrating that change can truly be discontinuous—not just faster rates of change, but change without temporal duration. For our discussion, a construction of the Major Arcana may also be built from a non-linear, non-continuous perspective.

Non-linear psychological approaches tend to focus on three cardinal factors of psychic reality: the here/now, simultaneity, and interdependency. They place primacy of importance not on the (linear) past or even the probable (deterministic) future, but rather on the lived present. In this sense, they are more reflective than predictive. Although the importance of the past and the directionality of events ("time's arrow") are not denied, holistic and structural thinkers differ with linear theorists as to which time dimension exerts the most influence upon events. The distinction becomes a question of linearity versus simultaneity. Holists look primarily to the events which are simultaneous (i.e., concurrent) with the events under study, rather than those that precede them in linear time. This parallels the approach divination takes, asking the question: what seems to gather together in this moment of time? Other examples of important Western constructs that have emerged from emphasizing the primacy of the present include: context, system, synchronicity, interpersonal field, and implicate order.[10]

Interestingly enough, so-called 'futurists' also focus intensively on the present to make their predictions. This because as Ralph Waldo Emerson noted: "What lies behind us and what lies before us are small matters compared to what lies within us." Peter Schwartz, cofounder of Global Business Network, who advises the Pentagon and large corporations on adapting to the new realities of an information-based world, notes:

> The most successful futurists don't predict the future. They make their fortune by interpreting the present in a new way—a way that makes more sense and seems more conventional the farther into the future one goes.

Moreover, as will be discussed in greater detail in the next chapter, Jungian synchronicity emphasizes the impact that "meaningful coincidence" has on a subject's experience of the here/now. Jung like Einstein saw space and time as mental constructions, psychic in origin, and not existent in themselves. In reality, Jung believed space and time are created by the intellectual needs of the observer, caught beneath the spell of collective and archetypal belief. Jung anticipated what has already happened in modern physics, namely, that as intellectual needs radically shift, constructions of 'spacetime' have also begun to radically shift.

Wolfgang Pauli, the brilliant Nobel laureate and professor of theoretical physics, who together with Niels Bohr, Werner Heisenberg and Paul Dirac was a principal creator of quantum mechanics and quantum field theory, found in Jung's theory of synchronicity the promise of a new scientific paradigm applicable to nature in its entirety.

Pauli wrote:

> The ordering factors must be considered beyond the distinction of 'physical' and 'psychic'—as Plato's ideas share the character of a notion with that of a 'natural force.' I am very much in favour of calling these ordering factors 'archetypes', but then it would be inadmissible to define them as contents of the psyche. Instead the inner images are psychic manifestations of the archetypes, which, however, also would have to create, produce, cause everything in the material world that happens according to the laws of nature. The laws of the material world would thus refer to the physical manifestations of the archetypes.... Each natural law should then have an inner correspondence and vice versa, even if this is not always immediately visible today.[11]

Still today, regrettably and almost by definition, most accepted Western theories of psychological development (Freud, Piaget, Eric Erickson, Margaret S. Mahler, etc.) continue to lag behind such shifts of perception and vision, remaining intimately locked to realism and the linear passage of time which places primacy on the past, is continuous, causative, and flows equably without regard to anything external.

The Buddhist Traveler

For non-linear thinkers, as promised, another approach to the Major Arcana is at hand. While passage through consecutive doors on The Fool's linear journey (even allowing for fixation, arrest, and regression) may appeal to the rationalist constructions of conventional developmental theorists, this paradigm defuses the essential synchronistic nature of the Tarot method. It is one thing to didactically illustrate the stages of human development through a coherent procession of causally-linked symbolic representations, but quite another to express the actual simultaneous, chaotic, and interdependent realities that operate in true experience. Certainly the Tarot method allows for both perspectives, but its greater force unquestionably comes with the latter. A reading will focus intensively on those archetypal patterns that are configured in the present moment simultaneous to the querent's conscious concerns.

Perhaps the clearest expression of psychological development along non-linear avenues comes not from Western models of personality development but rather from Eastern models, and in particular, the ancient Buddhist doctrine of "dependent co-origination" *(pratitya samutpada/paticca-samuppada)* which states boldly that all physical and mental manifestations constituting individual appearances are interdependent; moreover, they condition or affect one another and are in a constant process of arising and ceasing to be.

Dependent co-origination (sometimes translated as "interconnected arising") subscribes to the three invariants of non-linear reality as we have discussed here: the primacy of the present (here/now), simultaneity, and interdependency. What further distinguishes Buddhism from other psychospiritual traditions is its key doctrine of the "emptiness of self" *(sunyata/sunnatta)* which states that "just as the individual is 'void' of a self, in the sense of an unchanging controlling agency, so too is the whole universe 'void of a self or anything belonging to a self."[12]

Scottish philosopher David Hume (1711-76), regarded today as one of the most enduring European thinkers of the 18th century, similarly was unable to find any introspective evidence of the self, a concept he attributed to a misinterpretation, a fantasy, or a fiction of the human imagination. Contemporary Western analysis in the science of consciousness has also tried to explain how it's possible that we still commonly experience a 'self' despite Hume's analysis. If the self is not a soul, not a Cartesian substance, if its psychological continuity is tenuous, then why do we still believe that we have a certain identity over time? A driving concern for modern theorists regarding the "problem of the self" includes assertions that there is no self; that the idea is a logical, psychological, or grammatical fiction. Rival views contend that the sense of self is properly seen and defined in terms of brain processes, or that it is merely a constructed sociological locus, or that it is the center of personal and public narratives, or that it belongs in an ineffable category all its own (this latter view comes closest to the Buddhist position). Notes Gallagher:

> Among these responses there is no consensus about how to approach the problems of self, much less what the appropriate resolution might be. In short, the modern philosophers have rendered both our commonsensical and our philosophical notions of self utterly problematic.[13]

As elaborate, and altogether mind-bending as the Buddhist view of psychological development is, we must limit our discussion to the traditional Buddhist doctrine of "radical becoming" *(Nagarjuna)* which is distinguished from the common Western view that regards change as pertaining to a core entity called 'self'. In the Buddhist view, the phenomenon which we call a 'person' is understood simply as a composite of factors or elements *(dharmas)* which are related in an orderly manner but which are continually in flux. The doctrine also denies the existence of an absolute universal essence and suggests that the proper place to gain an understanding of reality is with phenomenal existence, seen as a succession of constructions.

When a person passes through the stages of the lifespan, for instance, or through the doors of the Major Arcana, the common assumption is that some basic entity of selfhood continues throughout, what earlier was deemed 'agency'. The Buddhist view, to the contrary, is that the world and self are continually 'becoming'—yet 'are' in themselves nothing.[14] The nonlinear tarotist explores the interconnected arisings of phenomena through Tarot symbols, appreciative that interpretations are merely constructions and have no ultimate existence, are momentary reflections of the cosmic web of appearance, and that such is the nature of all human experience in general.

While contemporary quantum physicists have grown quite enthralled by ancient Buddhist metaphysics (see David Bohm, Frijof Capra, Gary Zukov, Victor Mansfield and others), this otherwise foreign and esoteric notion is made immediately intelligible to our psychological audience by the elusively simple parable given by contemporary Vietnamese Zen monk and international teacher, Thich Nhat Hanh. In *The Heart of Understanding: Commentaries on the Prajnaparamita Heart Sutra,* Thich Nhat Hanh speaks of "interbeing." To illustrate, he invites us to meditate on a blank piece of paper. Says the Buddhist monk:

> If you are a poet, you will see clearly that there is a cloud floating in this sheet of paper. Without a cloud, there will be no rain; without rain, the trees cannot grow; and without trees, we cannot make paper. The cloud is essential for the paper to exist. If the cloud is not here, the sheet of paper cannot be here either. So we can say that the cloud and the paper inter-are. "Interbeing" is a word that is not in the dictionary yet, but if we combine the prefix "inter-" with the verb "to be," we have a new verb, inter-be. Without a cloud, we cannot have paper, so we can say that the cloud and the sheet of paper inter-are (p. 3).

The author's meditation unfolds through layer upon layer of interdependencies. The sunshine is needed for the forest to grow, as is the logger who must cut down the tree, and presumably, the truck driver who must cart it to the mill, and the gas station attendant who must pump the truck with deisel. Without them, the paper cannot exist. In turn, the logger cannot log without his daily bread nor can the trucker truck without his cups of java, and accordingly, Nebraska wheat and coffee beans from Uganda must also reside within this single sheet of paper. The logic of 'interbeing' expands finally to include the logger's parents, the earth, the minerals in the soil, the river, the heat, the moon, the stars, and even our own minds, as obviously the sheet of paper is part of our perception. Thich Nhat Hanh concludes:

> The fact is that this sheet of paper is made up only of "non-paper elements." And if we return these non-paper elements to their sources, then there can be no paper at all. Without "non-paper elements," like mind, logger, sunshine and so on, there will be no paper. As thin as this sheet of paper is, it contains everything in the universe in it (p. 5).

The Circle of Interbeing

To properly imagine the Major Arcana from the perspective of 'interbeing' we must first unburden The Fool's Journey of its most defining symbol—the line—and replace it with the geometric form that best describes non-linearity, that is, the circle. That ubiquitous line, however impressive for structuring psychological explanation, has taken our poor unsuspecting Fool down a one-way dead-end street of diminishing possibility. What is needed instead is an approach that captures the spontaneous dance of universal energy whereby existence is created and extinguished in the here/now, carrying the simultaneous and interdependent flavor of unfolding, lived, subjective experience. That is, the realm of open possibility—The Fool's manifest destiny itself.

Suppose instead we choose this more circuitous route. The 'mandala', a Hindu term for circle, is an ancient circular map that describes "mental status" of one kind or another; it is entirely compatible with The Fool's Journey. Mandalas are used for contemplation and concentration, as in the well-known Tibetan Buddhist thanka mandalas, and are found throughout the Orient to this day. Buddhist scholar D.L. Snellgrove notes:

> The essential feature of a mandala is its regularity towards the various directions, for the first thing it must express is emanation from a centre into space. As the divinities in whose forms the process of emanation is expressed have the value of pure symbol, their forms and their number are relevant only to the categories in terms of which the meditator conceives of his own personality, for it is these two things, the divine nirvana forms and the components of his own self (samsara), which are to be identified.[15]

As such the mandala offers the proper conceptual and visual framework from which to approach non-linear subjectivity and interbeing. Thus for our purposes, placement of The Fool inside the circle represents a subjective, here/now emanation from a center into the imaginal doors of Tarot space.

Jung himself saw in the Eastern mandala the symbolic expression of the archetypal self. Apparently after visiting the Lamaist convent of Bhutia Busty, Jung's interest was heightened when a senior monk described to him the mandala as a "mental image which may be built up in the imagination only by a trained lama," and further maintained that "no one mandala is the same as another." This meant one thing: mandala heterogeneity mirrors the unique psychic condition of its author. Jung wrote:

> Although the centre is represented by an innermost point, it is surrounded by a periphery containing everything that belongs to the self—the paired opposites that make up the total personality. This totality comprises consciousness first of all, then the personal unconscious, and finally an indefinitely large segment of the collective unconscious whose archetypes are common to all mankind.[16]

With this in mind, as we construct a nonlinear map of the Major Arcana with The Fool at the centerpoint, we place equidistant at the periphery (and in no particular order) the remaining 21 trumps. No single card should universally be designated the "beginning" or "end point," more in keeping with the Buddhist cosmology of a beginningless and endless universe. Instead, the journey must unfold in the present moment according to the "unique psychic condition of its author," that is, subjectively, simultaneously, and interdependently. This spontaneous and unmediated order is, in fact, identical to the "empowered randomness" of the Tarot method itself elucidated in Chapter III.

The following configuration is a projected and spontaneous image of the psychic condition of this author at this moment:

Mandala of One Fool's Journey

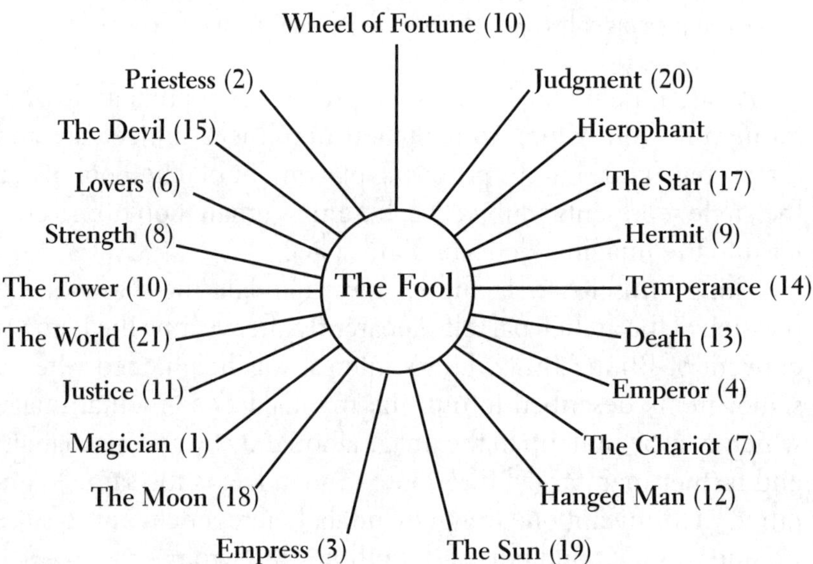

In this approach, wherever one's attention is drawn will mirror one's psychic condition in this moment, and thus becoming the journey's subjective starting point. As you can see, no arithmetic order or linear value is assigned the positions on the periphery, yet each trump on the circle nevertheless maintains its number symbolism as indicated in the parentheses after its name. The 2 of The Priestess card, for instance, maintains its numerological associations with two-ness whether the card appears second or seventeenth in one Fool's subjective journey. Its timing and placement is simply one patch on the self-created quilt from which one constructs subjective reality. Though no two stories are ever quite the same in Tarot, each human tale is spun from the same matrix of imaginal ideas (or Buddhist *samsara*) present in the material of the cards.

Now using Thich Nhat Hanh's allegorical logic, imagine each Tarot trump at the circle's periphery to be no more or less than one (symbolic) sheet of paper. If you are The Fool (and let's presume each of us is), and you are surrounded in all directions by the archetypal invariants of universal possibility (i.e., The Major Arcana), it matters little which arcanum calls your attention first or begins your journey, for in truth they all possess "inter-being" at all times.

Suppose, then, on this "Fool's Journey" you are drawn first to the balanced scales of Justice (trump 11), or perhaps the dire lunacy and howling mongrels of The Moon (trump 18), or even the ominous facade of The Lightning Struck Tower (trump 16), with its crumbling forces of destruction and its mighty walls of protection. Trump 16 (which seems, inexplicably, to catch my own attention in this moment) suffers the status of the besieged, leaving one feeling crushed apart in the mayhem of ruin and exodus. Pathologically, we may even equate The Tower card with the anachronistic "nervous breakdown," the decompensation of the ego complex. Here perhaps is as good a place to start as anywhere.

The Tower (New Palladini)

But look closer at this "Lightning Struck Tower" and you will soon discover many other things as well. You might glimpse (to your surprise) a noble Emperor within the edifice, unfazed in the fallen courtyard, and huddled proudly before his dismayed minions like the Great Alexander, now vigorously plotting their immanent escape. By the laws of opposition, naturally, without The Emperor's dominion, that is, without his strong structuring ego, there need be no mighty Tower built to contain him. Without The Emperor's command and impeccable sense of order and four-square reality, there can be no chaos and disorder now wreaking havoc. Without his formidable powers of construction and expansion, there is no counterforce of destruction and decompensation. In this sense, we can say that The Tower and The Emperor 'inter-are', that is, they share a quality of interbeing.

Looking deeper still beyond The Tower's facade, past the hysteria and exhaustion that comes with dramatic collapse, you will see sitting graciously at the imperiled Emperor's side his beautiful Queen, The Empress, radiant goddess of beauty and earthly abundance. There can be no Emperor without Empress. That is, without her gifts and abiding love, The Emperor grows weary and sullen, and forfeits The Tower. Without her passion and fertility, the Kingdom falls barren and empty, and admits of no children; without her sacred touch and feminine healing powers, the people grow ill and despondent. Therefore, we can say The Tower, The

Emperor and also The Empress share this interbeing. That is, all three *mutually co-arise*, all three inter-are.

But what about The Hierophant, upon whose wise counsel The Emperor so thoroughly depends? Without his subtle guidance and ethical wisdom The Emperor's command grows wooden and the people fall unruly and rebel. Or Temperance, who teaches The Emperor right pacing, patience, and the blending arts of a creative and benevolent leader? Or for that matter Strength, who conjoins her gentle kindness and good cheer with the ferocity of a lion, king of the beasts, and inspires the people's trust and confidence? The fact is, The Tower is made up of decidedly non-Tower elements. How could it be otherwise? Without such things, The Tower would hardly be recognized as The Tower (some medeival restoration project in the Balkans, maybe). And so we must also say as well that The Hierophant, Temperance, and Strength too have interbeing with The Tower, The Emperor and The Empress. All mutually co-arise. All inter-are. Without each constituent part, The Tower would not be The Tower, or The Emperor, The Emperor.

But if we look even closer at The Tower, without stretching terribly hard, we will also discover The Sun above it and The World around It, as far as the eye can see. The Sun, of course, energizes The Empress's vitality and passion and The Emperor's awareness and confidence. The four corners of The World hold the object of The Empress's aspiration to nurture and the boundaries of The Emperor's empire to rule. Without them The Empress grows alienated and disconsolate, and The Emperor falls unconscious and fragmented. This worries the people who in turn grow restless and agitated. Anxiety fills the land. The Tower feels shaky now, showing early signs of instability and chaos. The Kingdom is not well.

Gazing still further into The Tower, however, we may even catch the redhorned Devil, from whose outward manifestations of deception, ironically, The Tower itself was built to defend. Through his seductive forces The Devil now makes his diabolical mischief; he tempts the pale Empress pining and forlorn in The Tower to spin Fate's Wheel of Fortune (in the light of the Full

Moon and the zeal of The Lovers) to thus steal away to The Handsome Hermit, sitting alone beyond The Tower's gate, contemplating Hermit matters beneath his lucky Star. Trouble beckons.

The Magician is summoned to bring special spells and potions to sweeten the air for their immanent flight, and the sturdy steeds of The Chariot are made ready for two. But suddenly The Empress takes pause to reflect before The Hanged Man. Is this plan truly all that it seems? she asks. Gladly, by the trumpeted graces of clear and better Judgment, she reverses plans and is moved instead to secure her own private session with The Hierophant, a Kohutian, who at once assures her, naturally, that everything said in his inner sanctum will be strictly confidential!

The two discuss the advantages of delayed impulse gratification and the greater implications of drive theory for much of the 45-minute hour. Her eyes are opened to the beginningless web of interrelations that must account for any single action. The Devil, much as The Wheel of Fortune, The Moon, The Lovers, The Hermit, The Star, The Magician, The Chariot, The Hanged Man, and even The Hierophant himself, all share essential interbeing with herself. In closing, she agrees to bring The Emperor with her for regular weekly Hierophantic sessions. The people, as if by serendipity, now celebrate in great jubilation for the return of the Kingdom, and the sweet fragrance of luscious apples and pomegranates waft from The Tower's many orchards and lofty heights bringing a renewed spirit of joy to the land.

In this half-serious allegory, we see the laws of interbeing extending through most of the majors. The tale is a single example of the many forces co-arising in the present moment beyond (or better, 'within') a "presenting problem" or identified symptom. The psychological forces so outlined are present-focused, simultaneous, and interdependent. They are also crucial to the accurate assessment of the whole individual in his or her situational context. Most clinicians, if only through daily experience, will recognize such complexity lurking within any designated problem. But it should be emphasized again that the above interrelations were subjectively ordered and generated, reflected in experience, and not easily predicted along a linear or historical progression of events.

Alternate possibilities to our fable would appear indeed endless, given the unique outer concerns and particulars of the parties involved, yet it should be remembered that such possibilities were drawn from a finite pool of archetypal invariants: namely the 22 trumps of the Major Arcana. Interbeing, in fact, may explain why Tarot divination nearly always is perceived as meaningful and accurate to its subject. If everything indeed is interconnected and emerges from one cosmic vat of possibility, it would be impossible not to find or construct meaningful correspondence in any given reading. But one critical question remains. Why *these* particular cards? The answer will be addressed in the following chapter as we look closer at the so-called "synchronicity hypothesis."

I would like to close this chapter with still another metaphor of interbeing, also very ancient, and also coming from the East. I believe it elegantly encapsulates the notion of interdependency not simply in Tarot, or the spectrum of psychological possibilities as I have shown above, but also inclusive of the physical spectrums of existence as suggested earlier by Wolfgang Pauli. It is the Hindu notion of "Indra's Net." The net of the god Indra is a profound and subtle metaphor for the structure of reality. It leaves us holding a captivating image of the vast simultaneous, momentary, and interdependent nature of the infinite universe. Stephen Mitchell, in *The Enlightened Mind,* describes Indra's Net thusly:

> Imagine a vast net; at each crossing point there is a jewel; each jewel is perfectly clear and reflects all the other jewels in the net, the way two mirrors placed opposite each other will reflect an image ad infinitum. The jewel in this metaphor stands for an individual being, or an individual consciousness, or a cell, or an atom. Every jewel is intimately connected with all other jewels in the universe, and a change in one jewel means a change, however slight, in every other jewel.[17]

Notes

[1]O'Neill, Robert V., *Tarot Symbolism;* Fairway Press, Lima, Ohio, 1986.

[2]Greer, Mary K., *Women of the Golden Dawn: Rebels and Priestesses;* Park Street Press, Rochester, Vermont, 1995.

[3]Giles, Cynthia, *The Tarot: History, Mystery, and Lore;* Simon and Schuster, New York, 1992.

[4]Ibid., p. ix.

[5]Slife, Brent, *Time and Psychological Explanation*; SUNY Press, New York, 1993.

[6]Ibid.

[7]Ibid.

[8]Roberts, Richard, and Campbell, Joseph, *Tarot Revelations;* Vernal Equinox Press, San Anselmo, CA, 1982, pp. 59-80.

[9]O'Neill, Robert V., *Tarot Symbolism;* Fairway Press, Lima, Ohio, 1986, p. 298.

[10]For a fascinating discussion of this subject see Brent Slife's wonderful study *(op. cit.*, note 5).

[11]Atamanspacher, H. and Primas, H, "The Hidden Side Of Wolfgang Pauli" [*Journal of Consciousness Studies*, Vol. 3, No.2]; Imprint Academic, USA, 1996, pp. 112-126.

[12]Bowker, John (editor), *The Oxford Dictionary of World Religions;* Oxford University Press, Oxford, 1997.

[13]Gallagher, Shaun, *Journal of Consciousness Studies;* Vol 4, No. 5-6 *(Models of the Self)*, p. 400, 1997.

[14]Streng, Frederick J., *Emptiness: A Study in Religious Meaning*, Abingdon Press, 1967, p. 37.

[15]Snellgrove, D. L. *The Hevejra Tantra, Part 1*, Oxford University Press, 1959; [quoted in *Mandala: Path of Beauty*, Joan Kellog, ATMA Inc., 1978, p. 31].

[16]Jung, C. G., *Collected Works*, Vol. 9 Part 1: *The Archetypes and the Collective Unconscious;* Bollingen Series, Princeton University Press, 1969, p. 357.

[17]Mitchell, Stephen, *The Enlightened Mind;* Harper Perennial, New York, 1991.

PART THREE

EMPIRICAL STUDIES

Chapter IX

SYNCHRONICITY

> Science comes to a stop at the frontiers of logic, but nature does not—she thrives on ground as yet untrodden by theory.
>
> —C. G. Jung

> In all chaos there is a cosmos, in all disorder a secret order.
>
> —C. G. Jung

Strange Workings

Even after reading and accepting (albeit provisionally) the foregoing discussion pertaining to the meeting of Psychology and Tarot, the psychotherapist will still properly wonder: *How could these spiritually-based, randomly selected Tarot cards be reliable and valid in psychological treatment?* It is one thing to establish a Tarot lexicon based on sound psychological principles, or even stunning metaphysical insights, but quite another to actually bring this arcane instrument into one's livingroom, much less one's consulting room. Particularly as the Tarot method requires placing supreme trust in the natural intelligence that collects around sacred or 'empowered' randomness, many will feel hesitant, fearing the method's lack of reliability. Before being sufficiently comfortable to introduce so unorthodox a tool into actual practice, the therapist will need to better understand the mysterious mechanism of its operation. How on earth, he/she well asks, does it work?

Little assurance will be drawn from so unlikely an apologist as Fred Gettings, occult author and compiler of the voluminous *Fate & Prediction: An Historical Compendium of Palmistry, Astrology, and Tarot*, who himself allows an echoing, if not disconcerting, sentiment: "Although the Tarot method works," he writes, "it must be admitted from the outset that no one has ever been able to explain *how* it works [italics mine]."[2] Perhaps a more precise summation of Mr. Gettings' factually correct assertion would grant that although the mechanism behind Tarot has been speculated upon in multiple arcane and exotic ways, from nonlinear postulates of theoretical physics to ancient wisdom myths like Indra's Net (and everything in between), still no one to date has *empirically* demonstrated to any satisfaction how or even *that* the Tarot method works.

To do so scientifically, one must clearly demonstrate a causal relationship linking method and effect, a linkage that can be repeated under similar conditions by different observers. The inherent problematics of scientific proof for a subjective, invisible, and irregular effect present a real challenge to the would-be Tarot empiricist, much as is encountered with related depth techniques or even in the fierce "brain versus mind" debates brewing in the emerging science of consciousness. It is widely agreed that scientific study is not well-equipped to penetrate the subjective dimensions of the human mind. The problem with classical scientific method when dealing with intrapsychic states is that mental events are not always clearly distinguished, nor are they independent from each other. Subjective effects in some cases are not easily translatable into precise language, nor are they consistently or objectively reported. There is no clear flowing of influence from one event to the next as (allegedly) with outer behavior, and finally, "psychological time" is neither linear nor unambiguous, but irregular, observer dependent, and contextually shaded. All of which makes direct quantification and measurement especially troublesome.

The Theory of Meaningful Chance

Such inherent difficulties notwithstanding, I believe an empirical explanation for the Tarot method can indeed be demonstrated in Jung's theory of synchronicity. As we suggested earlier, many explorers today believe synchronicity carries the key not only to divinatory practices but to paranormal phenomena and certain anomalous physical phenomena as well. Herein lies a region we may refer to as 'metascience', the study of invisible, acausal, non-linear relationships between inner and outer worlds.

As was briefly discussed in Chapter IV, the term 'synchronicity' made its first introduction into the world's lexicon in 1938 by Carl Jung, in his quite famous foreword to sinologist Richard Wilhelm's classic translation of the *I Ching*. For those not familiar with the Book of Changes, it has been without rival the fundamental text of traditional Chinese culture and continues to capture the imagination of intuitively-inclined Westerners today. The text is a divinatory system with 3000-year-old roots in the traditions of magic and shamanism. Nearly all that was significant in traditional China—philosophy, science, politics and popular culture—was founded on interpretations and adaptations of the *I*. The core of the book is considered the oldest and most complex divinatory system to survive into modern times.

Perhaps more than any other divinatory tool, the *I Ching's* mechanism of operation parallels that of Tarot. The Chinese term *I*, reminiscent of our description of the Tarot method, emphasizes "imagination, openness and fluidity" as contemporary *I Ching* scholars Rudolf Ritsema and Stephen Karcher note:

> [*I*] suggest the ability to change direction quickly and the use of a variety of imaginative stances to mirror the variety of being. The most adequate English translation of this is *versatility*, the ability to remain available to and be moved by the unforeseen demands of time, fate, and psyche.[3]

The authors further summarize:

> The *I Ching* offers a way to see into difficult situations, particularly those emotionally charged ones where rational knowledge fails us yet we are called upon to decide and act.... [It] is able to do this because it is an oracle. It is a particular kind of imaginative space set off for a dialogue with the gods or spirits, the creative basis of experience now called the unconscious. An oracle translates a problem or question brought to it into an image language like that of dreams. It changes the way you experience the situation in order to connect you with the inner forces that are shaping it. The oracle's images dissolve what is blocking the connection, making the spirits available.[4]

From highly personal divinatory experiments with the *I*, Jung advanced the synchronicity hypothesis. In his later works, however, he more generally describes synchronicity in its relation to certain strange curiosities of nature operating in various rare instances of inner/outer 'crossovers' which defy normative constructions of reality. Such anomalies as prophetic dreams, unconnected parallel processes, paranormal oddities and chance occurrences in which subject and object mysteriously seem to collide are included in this brave literature of 'acausal' connection. According to Jung, synchronicity is a special case of 'acausality' that additionally produces in the observer some intimate, self-deepening, or spiritually-enhancing meaningfulness, or put in the Jungian vernacular, "unconscious compensation in the service of individuation."

By this definition, not all acausal phenomena are necessarily synchronistic. As its name implies, 'acausality' simply means that no exchange of energy (the hallmark of Newtonian causality) is transmitted between related events. Examples have been shown, for instance, by experimenters like Robert Jahn, et al., at the Princeton Engineering Anomalies Research Laboratory (PEAR) that certain acausal phenomena occur naturally and can be scientifically demonstrated as such. Through studying the interaction of human consciousness and complex machines ("sensitive physical devices, systems, and processes common to engineering practice") Jahn has been able to show that a test subject's conscious intent could influence a machine's operation. Such effects, though usually quite small, have nevertheless been proved to be statistically repeatable and appear to be operator specific in their details.[5]

Technically, however, these extraordinary findings of 'acausal connection' are not purely 'synchronistic' as they carry no particular meaningfulness to the subject unless, of course, the test subject is lucky enough to be a racecar driver, a machine gun mercenary, or even a high-speed computer user with minimal technoskills (like myself), in which case any clairvoyant repartee with one's machinery would prove meaningful indeed. Be that as it may, one point is certain, as put succinctly by Hall: "Science without parapsychology is two-dimensional. Parapsychology without synchronicity misses psyche."[6]

Therapists in all their sophistication should take heart as they search for alternative explanations for the synchronicity hypothesis. Jung stipulates clearly that acausality requires not merely the absence of physical energy exchange between events, but equally the absence of *psychological* energy exchange as well. Victor Mansfield, an astrophysicist and synchronicity author, further specifies this point: "just as gravity *causes* the apple to fall, anxiety *causes* the head to shake." Both events are easily explained by ordinary causation. Psychological causation will likewise contradict the elusive precondition of acausality, as Jung carefully stressed that neither repressed contents, defense mechanisms, complexes, nor archetypal constellations could cause such coincidences, thereby ruling out subtler mechanisms like projective identification or conversion from slipping through the cracks.[7]

Examples of synchronistic phenomena are easily illustrated in collective events, as for instance, the Oklahoma City bombing of April 19, 1995. But first, let's examine (hypothetically) the more likely cause and effect scenario of this incident, which must be ruled out should we find the genuine article. Suppose several research psychologists attempted dream studies in Oklahoma City following the event. They discover significant numbers of subjects reporting dreams and fantasies involving sabotage and destruction, of buildings exploding, hidden bombs or mass death—that is, dreams occurring shortly *after* reports of the tragedy. These parallels would hardly be considered 'synchronistic' or even 'acausally-connected'. The psyche of such dreamers has obviously been affected by psychological causes churning throughout local and collective awareness. Anxiety dreams following shocking events of this nature are quite common. To the contrary, after the tragic news one might rather expect a great many people in all parts of the country to incorporate this upsetting imagery in their dreams. We would then obviously rule out 'synchronicity' to explain such clearly 'caused' correspondences.

If, on the other hand, a particular dreamer reports: (1) the same sort of mayhem and destruction in his dream, perhaps with lucid details of the Ryder truck, the screaming panicked government employees, The Murray Building collapsing, etc.; and (2) this startling dream occurred on the night *preceding* the catastrophe; moreover, (3) we can be certain this dreamer bears no possible relationship to the conspirators themselves and has not been made privy in the slightest way to their goings on; then, (4) it safe to conclude that those clamoring headlines discovered on the morning *after* the event (by said dreamer) must reasonably be considered 'acausally-connected' to the dream. This is simply because the actual event for which said dream content was referent had not yet taken place.

No exchange of energy can therefore connect these two events or account for their mutual co-arising, neither physical nor mental energy. An acausal connection is thus clearly established between dream and event. But note: synchronicity has not yet technically occurred. If then, (5) upon reading the dreadful report in the newspaper on the morning after, this second dreamer is struck meaningfully (i.e., in regards to his own individuation) by such eerie coincidence, and encouraged, perhaps, to reevaluate his core beliefs (say, of the importance of family) due to this strange coincidence, at that point, officially, these two events have produced a synchronicity. They are now "acausally connected through meaning."

Of course, the parapsychologist might beg to differ. His argument would insist that a causal exchange did in fact occur: the second dreamer was simply prescient, his psychic foreknowledge (precognition) can be seen to account for (i.e., caused) the seeming dream coincidence as such. It was simply a case of prescience or clairvoyance; one might say, 'the future' caused the dream! It's simply that we have not yet the technology to measure such invisible forces. Jung himself, with his great fascination for J.B. Rhine's groundbreaking ESP experiments at Duke University in the 1930's, entertained the impressive parapsychological evidence contributing to synchronistic phenomena. Many in the Tarot community as well believe divination to be a psychic phenomenon, with the cards acting as "psychic springboards" or triggers for telepathic, clairvoyant, or precognitive phenomena. Paranormal research, in fact, may one day isolate certain subtle causal energy fields operating between Tarot cards, readers and subjects, and require major revisions of the synchronicity hypothesis.

More recently, however, Mansfield challenges this argument by making a compelling case against such paranormal attributions which, in effect, violate the technical specifics of Jung's own treatise. Psychic causes, Mansfield contends, suggest some transfer of energy between bodies, albeit to date, not an 'energy' clearly isolated, measured, or demonstrated as such. Psychic causal agents, of course, even unseen hypothetical ones, would veer away from Jung's central notion of 'acausality'.

Absolute Knowledge

Suggested in Jung's theory of synchronicity is the presence of some underlying interior intelligence at work, some non-personal agency of wisdom which purposively guides each individual psyche towards its predestined objectives of balance and wholeness (equilibrium and individuation). Empty of the sentiment that normally muddies human perception, this higher logic flows more like a fresh running river. It is deep and clear, cool and nonpersonal, unfixed and nonlocalized. Though accessed from a mysterious source, it is nonetheless closer to the natural order. It is immune to those arbitrary habits of conventional thinking which, in the final analysis, may rest on no logic at all.

For Jung, such transcendent intelligence is viewed as the very matrix from which all psychological development and transformation unfolds; it operates through a system of compensatory self-regulation for the purpose of linking conscious and unconscious worlds with the purpose of psychological wholeness. This view is quite distinct from the determinist constructions of evolutionary psychology which place more emphasis on the role of social and cognitive factors of adaptability without reference to teleology.

From a depth psychological perspective, the bridge that this transcendent intelligence uses to link conscious and unconscious worlds is the symbol. After all, one might pause to consider this: given the generally accepted hypothesis that dreams and dream symbols are significant and meaningful, and moreover, that these spontaneous unconscious narratives are revealing, multifaceted, intricately crafted, economical, restorative, poetic, and even comical—then by whose masterful intelligence are they authored? The sleeping child? Your snoring, comatose "creative side"? Who is it really, in the final analysis, that speaks to us (or through us) when we sleep? After studying thousands of such dreamscapes captured from his patients' and his own mind, Jung was moved to formulate the concept of "absolute knowledge" to account for their true creator:

> Final causes, twist them how we will, postulate a foreknowledge of some kind. It is certainly not a knowledge that could be connected with the ego, and hence not a conscious knowledge as we know it, but rather a self-subsistent "unconscious" knowledge which I would prefer to call "absolute knowledge."[8]

Habitual Causality

One needn't be a behavioral psychologist to know that old habits die hard. These learned patterns of activity through chronic repetition become automated, fixed, and effortlessly carried out much like putting one's left sock on first each morning. As author Umberto Eco laments:

> I believe that you can reach the point where there is no longer any difference between developing the habit of pretending to believe and developing the habit of believing.

Given the undeniable fact of our own nearly intractable, causally pre-conditioned, modern habits of explanation—the cognitive reflex that needs to discern "this is so *because of*_____," I think it is safe to surmise that many reading this brief synopsis of the synchronicity hypothesis will find it bordering on the ungraspable. I myself feel this way often. There will likely be a gnawing urge to restate the obvious, at least to oneself, as almost everything learned throughout our scientifically-constructed lives has taught us not to presume otherwise. Be it parlor trick, clairvoyant reader, psychological illusion, misattribution, projective identification, accident, meaningless coincidence, miracle, or loaded deck: *something* surely must be given credit (or blame) as the "real cause."

Jung's puffy phrase "absolute knowledge," a cause without a cause, will smack of fuzzy theology and leave the scientifically grounded and metaphysically squeamish (i.e., most therapists) whining about Oujia boards. His or her gut will continue to encourage rational assurances: *"There can be no reliable effects resulting from non-existent or indiscernible causes."* Of course, the corollary to this logic is equally tenacious: *"if no reliable cause can be established, then the effects of the reading cannot be valid."* A short while later, after the Tarot reading one has just witnessed does indeed appear to be unambiguously accurate, 'amazing' by some accounts, or at least, strikingly meaningful to its subject, then and there, as a matter of habitual reflex, the explanatory litany of accidental factors, suggestibility, projection, fraud, or 'coincidence' is causally assigned. We are relieved. Phew! It was merely an instance of ______.

But no matter. In defiance of our reassuring rationality, the synchronistic hypothesis reasserts its ugly head: All energetic exchanges between reader/querent/card are categorically ruled out and unrelated to the effect! That is, no parlor trick, no clairvoyant reader, no psychological illusion, no misattribution, no projective identification, no accident, no meaningless coincidence, no miracle, and no loaded deck has caused the reading's accuracy. Indeed, *there are no becauses.*

To the contrary, one finds instead only the disquieting reminder that the world moves in mysterious ways. Meaning has arrived *acausally* as a function of the method itself, involving no extrinsic influence whatsoever. Instead, an agent presumably of "higher intelligence" or "absolute knowledge" (at least from our limited vantage points) has delivered the correct cards for this moment much as it delivered the correct dream in all its well-crafted complexity last night. However, in Tarot, unlike the dream, the agent is deliberately called forth. Sagaciously, and in concert with the emotional motivation of the querent, the Tarot method itself creates conditions for the probability of synchronicity to occur. And as mentioned in a previous chapter, psychologists will likely locate this innate, guiding agency as residing within the psyche, while metaphysicians, theologians, and perhaps quantum physicists will place its residence in nature or in god.

In the Tarot method, a procedure that intentionally disrupts and confounds linear assumptions, the meaningful coincidence that occurs between cards and querent cannot be causally explained, because in the final analysis, there is no conventional causality operating. A linkage between mind and matter, subject and object, has been facilitated by what has been deemed "empowered randomness," the vehicle of oracularly-intended synchronicity. This phenomenon is likely to be simply an occurrence of nature—related perhaps to "The Force" of *Star Wars* fame—though typically unrecognized due to our vast inculcation of scientific realism and habitual causality. When it occurs spontaneously we deem it either fraudulent or else categorize it as "some religious miracle." Such describes the so-called "apex problem" of the Tarot practitioner, mentioned earlier with Thought Field Therapy. We simply don't want to believe.

We should regard such things in keeping with our previous theme of opposition: that is, so-called "acausal/synchronistic" phenomena are merely the other side of conventional causality, "like the different, but inseparable, sides of a coin, the poles of a magnet, or pulse and interval in any vibration."(Watts) The apparent rarity of synchronistic occurrences reflects more than anything the gluttony of our habit for causal explanation. If we can't explain it, it probably doesn't exist. But it is important to remember that the concept of so-called 'randomness' is itself a modern invention that developed out of the dogma of causation. Of course, that well-oiled band of naysayers—the professional skeptics and debunkers—who bravely embrace the scientific realism of the 19th-century will not be deterred by such unbridled "metaphysical hogwash" but instead will salivate over such claims like greedy jackals over wounded rabbits. "Blatantly unscientific!" they hoot and snarl with great assurance. "Prove it! Prove it! The method is flawed, it's entirely random. It can never be re-peat-ed!"

Little do these smug evaluators realize that Tarot's random selection is precisely what makes it Tarot. Repeatability is hardly the point. Like each unique fingerprint or signature of human identity, no two Tarot readings are ever identical or repeatable *per se*. Though what does repeat, should we call it that, is the consistent and striking experience of meaning for the subject. John Van Eenwyk notes in *Archetypes & Strange Attractors: The Chaotic World of Symbols*:

> If a dynamic repeats over and over (orbits, chemical reactions, symbols), it is possible eventually to figure it out. That which occurs just once, however (miracles, the creation of the universe, a crank telephone call) is infinitely more difficult to decipher. Repetition creates patterns that can be scrutinized. Single occurrences are incomparable, hence they tend to be labeled "random."[9]

Yet the serious scientist, on the other hand, without need to prejudge or "debunk" to make his living, does nevertheless indeed hold forth a legitimate challenge for objective verification. To my mind, solid scientific verification of the synchronicity hypothesis is an unrivaled and worthy challenge for the very best scientific explorers. But as the imaginative, and indeed highly regarded scientific thinker Arthur C. Clarke recently noted from his home in Sri Lanka:

> We need more scientists...to push the limits of knowledge and understanding. Science, unlike politics or diplomacy, does not depend on consensus or expediency—it progresses by open-minded probing, rigorous questioning, independent thought and, when the need arises, being bold enough to say that the emperor has no clothes.[10]

In this case is the Emperor clothed or butt naked? The scientist is quite right to wonder: Could this synchronistic hypothesis using the Tarot method be demonstrated experimentally? Could it empirically be shown to have practical value and application? Regardless of Tarot's inherent difficulties with scientific measurement, could a pilot study of sorts be designed to demonstrate sufficient consideration of this approach, in the least to initiate a path of further research and experimentation? The following chapter describes one of several such pilot studies conducted by the author wherein the synchronicity hypothesis was tested.

Notes

[1]Jung, C. G., "On the Nature of the Psyche." Reprinted in *Collected Works Vol. 8;* Second edition (Princeton University Press), Ziff, 246, p. 167.

[2]Getting, F., *Fate & Prediction: An Historical Compendium of Palmistry, Astrology, and Tarot;* Exeter, New York, 1980, p. 157.

[3]Ritsema, Rudolf, and Karcher, Stephen [trans] *I Ching: The Classic Chinese Oracle of Change;* Element Books Limited, Great Britain, 1994, p. 10.

[4]Ibid.

[5]Jahn, Robert, and Dunne, Brenda, *Margins of Reality: The Role of Consciousness in the Physical World;* Harcourt, Brace, Jovanovich, New York, 1987.

[6]Personal correspondence, 1998.

[7]Mansfield, Victor, *Synchronicity, Science, and Soul-Making,* Open Court. 1995, pp. 22-36.

[8]Jung, C. G., *Synchronicity* [*Collected Works,* Vol. 8]; Princeton University Press, Princeton, N.J., 1978, p.493 "

[9]Van Eenwyk, John, *Archetypes & Strange Attractors: The Chaotic World of Symbols;* Inner City Books, Toronto, Canada, 1997, p. 42.

[10]Clarke, Arthur, C. quoted in the *San Diego Union Tribune* [*"La Jolla Nobelist Rocks the Scientific Boat", Graham, David E.),* September 15, 1998, p. A13.

CHAPTER X

The Tarot Research Project

A Very Strange Onion

Synchronicity, if credible, would seem to blaze a trail of untold psychological possibility and therapeutic value. Particularly with the versatile Tarot method as its medium, the possibility of synchronistic anomalies converted into therapeutic regularities suddenly becomes relevant to clinical practice. A non-linear, non-causal explication of life's events leads one on quite a different journey of exploration. The so-called 'absolute knowledge' or transcendent intelligence that informs such a method may conceivably be tapped for its potential psychological value, even as spiritual traditions have universally cautioned against the dangers of putting such powers towards false pursuits. But would such an application be false or otherwise ethically impeachable?

One would think that harnessing such wisdom, were it possible, in the service of society's psychological health and understanding would be a most worthy pursuit indeed, though unquestionably contrary to many standard practices. As a clinician I have often wondered whether an experiment could be designed that addressed certain critical social problems using the unorthodox Tarot method. How would Tarot handle complex issues that were inherently perplexing but of immediate concern to a wide cross-section of the scientific and psychological communities, for which subtler knowledge might be appreciated if only for its practical relevance to the problem?

After considering many of the stickier "real world" subjects and arenas, I was quite excited to discover calling out from my piles of psychological journals, magazines, and newspapers the glimmer of what seemed the perfect "Tarot challenge," so to speak. Domestic violence. Dark and decidedly not mystical, corporeal and troubling, the topic seemed at first eminently unTarot-like, and therefore in a curious sort of way, the perfect test case topic for my purposes. In a comprehensive survey article in *Psychology Today*, an intriguing sentence jumped out:

> Researchers and clinicians (many of them hard-core feminists) now peering into the very heart of domestic violence find, even to their own surprise, that it is far more complex, and far less dark, than most had imagined.[1]

The article claimed that in the emerging new picture, researchers were finding that spousal abuse was like "*a very strange onion—the product of many forces operating and interacting at many levels between an individual and his environment* [italics mine]." The description had striking resemblances to the kind of process dynamics and multilevel interpretations that are reflected in a Tarot reading.

At that historic juncture on the American scene, the O.J. Simpson "trial of the century" had only just resolved, yet was nonetheless still pushing buttons daily in the aftermath of the civil suit, catapulting a new collective awareness of the potential dangers of violence in all walks of American society. The issue's inherent paradoxical nature—the admixture of love and aggression—was a phenomenon that both horrified and fascinated across the board, transcending any exclusive lock on race, class, education, or status. Moreover, the assignment of innocence or guilt raised as never before the subjective forces underlying much of American jurisprudence. In a *Los Angeles Times* editorial, author Neal Gabler comments:

> In some respects, the O.J. Simpson criminal verdict was deconstruction's coming-out party. To those who thought Simpson clearly guilty, the evidence provided objective proof that he had committed the murders: the bloody glove, the DNA analysis. On the other hand, to those who found Simpson innocent, this so-called proof was a collaboration between the L.A. Police Department and white Americans to provide a "text" in which Simpson would seem guilty. In other words, there was no one objective truth; there were only different versions of the truth. [*Los Angeles Times*, January 3, 1999, Opinion, p. M1]

Spousal abuse had now catapulted into national focus, enjoying the strange status of a hot and steamy tabloid story, the perfect dream topic for talk show hosts and paparazzi, as if mainstream America had just made its first shocking acquaintance. Of course, the paid professional experts were out in full force. Unfortunately, so-called expert opinion seemed to diverge along a wide body of conflicting hypotheses and conjecture. In the table that follows, I have listed a sample of the accepted theories (at the time of this writing) regarding the psychological causes of domestic violence.

Causes of Domestic Violence

INDIVIDUAL	RELATIONAL SYSTEM	SOCIAL-CULTURAL
Anger Management	**the "battering couple"**	**Power Differentials**
impulsivity	inability to de-escalate conflicts	male dominance
failure to delay gratification	codependency	enculturated sexism
alcoholism, rageaholism	enmeshed boundaries	gender discrimination
	power and control issues	pervasive misogyny
Cognitive deficits	false and failed expectations	male machismo
misread social cues	communication breakdown	media pictures of women
poor communication skills	family of origin patterning	sexual politics
low emotional intelligence	values differences	glorification of violence
	unfair fighting	women coming to power
Intrapsychic deficits	gender differences	
shame		**Race/Class**
poor mirroring in childhood		dynamics of poverty
child abuse		stresses of underclass
battering parents		racism/minority pressures
character pathology		
Biological causes		
insufficient serotonin levels		
high testosterone levels		
brain damage due to head injury		

The Myths of Domestic Violence

As the above list makes clear, no single theory seems to dominate or encompass the field. Predictably, some months later after Orenthal J. Simpson's civil trial had settled, once again the shadow issue of family violence began to recede from the public spotlight, while no definitive answers regarding its psychological nature were agreed upon. Then another newly released Justice Department study (1996) asserted that domestic violence was still seriously under-reported, that a quarter of a million people were treated in hospitals for injuries inflicted by an intimate partner in 1994, four times more than previously estimated.

Other related myths continued to unfold. The incidence of domestic violence, contrary to perception, is not increasing—but has always been high—although an idealized view of the American family has prevented us from seeing it otherwise. Surprisingly, violence often occurs in highly romantic and deeply loving relationships where partners are drawn by the fantasy and reality of having found acceptance for the first time and feel their relationship is "special" because of it—the "urge to merge" phenomenon as I've called it. Although black females were more than twice as likely as white females to be robbery victims, there were no significant racial differences in per capita rates among female victims of rape or assault. And finally, the rather shocking fact that in the first year after divorce, a woman's standard of living on average drops by 73 percent while a man's improves an average 42 percent (US Justice Report, 1996).

What was the deeper nature of this disturbing problem, I wondered? Were we missing something here? What might Tarot tell us? After all, no satisfactory consensus had been reached through conventional behavioral study. Depth approaches to the puzzle, including psychoanalytic and Jungian speculations, rested heavily on theoretical hypotheses that were hard to test under experimental conditions. Why not approach the phenomena through a method that might satisfy both experimental and depth concerns? Why not employ Tarot? To properly launch such a study, I would need to go straight into the eye of the hurricane and administer readings to actual offenders and victims themselves. Would certain meaningful patterns or tendencies emerge through this synchronistic method? Would certain unconscious factors or hidden trends stand out that advanced our understanding of the issue? Could a Tarot case study of sorts be shown to represent such trends (if they existed) in the meta-psychological flesh?

Naturally, I would need to proceed from a deliberately naive standpoint regarding the issue itself. Beyond my sketchy inventory of known facts and experience that is familiar to most generalists lay an open precipice of uncertainty and unclarity around this unstable brew of passion and violence, perhaps an advantage for a study of this nature. In fact, in the context of divination a certain level of preferred ignorance empowers an oracle to work from its own side. As Giles notes: "For a true reader of Tarot, the object is to get the least possible information about the client from sources other than the Tarot, for not only is such outside information of little help in obtaining a good reading, it may actually be of harm."[2] Instead, after posing the general query, the tarotist will focus exclusively on the execution of the procedure itself, approaching the cards reverently and intuitively, while asking in his indefatigable non-linear style: *What tends to collect meaningfully together here, in this moment of time, around this issue?*

The Pilot Study

The Tarot Research Project formally began in late August of 1996 when in the spirit of both researcher and tarotist (and using some advantage as a clinical psychologist) various treatment centers were contacted in my own Southern California locale that provided community-based services for recovering perpetrators and/or victims of spousal abuse and family violence. Two such programs were receptive enough to allow this atypical pilot study.

Our purpose was to solicit volunteers among active clients who would willingly serve as research subjects, and thereby receive free, taped, standardized, one-hour Tarot readings given by me in exchange for consent to use such data in the findings. As guest speaker, I made initial 30-minute presentations to each recovery group, offered short demonstrations of the cards, and answered questions regarding the research project in general. For those interested in participating, individual hour sessions were then scheduled on premise as time allowed. No personal or historic information would be taken before readings. The one stipulation for subjects was this: *Tarot readings must address some personal aspect of their own lived experiences with domestic violence.*

At *Homepeace* in Orange and San Diego counties, a program that treats court-mandated male offenders of domestic violence, seven groups of male clients were visited, totaling an approximate 75 men in all, from which 24 individuals expressed interest. Curiously of those 24 volunteers, despite strong face-to-face assurances, only 13 men actually showed for their scheduled consultation times. The relatively low participation and high "no show" rates are believed significant in themselves, particularly as all readings were scheduled well in advance, free of charge, and "friendly reminder" calls were even made by the Program Director on the day before appointed consultations.

One suspects that for this population, when confronted with the reality of the task, i.e., a private, unknown, encounter using a method preconceived as 'metaphysical' or 'occult' and directed towards, of all things, one's personal violence and abuse issues—convenient 'forgetfulness' and other mechanisms of defense were likely to account for many of the absences. While many clients may be less defensive before Tarot than before conventional therapy under normal conditions, as Giles has suggested, under other less voluntary circumstances, another type of client (typically possessing antisocial features) may harbor fears that a divinatory source of counsel is less defensible, less ambiguous, less manipulated, and potentially more threatening than the predictable concerns and confrontations of an otherwise (merely mortal) therapist. The perception of a faceless synchronistic method most likely cuts both ways.

As our purpose was to penetrate the hidden individual dynamics of domestic violence, simply testing the "offending side" of the equation, the so-called perpetrators, seemed unsatisfactory. Instead, a more systemic approach was sought, and to this end, several licensed programs were contacted that sheltered female victims of domestic violence as well. One such program, *Libre! Services*, a community-based agency in North San Diego County, also expressed interest in the project. Pair-testing (offender/victim couples) was deemed untenable, as the prospect presented not only logistical complications, but seemed clinically inappropriate, risky and potentially quite dangerous. Experimental considerations deemed pairs unnecessary as well, in that individual experiences of perpetrator and victim were primarily sought, not the "battering couple" unit *per se*.

At Libre, initial presentation was given before three residential groups, totaling perhaps 35 women in all. By contrast, interest, participation, and attendance with this group appeared generally strong and receptive. For women living in shelters, one might conjecture, the free offering of such readings may conjure certain magical fantasies of intervention, predestiny and fate as several subjects suggested—an attractive prospect to the vulnerable and uprooted victim who feels she may have little more to lose than she already has, and who may not carry the same issues of shame and remorse as her male counterpart. Of course, such is merely speculation.

Subjects

In the Tarot Research Project, 26 volunteers in total consented and were accepted to participate in experimental taped readings. Male subjects and female subjects bore no relationship to each other. Only four reported previous familiarity with Tarot divination. The median age for the 13 male subjects was 36; 9 were Caucasian, 3 Latino, 1 African-American. The median age for the 13 female subjects was 29; 6 were Caucasian, 7 Latino. Socioeconomic status for men was wide ranging and reflected the population at large. For women, the sample comprised a majority of low- to middle-income individuals, including several who spoke no English (and required a translator). Six of the women had children living in the shelter as well.

Measurement

All readings used a standardized card configuration comprising 11 pre-designated spread positions. Readings in this spread are described as "*a general reflection of your present state of mind or consciousness: an indicator of emotional, physical, and spiritual considerations.*" Reversed cards, which as we have said, typically point to the card's compromised state, were treated as unique and whole in their own right, making for 156 possibilities (78 x 2) in total within each full deck. For example, the Ace of Cups (Acp) and the ***Ace of Cups reversed*** (i.e., abbreviated in bold italics ***Acp***; see Appendix) were treated and interpreted as discrete, separate, and independent (albeit related) entities. Reversed/upright showings of the same card would *not* be considered 'repeats' if appearing in parallel readings, though their related significance would be noted.

Thorough randomizing of the deck preceded each reading through repeated shuffling by the reader (10x plus), the subject's further card mixing ("finger-painting" method), cutting the deck 6x, and selecting individual cards from a face-down fanned full deck. The 11th card, designated 'gift and guide', was (blindly) selected by the reader himself. In terms of decks employed, a freshly purchased unmarked *The Original Rider Waite Tarot* was used for all readings, but we suspect many standard decks would have served equally well. Ultimately, the particular artistic style or 'execution' of a deck is secondary to the universal conventions and archetypal roots inherent in all Tarot.

Interpretation Procedure

Collected data via spreadsheets and taped transcripts were analyzed for content. Exhaustive frequency breakdowns of Tarot cards were made for both groups (Homepeace/Men and Libre/Women) in the following areas: Spread Position, Element/Suit, Card Number, Court Cards, Trump Cards, and Reversals. Trends of statistical significance were earmarked in order to compile an initial Composite Profile for each group. From these composite sketches the most representative individual reading of each group was selected for case study.

Hypothesis

As an acausal, synchronistic reflector of human experience, the Tarot will reveal certain meaningful underlying group trends that are consistent in the personalities of perpetrator and victim.

Findings

It is acknowledged from the outset that a pilot study of this nature is obviously atypical. It carries no real precedence for comparison and utilizes a method and mechanism which are foreign if not controversial to conventional research. Moreover, the sample size is not sufficiently large nor is the design adequately specific to offer meaningful statistical analysis. These I believe may be some of the occupational hazards that accompany the mixing of such strange bedfellows as science and metaphysics that still need to be ironed out.

Nevertheless, certain trends have emerged from the data that deserve further consideration. As will be explored later in depth, for men the most significant finding was the repeated presence of The Hermit (reversed) in the 'present situation' position. Strikingly, in the first seven (of 13 total) readings this singular event occurred three times, that is the same card, reversed, in the same slot, where of course any of 156 cards (allowing for reversals) was available for selection. The psychological implications of The Hermit reversed will be discussed in the next chapter when we interpret case study readings in depth.

For women, the most significant finding (statistically, for the entire study) was the appearance of Knights in the 'obstacle' position. There are, of course, only four Knights in the deck. That a Knight occurred in five out of the 13 readings in position 2, the 'obstacle,' is significant and revealing as well. The inference of this event related to the psychology of female victims in recovery will also be explored in the next chapter.

The two tables that follow show all individual card breakdowns by spread position both for male offenders and female victims. Noteworthy trends from this data are placed below each table and were considered in the determination and formulation of the Composite Profiles that follow afterwards. I have added a chart of abbreviations below to aid in deciphering these tables.

THE DECK OF TAROT

Major Arcana
TRUMPS

No.	Trump Card	Abbreviation	No.	Trump Card	Abbreviation
I.	**The Magician**	Mag	XII.	**The Hanged Man**	HgMan
II.	**The High Priestess**	Hprs	XIII.	**Death**	Death
III.	**The Empress**	Emprs	XIV.	**Temperance**	Temp
IV.	**The Emperor**	Empror	XV.	**The Devil**	Devil
V.	**The Hierophant**	Hiero	XVI.	**The Tower**	Tower
VI.	**The Lovers**	Lovers	XVII.	**The Star**	Star
VII.	**The Chariot**	Char	XVIII.	**The Moon**	Moon
VIII.	**Strength**	Strgth	XIX.	**The Sun**	Sun
IX.	**The Hermit**	Hmt	XX.	**Judgment**	Judge
X.	**Wheel of Fortune**	WhFo	XXI.	**The World**	Wrld
XI.	**Justice**	Just	0	**The Fool**	Fool

Total: 22

Minor Arcana
SUITS

	Card (of)	Pentacles	Wands	Cups	Swords
PIPS	**Ace**	Apnt	Awd	Acp	Asw
|	**Two**	2pnt	2wd	2cp	2sw
|	**Three**	3pnt	3wd	3cp	3sw
|	**Four**	4pnt	4wd	4cp	4sw
40	**Five**	5pnt	5wd	5cp	5sw
|	**Six**	6pnt	6wd	6cp	6sw
|	**Seven**	7pnt	7wd	7cp	7sw
|	**Eight**	8pnt	8wd	8cp	8sw
|	**Nine**	9pnt	9wd	9cp	9sw
|	**Ten**	10pnt	10wd	10cp	10sw
COURTS	**Page**	Pgpnt	Pgwd	Pgcp	Pgsw
|	**Knight**	Knpnt	Knwd	Kncp	Knsw
16	**Queen**	Qpnt	Qwd	Qcp	Qsw
|	**King**	Kgpnt	Kgwd	Kgcp	Kgsw

Total: 56

Table 1

TAROT CONTENT ANALYSIS

(ELEVEN-CARD SPREAD)

Designated Sample: Homepeace (HP) (Male Offenders)
Number: 13
(Note: ***Italicized*** words indicate reversed cards)

Breakdown by SPREAD POSITION

(Position) (Subjects)

	HP1	*HP2*	*HP3*	*HP4*	*HP5*	*HP6*	*HP7*	*HP8*	*HP9*	*HP10*	*HP11*	*HP12*	*HP13*
Situation:	***Hmt***	Kgpnt	Kgpnt	***Hmt***	***Hmt***	9cp	***Kgsw***	7pnt	9wd	***9sw***	***2wd***	***Hprs***	***Knwd***
Obstacle:	***7sw***	10sw	9cp	***2pnt***	10sw	Qwd	Awd	***Apnt***	Star	***5sw***	5sw	Devil	4pnt
Foundation:	***10cp***	9sw	***Hprs***	***Knpnt***	8sw	Pgwd	4cp	***Qpnt***	2sw	Moon	2sw	***Hmt 1***	***0pnt***
Cause:	Pgsw	***5cp***	4cp	HgMan	6sw	***Hmt***	***Emprs***	***6wd***	10cp	Kgpnt	***Kgcp***	3cp	***Char***
Goal/Ideal:	***6cp***	***Qcp***	6wd	Qpnt	***8cp***	10wd	Devil	***Awd***	Pgwd	5pnt	***7wd***	***Qsw***	Hiero
Effect:	***Kgcp***	Sun	Kgcp	***Acp***	Star	9wd	Empro	5pnt	Qwd	***Knpnt***	***8cp***	***Kncp***	Awd
Ego:	Judge	***2pnt***	6pnt	Awd	***Emprs***	***2sw***	***Apnt***	***Char***	***Hiero***	9pnt	Sun	***Kgcp***	8sw
Object:	8wd	Qpnt	***Qsw***	Death	***Lover***	***Apnt***	***5cp***	4sw	***6sw***	***Sun***	***Qpnt***	***10cp***	***6pnt***
Anticipation:	***3pnt***	7cp	***9wd***	***Qwd***	***7wd***	Awd	Moon	Pgsw	Strgth	9cp	6sw S	tar	7wd
Outcome:	***Towr***	7wd	Kgwd	3sw	Pgwd	***Hiero***	***7wd***	***Asw***	***Char***	***4sw***	***Knpnt***	2sw	Pgcp
Gift/Guide:	Moon	***Temp***	Fool	10cp	4sw	5wd	***Knwd***	10cp	***9cp***	7pnt	8sw	Kgwd	***8pnt***

Noteworthy Findings (in 13 readings):

1. **The Hermit reversed** ***(Hmt)*** appeared 3x as **'present situation'** plus 2x more (**'past cause'** and **'foundation'** positions).
2. The **King of Pentacles (Kgpnt)** appeared 2x as **'present situation'.**
3. The **10 of Swords (10sw)** appeared 2x as **'obstacle'.**
4. The **10 of Cups (10cp)** appeared 2x as **'gift/guide'** position, 5x total (2x reversed).
5. The **7 of Wands (7wd)** appeared 5 x overall (3x reversed). In **'outcome'** position, up and down.
6. Likewise, the **King of Cups (Kcp)** appeared 4 x (3x reversed). In **'past effect'** position, up and down.

Table 2

TAROT CONTENT ANALYSIS

(ELEVEN-CARD SPREAD)

Designated Sample: Libre! Services (L) (Abused Women)
Number: 13
(Note: ***italicized*** cards indicate reversals)

Breakdown by SPREAD POSITION

(Position)	(Subjects) *L1*	*L2*	*L3*	*L4*	*L5*	*L6*	*L7*	*L8*	*L9*	*L10*	*L11*	*L12*	*L13*
Situation:	Qwd	Awd	5pnt	***5pnt***	***WhFo***	7wd	***2cp***	Hmt	5cp	***8sw***	Awd	6cp	4sw
Obstacle:	Knpt	***4wd***	9wd	Knwd	Knpnt	Knwd	***2wd***	***Wrld***	5sw	***Kncp***	***4sw***	Judge	6wd
Foundation:	***Moon***	6wd	6cp	***Mag***	***Wrld***	Apnt	***7wd***	***4sw***	***2cp***	Hiero	***Kgwd***	Lovers	9sw
Cause:	9sw	Hiero	Pgpnt	***6sw***	Acp	2cp	***9sw***	Emprs	10pnt	3sw	***7pnt***	10cp	4pnt
Goal/Ideal:	***6wd***	***10pnt***	Apnt	Qcp	***Death***	4sw	3pnt	Judge	4cp	2cp	6wd	8pnt	Pgpnt
Effect:	***Acp***	***Devil***	***Moon***	8sw	7wd	***3cp***	Char	3sw	***Kgpnt***	7pnt	Pgcp	***Mag***	8sw
Ego:	***Strgth***	***Death***	***10sw***	5cp	Kgsw	***Qpnt***	***7pnt***	5sw	***Sun***	9cp	***Star***	***Kncp***	***Just***
Object:	***7wd***	Char	***5sw***	Sun	6pnt	Knpnt	Pgpnt	7wd	***Death***	***Just***	Qsw	***Tower***	***2pnt***
Anticipation:	***6cp***	Qcp	Kgwd	Pgwd	***Judge***	8sw	***4cp***	***Asw***	***4sw***	***5sw***	9pnt	Sun	10cp
Outcome:	***5wd***	7cp	7cp	Devil	5sw	***WhFor***	***Tower***	***Sun***	Hmt	4pnt	***6cp***	7sw	Mag
Gift/Guide:	***10wd***	8sw	Empror	8wd	Kgwd	***10cp***	9cp	***Temp***	7cp	3cp	2pnt	***6pnt***	Empro

Noteworthy Findings (in 13 readings):

1. In the **'obstacle'** position, **Knights** appeared 5x (in Pentacles 2x, Wands 2x, Cups 1x).

2. The **7 of Cups (7cp)** appeared 2x as **'outcome'**.

3. The **8 of Swords (8sw)** appeared 2x in **'future effect'** position, 5x total (once reversed).

4. **The Emperor** appeared twice in the **'gift/guide'** position.

5. The **9 of Swords (9sw)** appeared 2x in **'past cause'** position (1x reversed).

6. The **5 of Pentacles (5pnt)** appeared 2x in **'present situation'** position (1x reversed).

Composite Profiles of Perpetrator and Victim

As suggested, the purpose of this pilot study was to determine whether or not the use of the Tarot method as a tool of psychological assessment could effectively "peer into the very heart" of specific collective phenomena (in this case, domestic violence) as carried by relatively small representative samples of the population in question. However striking or personally meaningful any single reading may have been to its subject, which was virtually so (as self-reported) in every case, for our purposes here its inclusion will depend more upon its consistency with group trends as a whole. In effect, the Composite Profiles narrow the field from which the most representative cases can then be selected for deeper analysis.

What follows now in Table 3 are Composite Profiles of Perpetrator and Victim based solely on synchronistic Tarot card tendencies analyzed quantitatively from the whole sample. Where no 'repeats' were to be found at specific positions, criteria for card selection was based on other noteworthy trends, such as overall Suit, Number, Court, Trump, or Reversal frequencies otherwise dominating the position under examination. While such secondary trends are less conclusive, they serve much like the imperfect sketch of a police composite, providing best 'guesstimates' that help round out the more clearly established salient features in evidence, serving to better create a full impression or facsimile of the whole individual. As earlier noted, these composite profiles became the norms from which specific case material was chosen. The Case Studies that follow in the next chapter are those single readings for each group that most resembled their respective composite profile on the next page.

Table 3

COMPOSITE TAROT PROFILES

Position	**The Male Perpetrator** *Card*	**The Female Victim** *Card*
Present Situation:	HERMIT reversed	5 of PENTACLES
Obstacle:	10 of SWORDS	KNIGHT of WANDS
Foundation:	2 OF SWORDS	THE WORLD (reversed)
Past Cause:	EMPRESS reversed	9 of SWORDS
Goal/Ideal:	QUEEN of CUPS	6 of WANDS
Future Effect:	KING of CUPS reversed	8 of SWORDS
Ego:	JUDGMENT	DEATH reversed
Object:	QUEEN of PENTACLES reversed	7 of WANDS
Anticipation:	7 of WANDS reversed	PAGE of WANDS
Outcome:	THE TOWER reversed	7 of CUPS
Gift/Guide:	10 of CUPS	EMPEROR

General Comments

Like human fingerprints, handwriting, and snowflakes, each Tarot spread is a unique variation on primary materials, and the Composite Profiles above are no exception. Before we turn to individual cases selected from the above, several general points can be observed and noted from our list.

First, as we are dealing with failed conjugal relations, it is not surprising that certain contrasexual themes stand out. For male perpetrators, the archetype of the nurturing female (Mother/Goddess) is notably represented in various dynamic permutations and complexes. As the archetypal Empress, the image appears "reversed" (i.e. compromised) in the 'past cause' position as we see in Table 3, extending backwards in time (due to its magnitude of psychic energy as a trump card) perhaps even to infancy. In Court cards, typically viewed as intermediary stages between ego and archetype, the mother imago appears in various realms and elements. As an idealized fantasy object, she is regally imagined in the all-nurturing Queen of Cups ('goals/ ideals'). As primary partner, the archetypal feminine again appears inverted in the more practical Queen of Pentacles ('object'), a humanized earth goddess who has lost her daily rhythm and basic trust.

For female victims, similarly, the archetype of the Father/Protector is likewise highly visible in his various aspects. As the archetypal Emperor, bearer of logos and orderly benevolence, he is the philosopher king appearing as good father and spiritual friend ('gift/guide'). As a mere mortal, he comes as the rapacious warrior in the persona of the ever-fiery Knight of Wands (here stuck in the 'obstacle' position); yet in his younger, kinder and gentler incarnation, he is the romantically yearned for (but secretly feared) charismatic and innocent puer, the Page of Wands ('anticipation' position).

With these brief introductions of those selected cards which best reflect the samples of this study, we are now ready to move to the next chapter for a closer and more detailed gaze through the synchronistic portholes of two actual cases, our so-called prototypes or composite profiles of the male perpetrator and female victim of domestic violence.

Notes

[1]*Psychology Today*, November/December 1993, "Marital Violence," p. 50.

[2]Giles, Cynthia, *The Tarot: History, Mystery, and Lore;* Simon and Schuster, 1992, p. 131.

Chapter XI

CASE STUDY: THE HERMIT REVERSED

> I was not getting the loving touching that I needed.
>
> —Andrew, age 48

Format

The structure of the studies that follow, like much of our discussion in general, is slightly unconventional. As we have noted, contrary to the usual practice, the less history and circumstance a Tarot reader is given about the subject preceding a divination, the more powerful that reading becomes, as full attention can be focused without distraction or bias. Consequently, in all cases of this study, absolutely no personal information was given beforehand beyond the subject's first name, age, and previous exposure to Tarot, if any. This practice allows the reader to properly attend to the execution of the procedure itself, placing trust in what randomly gathers in the moment and thus encouraging, as it were, the cards themselves to speak. In order to preserve this divinatory integrity in the case studies that follow, a reading's validity was determined not by correlations with biographical or circumstantial data, but by convergence with tendencies that were seen in the group as a whole.

Nonetheless, six months after the experimental readings were conducted and analyzed, the two individuals selected for case study were contacted and interviewed by the experimenter for the first time. These contacts, it should be noted, were made immediately *after* the transcribed interpretations that follow were fully formulated as such. The purpose of delayed post-test interviews was twofold: (1) to obtain non-contaminating data intentionally withheld at the time of the reading, and (2) to obtain any information regarding future developments that was pertinent to the initial readings. The considerable interval of time between readings and follow-up interviews was judged necessary to guard against experimental bias in the subject's reporting of biographical and circumstantial information, as well as to allow sufficient time for the prognostication itself to unfold.

For the sake of coherency I will first offer brief biographical sketches (not originally available) based on my interviews six months afterwards. Then as analysis of the subject's Tarot spread is presented, I will include parenthetical remarks (where relevant) obtained from the follow-up interviews. This procedure, while perhaps slightly awkward, best captures the actual Tarot process. We begin now with an examination of the most representative individual in the group of male perpetrators of this study. For obvious reasons, his name has been changed to preserve confidentiality.

ANDREW

Andrew, age 48, is a soft-spoken, Caucasian, middle-school science teacher of 23 years. He has the blonde hair and tall, wiry physique of a Southern California surfer, which indeed is a long-time, favorite pastime. Andrew has been married to Amy, a respiratory therapist, for 20 years. They have a son who is currently in junior high school. At the time of this reading, Andrew and Amy were separated. Andrew was the oldest of two boys, and his parents were deceased. He later explained that it was shortly after his father's death and while his mother was then herself in the hospital terminally ill, that the incident happened which ended in domestic violence.

In response to perceived badgering from his wife, Andrew reports he 'pushed' an antique table at Amy in anger and frustration, cutting badly and breaking her arm. Amy required emergency medical care to mend the wound. Andrew's mother died several days afterwards. Because of the pervasive chaos and grief of the moment, Amy agreed not to press formal charges on the condition that Andrew seek immediate help. Unlike the other Homepeace subjects, Andrew had not been arrested and subsequently court-mandated into a one-year recovery program, but instead chose to participate voluntarily. The following configuration shows Andrew's Tarot spread:

Andrew's Query: What does my relationship path hold for the future?

Present Situation: Hermit reversed
Obstacle: 7 of Swords
Foundation: 10 of Cups
Past Cause: Page of Swords
Goals: 6 of Cups reversed
Future Effect: King of Cups reversed
Ego: Judgment
Other: 8 of Wands
Anticipation: 3 of Pentacles reversed
Outcome: Tower reversed
Gift & Guide: The Moon

Interpretation by Cluster

As we initially noted, Tarot interpretation is more art than science. In Chapter III, Greer's interpretative styles (analytic, therapeutic, magical, psychic) were discussed along with my suggestion for a 'global method' appropriate for research of this nature. For our purposes here, we will use primarily the analytic method in a global context which is based on analyses and correspondences of each card in its respective position. It assumes that everything in a spread stands for something in the individual psyche, and that multiple levels of meaning can be found within each card. As will become obvious, my own theoretical style will be reflected in the interpretation (it's unavoidable), but *unquestionably* other *interpretations* may be considered. When deciphering symbols of psychic origin there can never be only one interpretation.

As the Tarot method is essentially an oral tradition, I've tried to streamline this written presentation by delineating six dynamic spread clusters (as laid out in Chapter III), each of which will be interpreted before general summation is offered. Typically, cards are analyzed individually in spread sequence before any attempt at cluster summation or general synthesis is made. In the condensed version below, established card phrases are placed in quotations, while pertinent follow-up disclosures (learned well after the reading) are italicized. Furthermore, it should be kept in mind that the following interpretations were not directed to the client himself in this manner, but are presented here for the audience. How one shares such material directly with a client, as we have suggested, varies by therapeutic style, intent, context, and receptivity of the client.

Cluster 1: *The Core* (1-2)

Hermit reversed/7 of Swords. *[The central dynamic of the reading involving the interface of 'present situation' and 'obstacle' positions]*

For Andrew the recovery situation itself is personified by **The Hermit reversed**, a time of "social isolation, introversion, and fearfulness." As earlier mentioned, in three of the first seven men's readings this card appeared reversed in the same position. When The Hermit is reversed, notes Tarot author Rachel Pollack, "we corrupt the idea of withdrawal."[1] The Hermit's healing properties associated with retreat and refueling are turned instead to their opposites, self-absorption and self-pity. The combination is rife for depressive affect and distancing behaviors, that is, The Hermit's shadow side. *[In our follow-up interview, Andrew confirmed this description of his marital estrangement, recalling half-hearted attempts to engage other women while feeling predominantly lonely, needy, and anxious.]* Although we are exploring the individual reading of Andrew, as it is derived from the composite, we are additionally speaking of this population of recovering perpetrators in general.

While The Hermit reversed may serve as the 'signature' card of the male of our study, inferred in any card's reversal is its opposite, that is, its upright significance which points to the card's healthy expression and potential. As we have seen in Chapter V, opposition is a key theme running throughout Tarot. In analytic terms, the reversal of a trump represents the pathologized complex that shrouds the image's archetypal core. In its unique spectrum, **The Hermit** stands for "intentional withdrawal" for the purpose of activating the unconscious mind, that is, "soul-making." However thwarted here (i.e., reversed), this possibility remains a shadow potential for Andrew, and by extension, for men in general at risk for striking out violently. In principle, I believe this theme carries the proper psychological function for treatment programs such as Homepeace et. al.: psycho-spiritual restitution by way of embracing the solitary, self-reflective and authentic path of The Hermit.

Next, crossing Andrew's forward movement and lying sideways in the 'obstacle' position (thus obstructing the spread's proper flow) is the **7 of Swords**, a card meaning "mental struggle over the dissolution of some former relationship, loss of trust or friendship." *[In our follow-up interview, this was the only card still recalled in detail by Andrew after six months.]* The card's imagery, showing a division between swords held and those relinquished, suggests the discarded two swords remain "split off" contributors to Andrew's otherwise overburdened anguish (the five swords he now 'shoulders'). Fives, like fingers on the human hand, stand for human complexity and grasping in general. In the seven, we see a broken combination of the two and five, that is, fragmentation and mental burden: Andrew is split off from the discarded two swords suggesting a loss of primary trust; and instead he is left to carry the mental burden on his 'hero's' shoulders.

Andrew's task, as always is the case, is to bring what is resisted and split-off into awareness before healing and integration can be possible. This is visually illustrated in the spread configuration itself: position 2 (the only horizontal placement in the pattern) must in all readings be corrected vertically before realignment with the others can take place. In effect, the healthy Hermit must be resurrected to painfully reexamine and reintegrate the castaway friend. This brings what is resisted into the unfolding pattern. *[In our follow-up, Andrew reports some recent progress here; three months after the reading, his wife had accepted him back home. He admits however: "I still think she may not be in love with me. I'm still trying to get it back."]* Unfortunately, the unhealthy Hermit who is now reversed in the present position misses the opportunity and stagnates in self-absorption and self-pity. In a reading proper, the therapist helps the client to explore ways to correct the problem and seize this opportunity. As earlier mentioned, a reading typically should not proceed until the cards of Cluster 1 are clearly established with meaningful referents to the querent. The reader must be flexible and careful to correctly identify where these cards are relevant to the query. This cluster is equivalent to the formation of a "therapeutic contract" between clinician and client in the early phase of treatment, one that identifies the areas and issues to be worked on. To simplify, we can describe the presenting problem as:

present situation: Hermit reversed ≅ **social isolation, fearfulness**
present obstacle: 7 of Swords ≅ **mistrust, loss**

Cluster 2: *Above and Below* (5-3)

6 of Cups reversed/10 of Cups reversed. *[Interrelates goals and foundations at the two poles]*

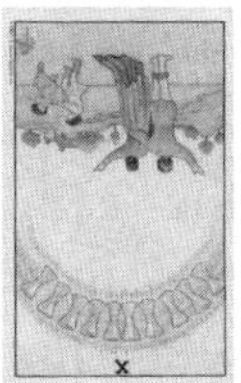

The **6 of Cups** 'above' traditionally signifies "sweet memories of childhood," nostalgia, and yearning, but in this case the card is again **reversed** and suggests the opposite. As we have seen, oppositions (when combined) carry the full spectrum of a given card, though when they are opposed or split in two, they invariably surface as neurotic disturbance. Not surprisingly, a reversal in this fixed position of 'goals and ideals' suggests that Andrew's limited ability to visualize and intentionalize (an essential prerequisite for behavioral change) is currently "disturbed by unpleasant and turbulent childhood memories" (6 of Cups reversed).

With no incorporated picture of early tenderness, no "object constancy," not only will Andrew lack the affect-imagery needed for self-soothing, or the mental focus to visualize future goals, but his ability to now ward off more immediate ideations surrounding his own transgressions may be further compromised. It would not be surprising to discover addictive substitute behaviors (drugs, alcohol, sex) operating for this purpose. *(In the follow-up interview, Andrew describes the troubled dynamics of his family of origin. Tempermentally, Andrew's father was reactive and hot-headed, (an "Italian rage-aholic" according to Andrew) who had himself suffered the premature death of his mother at age ten. Andrew's mother became alcoholic in response to this aggression, occasionally "bar-hopping and not coming home some nights"—subsequently, "angry outbursts, physical abuse, intense blaming, and threats of divorce" pervaded Andrew's household during adolescence. Of course, this information was not shared before or during the reading.)*

'Below' Andrew (in position 3), representing his 'ground of being,' we similarly discover a psychological 'foundation' that is submerged in the watery element of murky emotionality. When the otherwise "lovestruck, rainbows in the sky" emotionally rich ambiance of the **10 of Cups** is **reversed**, Pollack notes, "all emotion turns against itself. Some highly charged situation, usually romantic or domestic, has gone wrong, producing violent feeling, anger or deceit." [2] In this spread position we find that Andrew's connection to earth, that is, his emotional 'ground' and anchor, are imploded with aggressive affect. *[In the follow-up, Andrew reports early in the marriage that Amy had chosen abortion as she felt unready for a child. "I wanted to have the child. I think the abortion has always hurt our relationship. Also she was less interested than me in sex. I was not getting the loving touching that I needed."]* These resentful feelings apparently remain stagnant by the psychological reversal. In all, this cluster mirrors the mental poles above and below him, Andrew's psychological sky and earth, his sight and motility—both of which are perceived through cracked or inverted cups (feeling containers), leaving Andrew emotionally thwarted, angry, dry and thirsty.

This vertical line metaphorically represents the querent's "psychological space" with analogous "body centers" (chakras, energy points, meridians etc.) corresponding from top to bottom to:

(1) **head** (goals/ideals) @ **disturbed childhood memories**
(2) **eyes/mouth** (present situation) @ **isolation/fearfulness**
(3) **heart** (obstacle) @ **mistrust/loss**
(4) **legs/feet** (foundation) @ **violent implosion**

Cluster 3: *Cause and Effect* (4-2-6)

Page of Swords/7 of Swords/King of Cups reversed. *[Views linear progression and causal relationships]*

The **Page of Swords** in 'the past' suggests a former attitude of "mental detachment associated with spying and secrecy," perhaps a clue to the disturbed coping strategy of Andrew's troubled family years. The Page of Swords is cautious, cunning, and watchful, and one suspects in Andrew's case, slightly paranoid. Given previous dissociative tendencies which we have discussed in the 'obstacle' position (**7 of Swords**), compounded by the troublesome unwanted memories 'above' (6 of Cups reversed), the Page of Swords appearing in the 'past' alerts the therapist to assess for underlying paranoid pathology.

Accessed without verbal interview but through purely synchronistic means, now Andrew's past pattern of withdrawal and secrecy is hypothesized through the selected cards and the fixed positions of the reading. Now we are further shown the process and 'causative agents' producing the problematic effect, the **King of Cups reversed**. The formula, not conclusive by any means, holds the following equation: past cause (Page of Swords) ÷ current obstacle (7 of Swords) = future effect (King of Cups reversed).

At first glance, quite an impressive "King of Hearts" occupies the 'future effect' space, symbolizing the socially responsible mature man of service, emotional intelligence, and compassion. That is, until once again the card's reversal produces quite the opposite effect, namely, "vice, deceit, and corruption." Romantically, notes Pollack, the King of Cups reversed describes "a dishonest yet domineering lover, more often male, sometimes female."[3] Although the laws of opposition suggest the healthy King of Cups also resides within this spectrum of possibility, the emphasis of the reversal points to the opposite effect: deceit and corruption. *[Andrew reports: "I was always trying to get my needs set up, forcing the sexual issue. I was always the aggressor. I'd use disgusting language and abuse her verbally when I didn't get what I wanted."]*

Rather quickly then, with virtually no direct information offered, Tarot has captured some of the subtler dynamics operating within Andrew's marriage. To simplify this axis of cause and effect, we can say:

(primacy of) **past cause:** Page of Swords ≅ **secrecy and paranoia**
(through) **present obstacle:** 7 of Swords ≅ **mistrust, loss**
(yields) **future effect:** King of Cups (rev) ≅ **deceit, corruption**

Cluster 4: ***Self/Object*** (7-8)

Judgment/8 of Wands. *[Reflects the structural components of ego identity and object relations]*

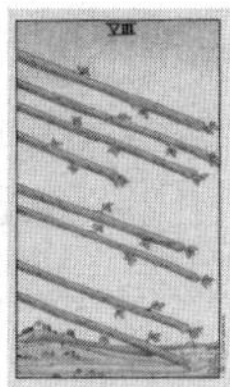

Judgment in the ego position (the second trump we've seen) is perhaps the most hopeful sign thus far in the reading. In general, when a Major Arcana card appears in a spread it is given more weight than a Minor for it is presumed to carry a vaster range of archetypic meaning and psychic energy. The Judgment card represents self-declaration and finality, "a deep call to take stock, a push from within to make a stand, to declare some important change or new commitment." Though Andrew's first association in the reading was to acknowledge his own self-judgmental tendencies, I believe Judgment here points more positively to Andrew's perceived stage of treatment and recovery: self-accountability.

Like the majority of those who consented to have their cards read in this study, Andrew's sincerity was not questioned so much as his ego strength. He frankly admitted the recovery program underway had been the turning point of his life, and this positive belief has carried into his current self-identity. **Judgment** here reflects Andrew's conscious commitment to psychological change (even as other dynamic forces make no such concession). With weaker or fragmented ego structures however, when a trump card appears in the 'ego' position one must guard against over-inflation (or deflation) manifested in overtly heroic (or villainous) self-perceptions. It is quite common in all types of recovery programs during a particular stage of treatment that clients will identify positively with the stated goals of the program. Cautiously, from the follow-up conversation with Andrew, it seemed indeed that a more realistic view of accountability was emerging in his developing commitment to the reconciliation process.

As for the 'object' card, the **8 of Wands** in this position reflects Andrew's current perceptions of significant others, and we may presume, his estranged wife Amy. It may also carry his experience of how others perceive him (internalized object relations). In the suit of fire, "swiftness and movement" are implied, psychologically 'red-flagging' rapid escalation. The 8 of Wands speaks to the rapidity with which domestic fires have gotten out of control in the marriage, and in particular, how distorted object relations have added fuel to those fires. What is lacking in this card is the ability to modulate, to contain, and delay the intensity of the affect.

At the more positive point of this card's spectrum of meanings, Arrien describes the 8 of Wands as a "spiritual bridge to wholeness using intuition and spiritual vision."[4] Seen in this context, Amy truly becomes the bridge over which Andrew's healing must pass. But a therapeutic expectation of this optimistic possibility (after distorted perceptions of self and other are corrected) should be tempered, in Andrew's case, by less 'magical' expectations for the reconciliation process. Interpretative emphasis is better served by underscoring the swiftness in which destructive perceptions and loss of control can strike again. *[Andrew freely reflects: "I was very abusive before mainly because of my expectations in that area" i.e., sexual.]* There is little evidence at this time that such expectations have truly disappeared. This card and issue will be revisited in our second study as well. A synopsis of the cluster is as follows:

self concept: Judgment ≅ **taking stock, accountability**
object concept: 8 of Wands ≅ **rapid escalation, spiritual bridge**

Cluster 5: *Anticipation/Resistance* (9-2)

3 of Pentacles reversed/7 of Swords. *[Shows the relationship between anticipation and resistance which is typically interdependent]*

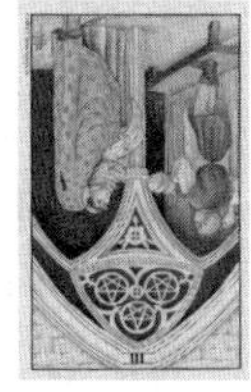

As we have already discussed the obstacle card (**7 of Swords**) in Clusters 1 and 3, we must assume the card's theme of basic mistrust and loss unconsciously affects the subject's hopes and fears as well. These hopes and fears are reflected in the **3 of Pentacles reversed**. Generically, any reversal in the 'anticipation' position points to the shadow spectrum of the card in question (i.e., fear and anxiety), while the card if upright points primarily to the positive spectrum (hope and optimism). Both aspects are typically involved in 'anticipation' though in this case, once again, the card's reversal underscores the negative side.

With the **3 of Pentacles reversed**, we find suggested a sense of "mediocrity, non-participation, apathy, and clumsiness" (Pollack). By contrast, when upright the **3 of Pentacles** carries a hopeful aspect, "hard work and effort, particularly in crafting and constructing of one's own sacred structures." By "sacred structures" we can assume Andrew's marriage is the referent. *[In the follow-up, Andrew said current reconciliation efforts were now directed mostly towards his completing certain long overdue home projects "like fixing the spa. This is the way men show their love, by doing things in the house."]*

But defended in such external efforts is Andrew's private fear: the self-perception of clumsiness and shame in relational tasks like intimacy, sexuality, communication, and marital rebuilding. This becomes the major contributor to his blockage and resistance. As a secondary effect, paradoxically, the hopeful aspect of the crafty **3 of Pentacles** (upright) may also animate Andrew's consuming wish, as we saw in the last cluster, and contribute to the false expectation for some 'swift' and magical rapprochement (the 8 of Wands). Such anticipation, particularly with its avoided fears of failure and humiliation, contributes severely to the anguish and dissociation of the reading's core issues: isolation and mistrust (Hermit reversed/7 of Swords).

Certainly, therapeutic support in relational skills would surely lessen Andrew's resistance. Tarot cards in general don't simply point to the active spectrum of a situation, but include hints and possibilities associated with the dormant side as well. The card, in its symbolic richness and multidimensionality always mirrors both sides of a polarity. As we see, Tarot offers a keen hand in correctly perceiving such psychodynamics, displaying visually (its unique talent) many possibilities and contraindications for the subject. With the added complexity of card reversals, the laws of opposition are strikingly amplified and well put to use. Thus we summarize this cluster:

anticipation:
- **fears:** 3 of Pentacles reversed ≅ **inner clumsiness, shame**
- **hopes:** 3 of Pentacles ≅ **outer resourcefulness, craft**

resistance: 7 of Swords ≅ **mistrust, loss**

Cluster 6: *Resolution and Wisdom (10-11)*

The Tower reversed/The Moon. *[Points to psychological destiny mediated by conscious choice and spiritual guidance]*

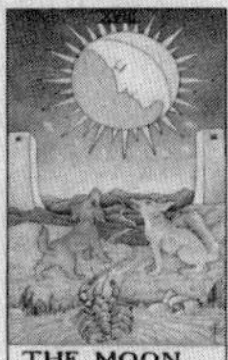

Completing the "karmic loop," to borrow from the East, **The Tower reversed** appearing in the 'outcome' position forebodes a dramatic ending, to say the least. The trump here indicates an "unequivocal, radical departure" will ultimately be required, as this least forgiving of all trump cards leaves little room for negotiation or half-measures. Andrew must "abandon the stale structures of his former self" lest this not-so "ivory tower" come crashing down upon his very head. The surroundings are stormy, and the lightning that strikes the Tower's facade (persona) is associated with "bolts of revelation" or "flashes of enlightenment." Its laser intensity must be converted into powerful directed action if Andrew is to survive the immanent collapse.

Yet **The Tower's** reversal , paradoxically, suggests milder outer conditions but greater internal danger, that is, the danger of 'self-imprisonment'. Pollack notes:

> When [the Tower is] reversed…we do not allow ourselves to undergo the full experience. By keeping a tight control on our reactions we lessen the

> pain; we also do not release all the repressed material...By shielding the Tower from the lightning we become its prisoners.[5]

The eventuality of this psychological "prison sentence" portends an outcome which from a treatment perspective obviously should be averted, or in the least, consciously prepared for. For Andrew, unfortunately, its early appearance has been already set in motion. He reports in the follow-up interview six months later:

> Since I returned home she's been ice cold, not receptive, still separate. We have little sex. I realize I've been an abusive person through many years. I got angry, I cussed a lot and called her names easily. I think I lost her love and I'm trying to regain it.

But what can be done? The forces of "pathological determinism" seem well-lodged in both Andrew's vulnerable personality and marital dynamics, not to mention the spread itself which offers little encouragement or resolution. With **The Tower reversed** in the outcome position we observe an imprisoned Hermit struggling within a high-pressured and closed marital environment, predictably setting the psychological conditions for repeated violent explosion. Although the core complexes have now been identified, the reading has not provided a compelling strategy for forward motion.

Yet an answer does come, mysteriously, via the final card selected as 'gift and guide', **The Moon**. This card alone was chosen ('randomly') by the reader. In real terms, a solution is waning. The Moon is the cardinal symbol of the unconscious itself and, as such, is organized around imagination, fluctuation, and aroused by emotion. The archetype of The Moon covers all symbolic moonlit realms including dreams and the numinosum, imagination and lunacy, receptivity, romance, and the magnetic forces of the feminine. As Marie-Louise von Franz wrote in *Man and His Symbols:*

> In the unconscious, one is unfortunately in the same situation as in a moonlit landscape. All the contents are blurred and merge into one another, and one never knows exactly what or where anything is, or where one thing begins and ends.[6]

Yet as the "creative matrix of consciousness," (Jung) the left-handed path of The Moon may ultimately direct Andrew's trouble-some recovery into longer term analysis, i.e., depth work, dream interpretation, divination, active imagination, etc. At least, this seems to be the advice of the reading. Though vague and obscure as it sounds, The Moon may offer the only effective medicine able to liberate Andrew from the incarcerating iron bars of the "Lightning Struck" Tower reversed, looming in the future.

In The Moon's numerology we find another confirming link: elegantly, its number value of 18 reduces to its root [1+ 8= 9], that is, to Trump IX, **The Hermit** himself. The correspondence underscores the central theme of this reading: The Hermit reversed must stand upright on his two feet. The Moon's suggested 'gift and guidance' powerfully returns the possibility of reuniting psyche with seeker [18/9]. For Andrew, this marks a meaningful return to the spread's beginning, The Hermit reversed. The logic of this synchronicity has paved a way back to what has been left undone: namely, as true Hermit, Andrew must now intentionally withdraw from his self-imprisonment [Tower, reversed] for the express purpose of activating the unconscious mind in the service of his own healing. That is, internally, he must take the true Hermit's path and embark on the long solo journey of "soul-making" by way of the deep unconscious.

While this result may have already been sensed even before the reading, it has now been efficiently and convincingly made transparent. Ingenuously, Tarot guides Andrew back to his original unrealized lesson—the path of The Hermit.

The summary below simplifies Cluster Six (though without the numerological operation that returns to The Hermit):

Outcome: Tower reversed ≅ **self-imprisonment**
Gift/Guide The Moon ≅ **psyche, depth, the feminine**

On the following page I have integrated each cluster summary into one table so that easy review is available. In the next chapter, a second case study is presented. This case reflects the single subject whose reading most closely resembled the composite profile of the female victim. A similar format is presented.

Summation of Andrew's Spread

The following table is a compilation of cluster summaries:

Cluster 1: The Core
presenting situation: Hermit reversed ≅ **social isolation, fearfulness**
presenting obstacle: 7 of Swords ≅ **mistrust, loss**

Cluster 2: Above and Below (spatial axis)
head (goals/ideals): 6 of Cups reversed ≅ **disturbed early memories**
eyes/mouth (present situation): Hermit reversed ≅ **isolation/fearfulness**
heart (obstacle): 7 of Swords ≅ **mistrust/loss**
legs/feet (foundation): 10 of Cups reversed ≅ **violent implosion**

Cluster 3: Cause and Effect (temporal axis)
(primacy of) **past cause:** Page of Swords ≅ **secrecy, paranoia**
(through) **present obstacle:** 7 of Swords ≅ **mistrust, loss**
(yields) **future effect:** King of Cups (rev) ≅ **deceit, corruption**

Cluster 4: Self/Object
self concept: Judgment ≅ **accountability/self-persecution**
object concept: 8 of Wands ≅ **rapid escalation/spiritual bridge**

Cluster 5: Anticipation/Resistance
anticipation:
fear: 3 of Pentacles reversed ≅ **inner clumsiness, shame**
hope: 3 of Pentacles ≅ **outer resourcefulness, effort, craft**

resistance: 7 of Swords ≅ **mistrust, loss**

Cluster 6: Resolution and Wisdom
outcome: Tower reversed ≅ **self-imprisonment**
gift/guide The Moon ≅ **psyche, depthwork**

Notes

[1]Pollack, Rachel, *Seventy-Eight Degrees of Wisdom* (Part 1): *The Major Arcana;* Aquarian Press, 1980, p. 71.

[2]Pollack, Rachel, *Seventy-Eight Degrees of Wisdom* (Part II): *The Minor Arcana*, p. 58.

[3]Ibid, p.51.

[4]Arrien, Angeles, *The Tarot Handbook: Practical Applications of Ancient Visual Symbols;* Arcus Publishing Company, 1987, p. 310.

[5]Pollack, Rachel, (Part I) *The Major Arcana* (as above), p. 106

[6]Jung, Carl G., *Man and His Symbols;* Doubleday & Company, Garden City, New York, 1964.

Chapter XII

Case Study: Lady of the Knight

He'd get on me, spit in my face, call me Chicano whore.

—Vivian, age 34

VIVIAN

The following historical information was taken in a one-hour interview, six months after experimental Tarot readings were administered. Vivian, age 34, is a dynamic, tall and rotund woman of Mexican-American descent. Currently she is completing her AA degree, works in community education, and hopes one day to become a registered nurse. Vivian is from a fifth-generation, middle-class Chicano family living in San Diego, California. English was primarily spoken in her home. Of her four sisters, she reports being "daddy's favorite," the "good child" who took on many of the maternal household responsibilities and stayed close to the fold. "My father was the king, my mother was the maid," she said. "He was always very controlling, very loud, while my mother was very private."

Vivian has been separated for a number of years from her husband Ernesto, a migrant worker, whom she met at age 16 near the Canadian border in Washington while visiting a family member, and whom she married at 17. She describes Ernesto as a "simple, traditional, illiterate Mexican farm worker," who was uncomfortable with her 'Americanized' ways. *["He was the first man I had sex with, the second man I kissed. I was now his woman."]* She describes Ernesto as mild mannered and passive until he began to drink, at which time a full "Jeckyll and Hyde" conversion ensued, one of brutish dominance, aggression and paranoia. A tragic scenario of violent beatings, fear of flight and banishment from her family, escalating to eventual mutual physical violence became chronic weekly events for many years. *["He'd get on me, spit in my face, call me Chicano whore."]*

Vivian survived in this climate for some 11 years, had two children, and 'adapted' as she said, matter-of-factly, while every weekend Ernesto would get drunk and reignite the vicious abuse cycle. Eventually, as the alcoholism and violence escalated to critical levels, Vivian feared for the safety of her children, left Ernesto, and moved into a shelter. Months afterwards, she found her own apartment and formally severed the relationship. At the time of the follow-up interview, Vivian describes a series of more recent (abusive) relationships which were to become the focus of the Tarot reading.

Vivian's Query: What does my relationship path hold for the future?

Present Situation: 5 of Pentacles reversed
Obstacle: Knight of Wands
Foundation: Magician reversed
Past Cause: 6 of Swords reversed
Goals: Queen of Cups
Future Effect: 8 of Swords
Ego: 5 of Cups
Other: The Sun
Anticipation: Page of Wands
Outcome: The Devil
Gift & Guide: 8 of Wands

Interpretation by Cluster

Cluster 1: *The Core* (1-2)

5 of Pentacles reversed/Knight of Wands. *[The central dynamic of a reading involving the interface of 'present situation' and 'obstacle' positions]*

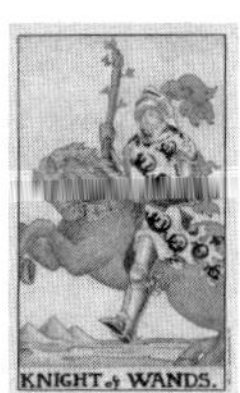

For Vivian, the **5 of Pentacles reversed,** as clearly shown in the card's composition, illustrates the daily struggle inside a women's shelter for victims of domestic violence. In our study, this card appeared in the first position twice (once reversed), though psychologically, either direction would seem most apt. The card's imagery and traditional meaning describe perfectly the experience of the victim in recovery: "reversal of fortune." In the classic Waite/Smith illustration (above), two beggars pass a brightly lighted church window, hurrying through the snow. The pentacles are incorporated into the stained glass windows. The wayward figures are clearly on the outside looking in. Reversed, Waite gives the meaning "chaos, disorder, ruin, confusion." The challenge for Vivian, as for all women living in her circumstance, is the lesson of humility, patience, restitution, and survival.

Crossing Vivian's path in the 'obstacle' position we find the object of her resistance and the center of her trouble: the **Knight of Wands.** The card echoes by far the most statistically meaningful finding of the study as a whole: namely, Knights in the second position of female victims—which in one suit or another appeared an extraordinary five out of 13 readings (twice in pentacles and wands, once in cups). Speculation over the uncanny repeat showings of so many "knights in shiny armor" as 'obstacles' for this group of women is itself an intriguing subject, but a topic we cannot do full justice to due to the constraints of our larger purpose.

In general, **Knights** are to be seen as questers and protectors, as outward masculine energies of mid-adulthood; but now standing sideways in the 'obstacle' position, these warriors seem a bit hampered in their missions. Indeed, they are significantly out of alignment. Traditionally, the **Knight of Wands** is seen as "a fiery conquistador of creative adventure." He is ambitious, charismatic, and magical. As the intense puer, he is often thought "overeager and overcharged, a hasty lover, lacking some needed grounding influence" to anchor his intensity in ordinary reality. *[Vivian associated this card with the type of man she has attracted since Ernesto. "They are like my father, very strong and independent, and very vocal. They have dual personalities, one minute they're nice, the next minute they get very aggressive."]* Although such remarks reveal important clues to Vivian's outer world, we must not overlook Vivian's own past tendencies. As such, the Knight can be equally understood as some internal contrasexual (animus) figure, or even more likely, a combination of both. *["With Raymond, the guy I was seeing at the time of the reading, I was also very dominant, controlling and aggressive. He has a history of battering girlfriends, and he knows my history. We would consistently bump heads."]*

Here stuck in the 'obstacle' position, the natural outward surge of the **Knight of Wands** is thwarted. His fire element which requires oxygen to increase its heat and flame now suffocates inside this boxed-in spread position. The combination becomes lethal: the Knight's fiery nature grows pent-up, frustrated, volatile, and indeed, combustible. Alcohol becomes a dangerous igniting agent. This describes another common energetic context that eventually explodes into domestic violence: fiery pent-up frustration coupled with alcoholism. The reading would indicate that all temptations towards such machismo (and 'marianismo') should be resisted at all costs. To summarize then:

present situation:	5 of Pentacles reversed ≅ **reversal of fortune**
present obstacle:	Knight of Wands ≅ **frustration, volatility**

Cluster 2: *Above and Below (5-3)*

Queen of Cups/Magician reversed. *[Interrelates air and earth elements at the poles]*

The **Queen of Cups** 'above' reflects Vivian's developing awareness and healing potential. Queens are nurturers and most at home in the element of water, which one suspects may be needed when knightly fires require extinguishing. Vivian now recognizes the values of "caring, trust, softness, and intimacy"—the Queen's perfected attributes of love—as worthy (and previously unknown) relationship goals. This is a positive sign. Most importantly, notes Rachel Pollack:

> The Queen of Cups joins consciousness to feeling. She knows what she wants and will take the steps to get it. Yet she acts always with an awareness of love.[1]

[Vivian at the time of our interview was becoming less willing to be emotionally manipulated. "I didn't want any more pampering, I wanted strength and equality." In her career she had begun to rededicate her efforts towards completing her AA degree. Her goal to study nursing, and her strength in community service, reflect the mature Queen's ideal of healing and nurturance.]

'Below,' however, Vivian's foundation is anchored to a troublesome inverted trump, **The Magician reversed.** For all his creative talents, his channeled will, and 'shape-shifting' potentials, The Magus when reversed is left lifeless and underachieving, 'mana-less' we might say, suggesting for Vivian that "transformative energies have been disrupted or blocked." She is not able to 'ground' her emerging accumulation of personal power into strong acts of will (though this remains through the laws of opposition a promising potential for the resurrected Magician).

Instead Vivian suffers from foundationlessness, the depletion, lack of concentration, and powerlessness that is suggested in this card when reversed. Although in the Queen (above) a healthier vision is achieved, the creative doer at her feet is left anemic and stymied. She has an idea of what she wants but lacks the means to pursue it. Consequently, Vivian's vulnerability and ambivalence before the Knight of Wands would seem relatively unchanged. *["I couldn't really trust Raymond. I would have sex with him and then pull away. I know him."]*

The vertical axis (as we saw with Andrew) that metaphorically structures Vivian's "psychological space" with analogous "body centers" from top to bottom is:

(1) **head** (goals/ideals) ≅ **awareness of love**
(2) **eyes/mouth** (present situation) ≅ **reversal of fortune**
(3) **heart** (obstacle) ≅ **volatile frustration**
(4) **legs/feet** (foundation) ≅ **lack of will**

Cluster 3: *Cause and Effect* (4-2-6)

6 of Swords reversed/Knight of Wands/8 of Swords. *[Views linear progression and causal relationships]*

The **6 of Swords** in the past cause traditionally suggests "passage through troubled waters to a new land." In the card image a boatsman is ferrying a shrouded woman (with child) across deep waters, symbolizing inwardly the ego's journey over unconscious change. The transition is delicate and potentially dangerous, but it will ultimately prove successful provided one and all keep their wits (the swords) about them and not rock the well-constructed though rather exposed 'boat'. Once more the Tarot image captures poignantly the female victim's challenge: to patiently transition through periods of turbulence, darkness and confusion to a new and unknown destination.

Unfortunately in Vivian's case, past attempts to evacuate were not so skillfully managed, as indicated by the card's **reversal**. Tragically, as has been well-documented, such is often the case for women who try to escape abusive marriages, and this fact is confirmed by Vivian herself. *[Vivian knew leaving Ernesto carried with it potentially lethal reprisal. "He came after me with a knife when I locked myself in the bathroom.... It eventually took four men to get him off of me." It was not until Vivian feared for the physical safety of her children that she would take another risk to leave. The experience has left her understandably terrified of future commitment, but also vulnerable to further engagement in non-committal, dangerous liaisons with fiery conquistadors like Raymond.]*

After enduring so extraordinary a toll to extricate herself from Ernesto, another rendezvous with an incendiary love object (as we discussed in position 2) would seem nothing short of suicidal, but such is forewarned (i.e., 'predicted') in the cards. The 'future effect' here illustrated by the captive woman bound and blindfolded in the **8 of Swords** shows vividly the predictable "hopelessness and paralysis" that will come with any repeat performance of the past, belying the dangerous "return effect" of abuse recidivism. Judging from the negligible interval of growth (numerically) in swords between the "troublesome 6" and the "depressive 8" (not to mention, the "anguished and splitoff 7" of Swords that was repeatedly seen in Andrew's pathology), secondary clues such as these leave an ominous impression of the classic reenactment between perpetrator and victim. ("Why would she go back?" the puzzled question so often asked by those outside this distorted psychological loop.) Still, one must look further before daring a full-blown prediction based on the clustering so far. To recap:

(primacy of)	**past cause:**	6 of Swords reversed ≅ **failed escape**
(through)	**present obstacle:**	Knight of Wands ≅ **volatile frustration**
(yields)	**future effect:**	8 of Swords ≅ **hopelessness, paralysis**

Cluster 4: ***Self/Object*** *(7-8)*

5 of Cups/The Sun. *[Reflects the structural components of ego identity and object relations]*

Here we turn to the 'ego' position, representing the way Vivian sees herself in the relationship. The **5 of Cups** depicts "sorrow, grief, but also acceptance and eventual renewal." Three cups lie spilled out, but two remain standing. In the three turned cups, Vivian grieves the loves (such as they were) and the losses, the trough of emotional investment now empties to its original source, the earth itself. *["I was two different people to two different men."]* The unseen two remaining cups situated behind the figure, that is, out of conscious view, symbolize a new romantic union in waiting. This may be either good news or bad, for whether the next involvement proves the more satisfying given the full context of the reading remains yet to be seen.

To Vivian's credit, **The Sun** that falls next suggests that she is able to differentiate the particular from the general. In contrast to the grief and sorrow she identifies for herself in the 5 of Cups, here the world outside is perceived positively, as a "great burst of energetic freedom" evidenced in the 'object' position by **The Sun.** This cardinal trump offers much needed optimism, energy, and light, particularly as a trump will always refer to a possibility greater than an individual's sphere of ego-based personality.

The Sun's vibrancy and vitality leave Vivian to entertain fresher, more sun-ripened possibilities for relationships of all kinds. The fire proclivity which has drawn so many charming arsonists in the past can now be enjoyed more universally in the natural abundance of The Sun's health, activity, and brightness; in this climate "love objects" as individuals become less sought to fan the flames. At least such is the possibility suggested by the card's dramatic showing in this position. Arrien describes **The Sun** as "the universal principle of teamwork, partnership, and collaboration."[2] In this light, it is suggested by the reader that work relationships, friendships, and community activities may provide more suitable networks of connection. The possibility gives the querent the image of healthy alternatives not quite considered previously. To summarize:

> **self concept:** 5 of Cups ≅ grieving before return
> **object concept:** The Sun ≅ community activity, health

Cluster 5: *Anticipation/Resistance Axis (9-2)*

Page of Wands/Knight of Wands. *[Shows the relationship between anticipation and resistance which is typically interdependent]*

As a younger version of our troublesome Knight of Wands in the 'obstacle' position, the **Page of Wands** standing modestly in the 'anticipation' position would seem a bit disconcerting, to say the least. Not so intense as his older brother the Knight, he is traditionally described as "an anonymous messenger of unseen possibilities," associated with the mercurial "traveling minstrel" or 'stranger' of earlier times.

Pages in general represent the quality of each suit in its simplest state; they are childlike in their innocence and sincerity. The dotted line that connects these fascinating "siblings of fire" (9-2) speaks to the hopeful side of Vivian's fantasy life: she dangerously wonders whether perhaps a kinder, gentler version of her man-type would do the trick. But would he be sufficiently charismatic? And then again, what should happen when this fireboy becomes a man? Deja vu all over again? These nagging "hopes and fears" suggest critical lessons are still to be learned and unlearned. Perhaps Vivian cannot fully make the necessary break from her self-destructive tendencies until a younger Prince is finally ruled out.

[In the follow-up interview, Vivian described still another two-year affair that was sandwiched in between Ernesto and Raymond. "Scott," a strong 6 foot 5 married black man fits the bill perfectly as her anticipated Page of Wands. "He was loud and dominant like my father, but he never tried to control me. He wanted me to see other men. We were each other's comfort stations." Synchronistically, Vivian mentions how the night before her Tarot reading (six months earlier) she had endured a violent verbal exchange with Raymond (the Knight) and to her surprise, "out of the blue" shortly afterwards came a phone call from Scott (the Page). They hadn't spoken in a year until then.] Such dangerous anticipations and obstacles are woefully active in the spread and would seem to animate her much troubled attachments to hot lovers and courtly wands. The hopeful signs of the Queen of Cups and The Sun may not be enough to counteract to potential web of Cluster 5:

anticipation:
- **hope**: Page of Wands ≅ **gentle messenger**
- **fear**: Page of Wands ≅ **controlling firebrand**
- **resistance**: Knight of Wands ≅ **volatile frustration**

Cluster 6: *Resolution/Wisdom (10-11)*

The Devil/8 of Wands. *[Points to psychological destiny mediated by conscious choice and transcendent guidance]*

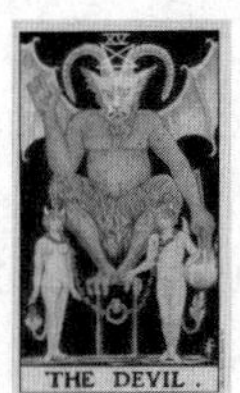

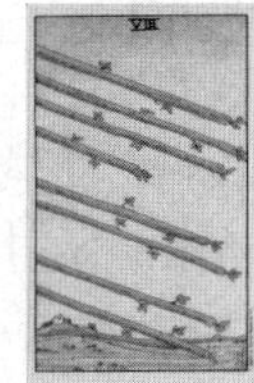

Traditionally, **The Devil** is viewed as a force of illusion, disruption, and oppression. Now occupying the 'outcome' position, its appearance is notably ominous. Its numerological dimension ties **The Devil** to its root in **The Lovers,** as Trump 15 reduces to Trump 6 (15=1+5=6). The Beast, perched between his captured demons on a block of stone, represents a perversion of The Lovers who themselves symbolize the harmonious union of opposites. As we have seen, this is quite a concern as Vivian has previously demonstrated an inability to differentiate the two. The Devil's chained male and female figures at his feet reflect his penchant for "attachment, abuse, deception, and bondage." From all that has gone before, his appearance in Vivian's future destiny is disturbing, but no real surprise. Like The Tower reversed was for Andrew, this outcome bodes poorly and should be averted or consciously apprehended if possible. The 'outcome' position itself is described to the querent during selection as "something you can work towards, or work against, though on some level it will emerge in your destiny and will need to be reckoned with."

Pollack notes, "On a wider sense [The Devil] symbolizes the life energy locked-up in the dark hidden areas of the self, *which cannot be entered by ordinary means* [italics mine]."[3] What progress Vivian has made to date has been notably external; we have seen this "locked up" life energy projected outwards onto **The Sun**, with the external world appearing to Vivian as a brightened playground. But the shadow work **The Devil** commands has not been truly forthcoming, but left stultified inwardly, perhaps, owing to the impassivity of **The Magician reversed**. Such, in fact, is reminiscent of our introductory assessment regarding the phenomena of domestic violence itself: "a very strange onion—the product of many forces operating and interacting at many levels between an individual and his environment." Sadly for Vivian, another tragic repeat performance hinted at in the reading is now more strongly suspected in her future.

Nevertheless, the 8 **of Wands** (our final card) marks Tarot's parting words—not only to Vivian, but to our case studies in general. As this card was explored in Andrew's reading, we have already discussed its "arrows of love" connotation (Waite), particularly in terms of the swiftness with which the fire element is known to flare and embroil. For Andrew, the card was deemed "rapid escalation." But as we are dealing with the final position, 'gift and guide', we may approach the card from a slightly more elevated angle, and return to the observations of Angeles Arrien, who of all contemporary Tarot commentators is first to hold forth the "wisdom dimension" of each card. As already suggested, Arrien describes the 8 of Wands as "a spiritual bridge to wholeness using intuition and spiritual vision."[4]

Such a description might apply to the Tarot method in general. Unquestionably, Tarot is a bridge to wholeness using intuition and spiritual vision. But for Vivian the card's guidance is specific and urgent: she must examine her struggles and patterns from the insights and warnings provided by the cards. The transcendent logic of this vision, i.e., 'spiritual bridge', provides a gift of liberation from the cycles of abuse Vivian seems bound to repeat. Synchronistically, Tarot gives and guides this vision.

A summary of Vivian's cards follows before general conclusions are offered. For those interested to learn how Andrew and Vivian might verbally interact through the vehicle of their Tarot spreads, I have included in Appendix B an imaginary "Tarot Dialogue" between male perpetrator and female victim; this is a device which translates each card and position into first-person narratives and gives license to let the cards "speak."

Summation of Vivian's Spread

The following table is a compilation of cluster summaries

Cluster 1: The Core

present situation:	5 of Pentacles reversed ≅ **reversal of fortune**
present obstacle:	Knight of Wands ≅ **frustration, volatility**

Cluster 2: Above and Below (spatial axis)

head (goals/ideals):	Queen of Cups ≅ **awareness of love**
eyes/mouth (present situation):	5 of Wands reversed ≅ **reversal of fortune**
heart (obstacle):	Knight of Wands ≅ **volatile frustration**
legs/feet (foundation):	Magician reversed ≅ **lack of will**

Cluster 3: Cause and Effect (temporal axis)

(primacy of) **past cause:**	6 of Swords reversed ≅ **failed escape**
(through) **present obstacle:**	Knight of Wands ≅ **volatile frustration**
(yields) **future effect:**	8 of Swords ≅ **hopelessness, paralysis**

Cluster 4: Self/Object

self concept:	5 of Cups ≅ **grieving before return**
object concept:	The Sun ≅ **community, health, play energy**

Cluster 5: Anticipation/Resistance

anticipation: (bipolar)	
hope:	Page of Wands ≅ **gentle messenger**
fear:	Page of Wands ≅ **controlling firebrand**
resistance:	Knight of Wands ≅ **volatile frustration**

Cluster 6: Resolution And Wisdom

outcome:	The Devil ≅ **abuse, deception, perversion, domination**
gift/guide:	8 of Wands ≅ **bridge to wholeness, vision and intuition**

Case Study Conclusions

In *Synchronicity, Science, and Soul-Making* author Victor Mansfield argues that in the final analysis, it is the meaningfulness of a synchronistic event that matters, while the means of arrival is secondary and contingent. He explains:

> We would not accept an interpretation of a symbolically rich and numinous dream as complete or satisfying if it merely reaffirmed the existence of the unconscious. That would hardly illustrate a specific expression of that person's individuation.[5]

Mansfield's observation would suggest that the Tarot method itself is ultimately of secondary importance, while the insights it stimulates and clarifies are themselves the primary value. From a pure synchronicity standpoint, I would have to agree. Tarot is a tool and a vehicle, not the finished product or destination. It is the clever seamstress who needles and threads the fuzzy nuances that gather meaningfully in time, the metaphysical mirror and teacher of the moment. It trades in meaning, and for that it must be considered as an instrument of potential psychotherapeutic value.

While other intriguing new methods in Psychology may seek to circumvent meaning entirely in their quest for symptom relief and so-called 'cure', in Tarot self-understanding, insight, depth, and expanded vision are gold. They above all else are what animates the human heart and transports it beyond the limits of our ailments and ordinary existence. In the final analysis, Tarot's validity on the journey can only be judged by the "quilt" of meaning that is experienced by its users. In the pilot study examined in the past three chapters, those answers can come, ultimately, only from the experience of the subjects themselves. But as we have seen, domestic violence is a very strange onion, with many forces operating and interacting at many levels. Obviously, each individual story carries particular themes and subplots unique to its narrator. Nevertheless, certain patterns accessed through the Tarot method have been clearly shown to be shared by many.

Mansfield's conclusion notwithstanding, at the heart of this book is the very method itself, and not the particular insights derived through it. Giving practical feet to this esoteric tool has hopefully allowed us to separate the essential Tarot from its countercultural packaging. In this study I have tried to provide a sound philosophical and empirical basis by establishing a rational application for an irrational method. In the particular focus of domestic violence, I am merely knocking on Pandora's Box. The possibilities of related travels through a synchronistic lens are bound only by the imagination itself, and the courage of those who would attempt such uncharted territory.

As we consider the hypothesis of our pilot study: *That as an acausal, synchronistic reflector of human experience, the Tarot method will reveal certain meaningful underlying group trends that are consistent in the personalities of perpetrator and victim*—I believe the careful reader would join me in support. The pilot study reported here is inconclusive, but suggestive. If so, the synchronistic hypothesis must be entertained, even though it will surely challenge the natural reflexes of one's "habitual causality."

As far as continued experimentation and scientific investigation, it is my hope that sufficient interest has been generated in the chapters of this book for others who are so inclined to join these efforts. Certainly this atypical attempt to empirically demonstrate and replicate synchronistic phenomena accessed through divination is vulnerable to methodological flaw and experimental error. No doubt a tighter design, use of control groups, correlation to other acausal and causal predictors, multiple replications and other measures would make statistical analysis and verification more manageable. Such is greatly needed if we are to bring to this work less notoriety and more respectability. The value in going down this difficult road of experimentation is simply that the greater scientific validity Tarot is accorded, in this age and undoubtedly the next, the greater too will be Tarot's potential contribution to the world.

But ultimately, whether or not the individual subjects of our study truly discovered deep, personally impactful meaning (the acid test of synchronicity) from the transcendent logic of the cards, we may never know. Collectively, however, from the symbolic patterns that gathered in time synchronistically before these specific groups of individuals, we as observers of the larger process are left to determine for ourselves whether the aforementioned experiments are indeed meaningful, not merely to our comprehension of the issue in focus, but to our wider conception of the mysterious cosmos we inhabit.

Notes

[1]Pollack, Rachel, *Seventy-Eight Degrees of Wisdom* (Part II) *The Minor Arcana;* Aquarian Press Limited, 1980, p.52

[2]Arrien, Angeles, *The Tarot Handbook: Practical Applications of Ancient Visual Symbols;* Arcus Publishing Company, 1987, p. 92.

[3]Pollack, Rachel, (Part I) p. 57.

[4]Arrien, Angeles (as above).

[5]Mansfield, Victor, *Synchronicity, Science, and Soul-Making;* Open Court. 1995, p 29.

Chapter XIII

WHEN PSYCHOLOGY MEETS TAROT

> Our doubts are traitors, and make us lose the good we oft might win, by fearing to attempt.
>
> —William Shakespeare
> *Measure For Measure*, Act 1, Sc.5

This book has invited you to 'attempt' a radically different approach from the standard procedure, to entertain a mode of perception that falls outside the familiar explanatory rules (habits) of causality, conventional wisdom and common sense. It has challenged you to trust the natural intelligence that gathers around so-called "empowered randomness" and put it to good use. It has encouraged the introduction of a complex, metaphysically-based instrument into everyday personal and clinical practice. It has acknowledged the seeming outlandishness and delicacy of this prospect.

The aforementioned are but a few of the adjustments that will be required when the practice of Psychology meets the deck of Tarot. Our discussion has also promoted the human imagination as Tarot's cunning ambassador who would speak wisely to us through encoded images via the strange workings of an unusual pack of mysterious pictures. A tall order for a small deck of "*those little cards used for fortune-telling.*" In truth, Tarot is no more fortune-telling than psychotherapy is personality-fixing. To the contrary, both disciplines primarily concern themselves with present difficulties, and are by nature exploratory, non-formulaic experiments in awareness and self-discovery with no guarantees for success. Additionally, for those in need of their offerings, both can be remarkably compelling and rewarding.

Navigating through the imaginal world of Tarot, we have highlighted this ancient art's unique vertical and horizontal topography of symbolism accessed through the elevator shaft of the mind, along with its constitutional laws of opposition and universality, its operating mechanisms of acausality and synchronicity, and its nonlinear avenues of simultaneity, present-centeredness, and interdependency. Throughout our travels we have sought to establish steady ground, an even hand and firm toehold, for skillful climbing over difficult terrain. Our mission, as stated from the outset, has been to blend the strange bedfellows of Psychology and Tarot, to get them to lie down together, as it were, without competing for the remote control.

We have made our disclaimers. The land of Tarot is not meant to replace the visible worlds we have come to know and cherish, nor disturb the settled territories we so staunchly defend and protect, though quite frequently (if we are honest) we blindly exploit and exhaust as well. Properly understood, Tarot is neither Old Age nor New Age, but then again such distinctions become quite meaningless when speaking of something that is ultimately formless, foundationless, and eternal. Tarot realms are merely complementary opposites of the more familiar worlds of sensation and intellect; they are their invisible counterparts, their dark matter and imaginary friends. And as we have suggested, only in combining the two realms are we likely to discover an "explicit duality expressing an implicit unity." As the Sufi scholar Henri Corbin wrote of imagination:

> There is a world that is both intermediary and immediate…the world of the image, the *mundus imaginalis:* a world that is ontologically as real as the world of the senses and that of the intellect. This world requires its own faculty of perception, namely imaginative power, a faculty with a cognitive function, a noetic value which is as real as that of sense perception or intellectual intention.[1]

In particular, we have described various regions or states of imaginative power as existing within discrete boundaries of psychological information called "spectrums of possibility." Spectrums have been defined as components separated and arranged along some special dimension. And of course, *possibility* in its purest sense suggests that which is naturally able or even likely to occur. That which, for better or worse, cannot be ruled out. In particular, the special dimensions of possibility discussed in this study have included: (1) spectrums of psychological experience known to coexist simultaneously in the moment, (2) spectrums of meaning within individual Tarot cards, and (3) spectrums of therapeutic intervention that Tarot facilitates for both clinician and client. These areas stand as possibilities worth pursuing when Psychology meets Tarot.

Throughout these pages we have observed how the human mind's 'infrastructure' appears greatly magnified under the complex lens of Tarot. Indeed, we all suffer from a multiple personality disorder of sorts. But for the real world of psychopathology, a realm about which most tarotists are regrettably unschooled, I have attempted to demonstrate a modest glimpse into Tarot's possibilities for research. The "perfect Tarot challenge" (as I've called it), implementing a synchronistically-based method in the unlikely study of perpetrators and victims of domestic violence, has yielded interesting and provocative, if inconclusive, results. More research in these "meta-realms" is certainly necessary and encouraged as our extraordinary claims unquestionably require strong if not extraordinary proof. Our pilot efforts are meant merely to open empirical channels of possibility.

In all, we have attributed Tarot's uncanny ability to reflect, predict, and indeed create subjective experience to its unique and mysterious assets, namely: (1) its essential visuality and nonverbality in the service of envisioning; (2) its economy, complexity, and condensation in the service of brevity; (3) its multidimensionality and simplicity in the service of "depth perception"; (4) its numinosity and evocative powers that stimulate emotional arousal; and, (5) its intentionality and extraordinary versatility in the service of therapeutic utility and efficacy.

Firmer ground for Tarot in the visible world has been sought. We have shown Tarot's natural affinity with the field of Psychology while acknowledging its own self-inflicted injuries, its confusion within ranks, its separation from scientific research and classification of mental disorders, its need for greater psychological sophistication, precision, empiricism, training, and ethical codification as it seeks wider acceptance and utilization. In doing so we have sought to undress Tarot of its misappropriated "gypsy garb" and to allow the cards to work their own phenomenological magic. We've also worked to establish Tarot's methodology more methodically, to classify its lexicon along sound and consistent psychological principles, and to direct its power more properly into psychological territory with the added advantages of a therapeutic container, professional training, and empirical research. But why have we labored to build such a bridge?

The simplest answers are: (1) "because it's there," and (2) because we need all the help we can get. The archetypes embedded in Tarot symbols, including image, color, and number archetypes, are fundamentally *a priori* psychical entities more likely to have been discovered by man in his search for truth than invented or constructed by him. Whether or not we choose to see them, THEY ARE THERE. What we lack are accessible tools for navigating through the deep invisible waters that lie within. The Fool's Journey, no matter the itinerary, is traveled (unconsciously) by all, and can indeed be guided by this higher source.

Oracles such as Tarot and *I Ching* are no more or less than special compasses that help us interconnect the two worlds. They change the way we relate to situations in order to show us the inner forces that shape them. They are based on a crucial insight into the workings of the psyche made most palatable in the 20th century by none other than Sigmund Freud: namely, the understanding that words, things and events, when properly approached, become 'omens' (signs) that open communication with a "spirit-world" (the unconscious) within—and that in every symptom, conflict or problem, an underlying, nonpersonal but highly intelligent voice is trying to communicate with us. It speaks to us not in words, but in symbols. WE NEED TO LISTEN. Divination gives this voice a special forum to be heard.

That we need all the help we can muster is indeed attested to simply by the provocative title of a recent book by James Hillman and Michael Ventura: *We've Had a Hundred Years of Psychotherapy and the World's Getting Worse.* Who would argue if not worse, then in the least, more complex and challenging? As we proceed into the 21st century, few practitioners of mental health and healing would not agree that the future of psychotherapy, indeed its very survival, is uncertain. On a more general level, one might conclude as well that the future of self-reflection and self-awareness, ominously, is likewise uncertain.

Traditional "talk therapy," for all its reported benefit, is currently undergoing a radical tracheotomy (some would prefer, 'lobotomy'), perhaps eventually for the greater good, though few therapists today relish the outlook. We've certainly noted the disconcerting fact that of the current estimated 400 schools of psychotherapy, to date there is no convincing evidence that one system is any better than the others. Making matters less certain still, today a squall of swirling interference marked by changing market forces and so-called health care reform, managed care, the corporatization and medicalization of therapy, an emphasis on brevity and targeted goals, cost containment, a rapidly changing client population, and the computer revolution have each demanded that conventional psychotherapy reconsider its standard practices. As I've suggested, perhaps these changing currents mark Tarot's clarion call, or in the least, this is a possibility and an opportunity. Tarot historian Cynthia Giles notes:

> Magical philosophy blossoms when old structures of cultural certainty start to crumble—much the way flowering vines will immediately insinuate themselves into the cracking walls of an abandoned building.[2]

But Tarot may serve a larger function as well. With its Western-based spiritual roots and cultural expression, its philosophical ties to both the golden Renaissance and the great wisdom traditions of the ancient world, Tarot may today serve as a complex and comprehensive map for healthy psychological functioning that brings continuity to bear from previous eras yet remains fresh and constantly reinvented and revitalized. It is uniquely multicultural and cross-cultural. The tremendous outpouring of newly-conceived Tarot decks speaks to the outstanding creative activity and fascination these cards continue to inspire in younger generations. And as noted, the timelessness and 'nonlocality' of Tarot images free them from the provinciality and territoriality that often hinders organized movements, making Tarot cards by contrast universally recognizable and accessible, cross-cultural, language-independent, and perennially contemporary. Few would argue that a map of higher possibility is notably absent in the Western psychological archives, which today encourages little aspiration beyond normalcy, adaptivity, and functionality.

Tarot offers this crucial missing piece of the psychospiritual puzzle: a tradition, a language, and an imagery, cast in a simple deck of cards, which reflect human potentials in their proper nuance, dimensionality, psychological development, and spectrum of possibility. As noted earlier by Arrien, the inherent value of Tarot used within a therapeutic context would be as a counterpart to the *Diagnostic and Statistical Manual of Mental Disorders* (DSM), a psycho-pathological handbook of diagnostic categories of dysfunctional behaviors. Tarot is a metaphysical 'picture' book which defines, divines, reflects, predicts, and creates spectrums of possibility and human potential. Through Tarot the healing powers of the human imagination are brought into fertile focus. Tarot is not a religion, but a sacred tool. Nor is Tarot a spiritual movement or a school of consciousness *per se*, but an exceptional catalyst of possibility. "Behind an able man," says the Chinese proverb, "there are always other able men."

In closing, I would invoke the words of the great French Tarot master of the 19th-century, Eliphas Levi. Perhaps the most influential of all Tarot theorists, and called "last of the magi," Levi saw the Tarot not just as a charming relic of some ancient symbolic system, but as an unparalleled practical tool, a key to the wisdom of the ages.

Levi wrote:

> The Tarot is a monumental and singular work simple and strong as the architecture of the pyramids, and in consequence as durable. It is a book which is the sum of all the sciences and whose infinite permutations are capable of solving all problems; a book which informs by making one think. It is perhaps the greatest masterpiece of the human mind, and certainly one the most beautiful things handed down by antiquity.

Notes

[1]Quoted by Donald Sandner in his foreword to R. Ammann, *Healing and Transformation in Sandplay;* La Salle, Illinois, Open Court, 1991.

[2]Giles, Cynthia, *The Tarot: History, Mystery, and Lore;* Simon and Schuster, 1992, p. 121.

Appendix A

Minor Arcana

Phrases and Proverbs

[Note: Images describe the standard Waite/Smith Tarot images and traditional descriptions are taken from Butler's *Dictionary of the Tarot* (1975). Meanings, however, are applicable to all decks. Phrases are those of the author. Reversals suggest compromised and/or 'inner' aspect of card. Spectrums of possibility are taken from the lexicons in this book.]

SWORDS *(Air, Clarity, Thinking)*

Ace of Swords

Phrase: ***"The sword of Wisdom (Prajna); cuts through confusion and emotional attachments; clarity, seeing things as they are; (reversed) confusion or inner clarity."***

Image: A heavenly hand holding forth a sword upright, the tip of which is crowned. The crown is garlanded with two branches, one of which has red berries. Solar 'Yods' are also in the card.

Traditional: Force, triumph, conquest, pure intellect. "**Measure a thousand times and cut once**" (Turkish Proverb).

Spectrum of Possibility: [**Intelligence**] idea/intellect, illusion/confusion, discovery/lucidity.

2 of Swords

Phrase: ***"Closeness without merging; friendship and respect; opposites; mutuality, and respect for difference; (reversed) broken trust, abandonment, betrayal, or self-trust."***

Image: A blindfolded figure seated beside the sea, its hands crossed and holding two upright swords. Above, a waxing moon.

Traditional: Conformity, friendship, concordance, opposition, balance, equilibrium. "**If you want to be respected, you must respect yourself**" (Spanish Proverb).

Spectrum of Possibility: [**Trust**] friendship/loyalty, doubt/betray, affinity/respect.

3 of Swords

Phrase: "***Heartbreak and sorrow; the mind penetrating the heart; painful insight; (reversed) denial, or boddhicitta.***"

Image: Three swords piercing the same heart.

Traditional: Sorrow, disappointment, tears, struggle, removal, division, delay. "**Where there is love, there is pain.**" (Spanish Proverb).

Spectrum of Possibility: [**Sorrow**] melancholy/heartbreak, shame/blame, suffering/introspection.

4 of Swords

Phrase: "***Rest and recuperation after long illness; withdrawal, renewal, (reversed) denial of illness or meditation, inner healing.***"

Image: The effigy of a knight praying displayed upon a tomb. On the wall three swords hang, point downward. Below him, on the side of the tomb, is another sword.

Traditional: Retreat, solitude, hermit's repose, rest, convalescence, meditation. "**A closed mind is like a closed book; just a block of wood**" (Chinese Proverb).

Spectrum of Possibility: [**Retreat**] rest/withdrawal, stress/isolation, mental cleansing/refueling.

5 of Swords

Phrase: "***Conflict between loyalty to self vs. friends; sadness over loss of two people or things; carrying forward after the change has been made; (reversed) dissociation, or consciously dividing attention.***"

Image: A man holding two swords over his left shoulder; a third points downward in his right hand. On the ground near him are two other swords. Two figures walk away in dejection. An expression of malicious triumph is upon his face.

Traditional: Defeat, loss, failure, slander, degradation and destruction, sadness, mourning. "**Love your neighbor, but don't tear down your fence**" (German Proverb).

Spectrum of Possibility: [**Despair**] strife/defeat, pessimism/disdain, division/dissonance.

6 of Swords

Phrase: "***Life journey and transition; crossing perilous deep waters seeking the other side; need to keep your wits (awareness) in the boat or risk capsizing into deep waters below (unconscious); the boatsman is your inner guide, the woman and child are important subpersonalities on the journey [the 'nurturer' and the 'vulnerable' within]; (reversed) failure to act, recklessness, or inner journey.***"

Image: Two hooded figures seated in a boat which also contains six swords, point downward. The boat is poled by a man.

Traditional: Success after anxiety, journey by sea, travel, journey of flesh or spirit. "**Smooth seas do not make skillful sailors**" (African Proverb).

Spectrum of Possibility: [**Transition**] passage/flight, escape/paralysis, journey/change.

7 of Swords

Phrase: "***Carrying a conflict at the expense of a friendship or relationship; martyrdom and betrayal; scheming while in confusion; (reversed) dazed and confused.***"

Image: A man stealing away from a crusader's camp with five swords. Two others remain, point downward, in the ground behind him.

Traditional: Design, attempt, new schemes, vacillation, uncertainty. "**Everyone thinks his own burden heavy**" (French Proverb).

Spectrum of Possibility: [**Defense**] futility/resignation, evasion/avoidance, stealth/deceit.

8 of Swords

Phrase: "***Self-imposed ego; cognitive distortions; to be bound and blinded by one's own negative thoughts; (reversed) clinical depression, immobilization.***"

Image: A blindfolded figure standing bound, three swords stand on its right, five on its left.

Traditional: Conflict, criticism, blame, obstacles, danger, indecision, imprisonment. "**When an elephant is in trouble even a frog will kick him**" (Hindu Proverb).

Spectrum of Possibility: [**Interference**] oppression/paralysis guilt/entrapment powerlessness/helplessness

9 of Swords

Phrase: "***Depression, worry, mental anguish, distortion, (reversed) self doubt, rumination, suicidality.***"

Image: A figure sits up on a bed, covers its eyes, weeping. Behind it nine horizontal swords. The bedcover is decorated with a design of squares which contain, alternating red roses with the planetary signs and those for the houses.

Traditional: Worry, suffering, despair, cruelty, desolation, death. "**He who has health has hope; and he who has hope, has everything**" (Arab Proverb).

Spectrum of Possibility: [**Distortion**] hopelessness/agony, depression/doom, shadow/demons.

10 of Swords

Phrase: "***End of your rope; paralysis leading to surrender; no more struggle; Hell Realm; ego death; return to the source; (reversed) fear of annihilation, fragmentation, or 'turning it over' to a higher source.***"

Image: A man laying face downward. His back is pierced with ten standing swords.

Traditional: Ruin, pain, desolation, karmic results, the beginning of harmony. **"If a man is destined to drown, he will drown even in a spoonful of water."** (Yiddish Proverb).

Spectrum of Possibility: [**Surrender**] ruin/rebirth, denial/repression, turning it over/release.

Page of Swords

Phrase: "***A student of the mind; detective or spy, making private notes based on subtle observations; checking things out, reality-testing; (reversed) hypervigilance or else keen self-observation.***"

Image: A young man standing on a windy hill, brandishing a sword.

Traditional: Vigilant, acute, subtle, deceit, spy or rival, secret service. **"Deceive the rich and powerful if you will, but don't insult them"** (Japanese Proverb).

Spectrum of Possibility: [**Observation**] detachment/cunning, suspicion/paranoia, calculation/caution.

Knight of Swords

Phrase: "***Moves fast, cuts through all nonsense, great skill in penetration; on the quest for clarity; seeker of knowledge; (reversed) obsession, over-intellection, or else Zen practitioner.***"

Image: A knight riding furiously, brandishing his sword, through the wind. His clothing is decorated with butterflies and red birds.

Traditional: Romantic chivalry, skillfulness, martial bravery, cleverness, capacity. **"Do not be in a hurry to tie what you cannot untie"** (English Proverb).

Spectrum of Possibility: [**Insight**] focus/discrimination, rationalization/obsession, evaluation/reduction.

Queen of Swords

Phrase: "***Independent, self-sacrificing woman of character; suffers in the service of honesty and clarity; sorrow in response to seeing things as they are; (reversed) animus ridden, manipulative, plotting, or deep penetrating insight.***"

Image: A stern queen, sitting on a throne decorated with butterflies and winged cherubs. Her crown is also decorated with butterflies. She holds firmly a sword in her right hand.

Traditional: Familiarity with sorrow, widowhood, dour, mourning, intensely perceptive and intelligent. "**There is no pillow so soft as a clear conscience**" (French Proverb).

Spectrum of Possibility: [**Accuracy**] penetration/honest, vindictive/self-righteous, congruence/consistency.

King of Swords

Phrase: "***Impartial and objective knowledge; the judge at court—makes unbiased judgments based on objective facts and presented information; command and authority; (reversed) judgmental, prejudiced, or crystallized awareness.***"

Image: A stern king seated on a stone throne carved with a waxing crescent, a waning crescent, butterflies and women. His crown incorporates the design of a winged cherub. In his right hand he brandishes a sword.

Traditional: Full of ideas, man in authority, judge or critic, intelligence, captain, lawyer, power. "**Examine what is said, not him who speaks.**" (Arab Proverb).

Spectrum of Possibility: [**Clarity**] precision/judgment, intellectualize/judgmental, crystallize/awareness.

CUPS *(Water, Heart, Feeling and Healing)*

Ace of Cups

Phrase: "***Emotional fulfillment on every level, happiness, abundance; (reversed) emotionally cutoff, or spiritual devotion.***"

Image: A hand from the heavens, holding a golden chalice which is also a fountain. From the fountain five streams of water and 'Yods' fall into a lotus pool. On the cup is inscribed the letter 'M' reversed. A white dove flies downward into the cup bearing a white circle with a cross in its beak.

Traditional: Transcendental love, joy, happiness, abundance. "**Love and eggs are best when they are fresh**" (Russian Proverb).

Spectrum of Possibility: [**Emotion**] receptivity/fluidity, despair/numbness, desire/ecstasy.

2 of Cups

Phrase: "***Emotional reciprocity—coming together on heart level; falling in love; union, the loving relationship; (reversed) relational friction, urge to merge, or soror mystica (spiritual union).***"

Image: Two lovers holding cups. Above them hovers the winged head of a lion with caduceus.

Traditional: Coming together, marriage, and healing. "**Love rules without rules**" (Italian Proverb).

Spectrum of Possibility: [Relation] union/intercourse, fusion/abandonment, attraction/appreciation.

3 of Cups

Phrase: "***Experience of joy; process of (feminine) relatedness; sharing, natural flow of spontaneous emotion; (reversed) bitterness, over-celebration, or shared ecstasy.***"

Image: Three women in an abundant field holding aloft cups.

Traditional: Pleasure, abundance, fertility. "**Shared joy is a double joy; shared sorrow is half a sorrow**" (Swedish Proverb).

Spectrum of Possibility: [**Expression**] celebration/joy, protest/bitterness, affection/sharing.

4 of Cups

Phrase: "***Trying to grasp or actualize the 'missing piece' (in relationships); discontentment owing to lack of structure, definition, or relational form; (reversed) unformed boundaries, or emotional intelligence.***"

Image: A dreamer sitting before a tree. On the ground near him are three cups. From heaven a hand offers a fourth cup.

Traditional: Discontent with present conditions, weariness and disgust, blended pleasures, new acquaintance. "**When we cannot get what we love, we must love what is within our reach**" (French Proverb).

Spectrum of Possibility: [**Expectation**] comfort/discomfort, apathy/lethargy, promise/probability.

5 of Cups

Phrase: "***Mourning the loss of some important emotional process; crying over spilled milk; a new love experience awaits completion of necessary grieving; (reversed) denial, shock, complicated bereavement, or separation-individuation.***"

Image: A man in black standing disconsolate beside a river. On the ground are three cups before him, overturned, and two behind him upright.

Traditional: Disappointment, separation, lack of harmony, loss of friendship or pleasure. "**We know the worth of a thing when we have lost it**" (French Proverb).

Spectrum of Possibility: [**Separation**] loss/grief, devastation/shock, clinging/letting go.

6 of Cups

Phrase: "***Reawakening the sweet scents of bygone dreams; nostalgia tied to childhood or adolescence; remembering; the tenderness of youth; (reversed) maudlin or fixated in past; deep yearning.***"

Image: Six cups with white, five-pointed flowers. A small boy offers a girl one of them. Six cups filled with assorted flowers.

Traditional: Working through the past, the faded past, memories, nostalgia. **"What was hard to endure is sweet to recall"** (French Proverb).

Spectrum of Possibility: [**Memory**] sentiment/nostalgia, regret/fixation, tenderness/yearning.

7 of Cups

Phrase: "***Overspeculation leads to indecision (Hamlet); many roads; overwhelmed by too many choices, best to pick one (or risk the pitfall of paralysis); (reversed) lack of options, failure of imagination, or active awareness of subpersonalities.***"

Image: Seven cups seen in the heavens by a silhouetted figure. From one cup arises the *head of an angel*. From another arises *a serpent*. From another, *a castle*. In a fourth, *jewels*. In the fifth, *a monster*. In the sixth is a *shrouded figure with a halo*. And in the seventh is a *wreath*. The seventh cup is doubly interesting in that the skull design on its side comments upon the contents. It is the only one of the cups to do so.

Traditional: Illusory success, imagination and vision, debauchery, external splendor/internal corruption. **"When in doubt, Gallop!"** (Proverb of the French Foreign Legion).

Spectrum of Possibility: [**Multiplicity**] fantasy/possibility, fragment/projection, choice/profusion.

8 of Cups

Phrase: "***Inner journey, dark night of the soul, instinctive pulls inward; outer world on automatic; follow your feelings; inner directed; (reversed) loss of control, loss of soul, loss of self.***"

Image: A desolate night scene. A man turns his back on eight cups and walks away under a waning crescent moon.

Traditional: Abandoned success, impractical in money matters, going inward.

Spectrum of Possibility: [**Retreat**] journey/withdrawal, decompensate/stagnate, descend/divest.

9 of Cups

Phrase: "***Pleasure and happiness; satiety and abundance, emotional satisfaction; (reversed) overindulgence, consumption, and addiction, or self-satisfaction.***"

Image: A portly merchant sitting in satisfaction before a row of cups.

Traditional: Material success, happiness, truth, loyalty, liberty. "**The dog's kennel is not the place to keep a sausage**" (Danish Proverb).

Spectrum of Possibility: [**Fulfillment**] pleasure/enjoyment, indulgence/addiction, sustenance/satisfaction.

10 of Cups

Phrase: "***Falling in love; intoxication, bliss, larger than life (inflation); 'rainbows in the sky' (impermanence); (reversed) emotionally empty, overflow, or the numinosum.***"

Image: A man and woman beholding a rainbow of cups in the heavens. Near them two children are dancing (W/R). A pair of lovers. She wears a rose in her hair. Above are nine small cups and a tenth larger one into which a rainbow is pouring.

Traditional: Perpetual success, happiness to come, contentment, friendship. "**Though a tree grow ever so high, the falling leaves return to the ground**" (**Malayan Proverb**).

Spectrum of Possibility: [**Inspiration**] affirmation/gratitude, inflation/deflation, excitement/infatuation.

Page of Cups

Phrase: "***Dreamy youth, all sounds good but nothing manifest; romance, poetry, jealousy, passion, moodiness often led by unconscious factors; (reversed) immaturity, lability, ambivalence, wearing one's heart on their sleeve, the puer aeternus.***"

Image: A page standing beside the sea. He holds a cup from which a fish is jumping.

Traditional: A bachelor dreaming of his pleasure; seduction, deception, artifice. "**Love tells us many things that are not so**" (Ukrainian Proverb).

Spectrum of Possibility: [**Vulnerability**] innocence/openness, moodiness/lability, affection/dependency.

Knight of Cups

Phrase: "***Seeker of the heart; quest for the holy grail; romantic hero; Braveheart; bodhisattva; seductive troubadour; (reversed) narcissism, effeminism, Don Juanism, quixotic, or bhakti devotion.***"

Image: A knight, wearing a winged helmet, rides over a desert toward a river and the mountains. He carries a cup. His clothing is decorated with red fish.

Traditional: Dreamer haunted in his vision; lover, rival, seducer; stranger, sailor, drug dealer; occultism, strong sexual tendencies. "**A full cup must be carried steadily**" (English Proverb).

Spectrum of Possibility: [**Heart**] romance/quest, narcissism/infidelity, passion/idealization.

Queen of Cups

Phrase: "***Healing nurturing Queen, works with psyche, heart, and emotion; Queen of Hearts; (reversed) helper syndrome, codependency, emotional reasoning, or goddess worship.***"

Image: A queen sitting on a throne by the sea. She holds an ornate cup decorated with angels. Her throne is decorated with cherub-mermen and incorporates a scallop motif in the heading. *Traditional:* Reception, reflection, illusion, a good fair woman honest and devoted, the watery part of water (Crowley). **"Wheresoever you go, go with all your heart"** (Confucius).

Spectrum of Possibility: [**Nurturance**] care/healing, smothering/punishing, giving/sending.

King of Cups

Phrase: "***The healing, feeling King; today's therapist, doctor, diplomat or social leader primarily involved with compassion and human service; (reversed) con artist, philanderer, or guru, inspirational poet.***"

Image: A king seated on a throne which stands on a stone block in the middle of the sea. A fish emblem is pendant from a chain round his neck, repeated as a jumping fish in the background. In his right hand he holds a cup, in his left a lotus scepter.

Traditional: Honest man, philosophical or idealistic; kindness, liberality, generosity. **"Enjoy yourself. It's later than you think"** (Chinese Proverb).

Spectrum of Possibility: [**Compassion**] wisdom/support, manipulate/betray, empathy/sympathy.

WANDS/RODS *(Fire, Spirit, Energy)*

Ace of Wands

Phrase: "***New beginnings, birth of creative spirit, creative essence, empowerment; (reversed) primal chaos, or spiritual enlightenment.***"

Image: A hand holding forth a wand in leaf from the clouds. Other leaves, in the shape of 'Yods" are also seen.

Traditional: Creation, invention, enterprise, energy, strength, powers of fire, birth, activity, initiative, male libido. **"Where there is no vision, people perish"** (Proverbs 29:18). *Spectrum of Possibility:* [**Aspiration**] initiation/creation, darkness/frenzy, individuation/adventure.

2 of Wands

Phrase: "***World/spirit split; new creative possibilities; imagination, power over others; creative partnership; (reversed) lack of imagination; or telepathy.***"

Image: A man standing on a battlement looking out over the sea. In his right hand he holds a globe, in his left, a wand. To his right, resting against the wall, is another wand. To his left, and upon the wall is a St. Andrew Cross, one transverse arm of which is white lilies, the other being formed from red roses.

Traditional: Dominion; influence over another; occult knowledge; love of battle and challenge; worldly riches.

Spectrum of Possibility: [**Choice**] synthesis/convergence, confusion/anxiety, possibility/resonance.

3 of Wands

Phrase: "***Potential expansion; choice between 'path of the one' or 'path of the two' (self or other), seeking direction; (reversed) loss of direction, loss of intention; envisioning.***"

Image: A man looking out over what could be the sea or a desert. The background color in this card is sometimes yellow, yielding a yellow sea. His right hand holds one wand, to his left stands another. Slightly behind him to his right stands a third.

Traditional: Established strength, effort, discovery. "**Fish or cut bait**" (American Proverb).

Spectrum of Possibility: [**Intention**] effort/action, ambivalence/impotence, visualization/direction.

4 of Wands

Phrase: "***Creative lifestyle, structuring energy; (reversed) writer's block, scattered resources, or inner discipline.***"

Image: Wands in leaf garlanded with flowers. Behind are people apparently celebrating.

Traditional: Domestic tranquillity, prosperity, peace. "**Where God has his church the Devil will have his chapel**" (Spanish Proverb).

Spectrum of Possibility: [**Creation**] freedom/passage, status-quo/inactivity, appreciation/integration.

5 of Wands

Phrase: "***Conflict or strife; competition; upsetting words without meaning; surface arguments without touching real feelings; (reversed) inner battle, inner critics, or inner judo.***

Image: Five youths playing with wands as staves.

Traditional: Quarreling, fighting, opposition, competition, lawsuits, strife. **"When you throw dirt, you lose ground"** (Texan Proverb).

Spectrum of Possibility: [**Conflict**] competition/struggle, passive-aggression/combat, division/multiplicity.

6 of Wands

Phrase: "***Marching into battle anticipating supreme success; mobilizing one's resources and supports; martialing confidence and optimism in the face of difficulty; (reversed) loss of confidence, fear of failure, or activating subpersonalities.***"

Image: Young person on horseback, riding in triumph. His wand has a victor's wreath. He is accompanied by other men on foot who bear wands.

Traditional: Victory after strife; attempt, hope, desire, expectation. **"To know the road ahead, ask those coming back"** (Chinese Proverb).

Spectrum of Possibility: [**Optimism**] achievement/victory, arrogance/defeatism, confidence/anticipation.

7 of Wands

Phrase: "***Valor in the face of difficulty; digging in and taking a stand; (reversed) entrenched, stalemate, persistence.***"

Image: An embattled man using his wand as a staff to fight off six attacking staves.

Traditional: Valor, negotiations, competition, caution, challenge. " **Good fences make good neighbors**" (American Proverb).

Spectrum of Possibility: [**Persistence**] tests/obstructions, stubbornness/inflexibility, loyalty/positionality.

8 of Wands

Phrase: "***Highly potent channeled energy; intentionality, assertiveness, goal-directed; intense psychic connections; potent love affair; (reversed) one-sidedness, jealousy, failure to focus, or clairvoyance.***"

Image: Eight wands flying through the air parallel to each other. Their flight is apparently terminating.

Traditional: Activity, swiftness, high energy, arrows of jealousy. **"It is not enough to aim; you must hit"** (Italian Proverb).

Spectrum of Possibility: [**Goal**] assertion/movement, aimless/dispersed, focus/direction .

9 of Wands

Phrase: "***Power and victory; strength in opposition; creative power; psychic alignment; (reversed) misuse of power, black magic, or channeling.***"

Image: A man leaning upon a staff. His head is bandaged. Behind him stand eight other staves.

Traditional: Preparedness, strength, power, health energy, realization of success. **"Do not throw the arrow which will return against you"** (Kurdish Proverb).

Spectrum of Possibility: [**Force**] power/dominion, domination/bullying, potency/alertness.

10 of Wands

Phrase: "***Overburdened; heavy load; burnout and exhaustion; too much on your pallet; (reversed) workaholism, overwhelmed, overstimulation or recharging, refueling.***"

Image: A man carrying a bundle of ten heavy wands.

Traditional: Oppression, cruelty, karma, exhaustion. **"We never know the worth of water till the well is dry"** (French Proverb).

Spectrum of Possibility: [**Oppression**] burden/overextension, entrapment/abuse, depletion/exhaustion.

Page of Wands

Phrase: "***The wanderer or messenger, anonymously bringing forth some secret information or inheritance of great consequence, the faceless envoy; Pied Piper, the stranger, (reversed) fear of commitment, inadequate personality, or Magician's apprentice.***"

Image: A young man, his clothing decorated with salamanders, standing in a desert with a wand.

Traditional: Dark young man, messenger, an envoy, communication. **"What the heart thinks, the tongue speaks"** (Romanian Proverb).

Spectrum of Possibility: [**Communication**] message/information, disguise/obfuscate, sharing/showing.

Knight of Wands

Phrase: "***Impetuous knight, hasty lover, charismatic fire starter; spiritual warrior; gets what he needs and splits; mania, hit and run; (reversed) frustration, rage, spinning his wheels, or alchemist, yogin, magician, or artist.***"

Image: A knight riding through a desert. His clothing is decorated with salamanders. A fiery plume streams from his helmet.

Traditional: Impulsiveness, pride, traveler, abandonment and flight. **"When anger rises, think of the consequences"** (Confucius).

Spectrum of Possibility: [**Determination**] pursuit/tenacity, impetuous/explosive, charisma/warrior.

Queen of Wands

Phrase: "***Female executive; the energizer; she runs the king's castle; directed psychic energy; creative projects; the catalyst; (reversed) explosive, catty, impulsive, dampening, or channeler, psychic, transformer.***"

Image: A queen on a lion throne. She holds a sunflower in her left hand, a wand in her right. A black cat is before the throne. The designs of lions and sunflowers appear behind her on the canopy.

Traditional: Dark woman, attractive power; passionate anger, fertility, persistent energy. **"When a thing is done, advice comes too late"** (Romanian Proverb).

Spectrum of Possibility: [**Energy**] conduit/catalyst, repellent/retardant, pacing/channeling.

King of Wands

Phrase: "***Self-possessed fiery ruler; mastery and effortlessness; at the center of his self-created universe; purification; (reversed) self-destruction, the tyrant, megalomaniac, or visionary; mystic.***"

Image: A king on a salamander and lion throne in the desert. His robe is decorated with salamanders. He holds a wand in his right hand. There is a salamander beside him.

Traditional: Married man, honest and conscientious, knowledge, spiritual force, courage, strength. **"Let every fox take care of his own tail"** (Italian Proverb).

Spectrum of Possibility: [**Vision**] empowerment/control, dictatorial/megalomaniacal, manifesting/envisioning.

PENTACLES *(Earth, Wealth, Solidity)*

Ace of Pentacles

Phrase: "***Bringing to fruition; solidification; seeding, planting, grounding; wealth and material comfort; (reversed) density, inertia, matter or anchoring and establishing roots.***"

Image: A hand from the heavens holding a yellow coin which is inscribed on a pentagram. Below it is a garden, hedged with red roses, filled with white lilies.

Traditional: Favorable conditions, material wealth, abundance and prosperity, profit. **"A journey of a thousand miles begins with a single step."** (Chinese Proverb).

Spectrum of Possibility: [**Manifestation**] conception/seed, inertia/chaos, ground/core.

2 of Pentacles

Phrase: "***The juggler; staying in balance; harmonious change; juggling two distinct parts; balancing opposites; (reversed) clumsiness, splitting, or tai chi, inner balance, attunement.***"

Image: A young man dancing near the sea. In his hands he is juggling two pentacles which are surrounded by the lemniscate.

Traditional: Harmony in the midst of change, change in all forms, the juggler, obstacles and difficulty. **"To change and change for the better are two different things"** (German Proverb).

Spectrum of Possibility: [**Polarity**] balance/change, splitting/onesidedness, grace/health.

3 of Pentacles

Phrase: "***Building your own temple; constructing your world from the ground up; craft and self-creation; individuation process (reversed) sloppiness, indolence, dependence, or taking responsibility.***"

Image: A monk and a hooded man observing a stonemason at his work.

Traditional: Construction, material gain, business, skilled labor, trade, craftsmanship. **"It is easier to pull down than to build up"** (Latin Proverb).

Spectrum of Possibility: [**Construction**] working/crafting, impeding/defiling, concretizing/building.

4 of Pentacles

Phrase: "***In need of solidity and earthly power; structuring your material and practical concerns, financial planning; (reversed) greed, hoarding, attachment to form, or ritualizing connection to earth, the four directions, grounding.***"

Image: A king sits brooding. On his crown rests one pentacle. He hugs another in his lap. The third and fourth are beneath his feet.

Traditional: Skill in physical forces, material benefits, acquisitiveness, security. **"A lean agreement is better than a fat lawsuit"** (German Proverb).

Spectrum of Possibility: [**Form**] power/gain, attachment/avarice, structure/shape.

5 of Pentacles

Phrase: "***Reversal of fortune; survival; on the outside looking in; paying your dues, feeling humility or humiliation, homelessness; begging; (reversed) depravity, shame, servility, or renunciation, non-attachment, initiation.***"

Image: Two beggars pass a brightly lighted church window. They hurry through the snow. The pentacles are incorporated into the stained glass windows.

Traditional: Material trouble, loss or reversal of fortune, disorder, chaos, ruin. **"Better a mouse in the pot than no meat at all"** (Romanian Proverb).

Spectrum of Possibility: [**Loss**] want/need, covet/envy, humility/adjustment.

6 of Pentacles

Phrase: "***Giving out and taking in; counting and accounting; measuring what you get in return; (reversed) score-keeping, overscrutiny, compulsivity, miserliness, or equilibrium, accountability; Tonglen (Tibetan Buddhism).***"

Image: A wealthy merchant giving alms to beggars. He holds a golden scales in his left hand.

Traditional: Prosperity, gifts, gratification, measurement. **"If you would be wealthy, think of saving as well as getting"** (Benjamin Franklin).

Spectrum of Possibility: [**Compromise**] give/take, obsess/compulse, measure/compare.

7 of Pentacles

Phrase: "***Delay before harvest; patience while waiting; time for consideration, assessment, appraisal, non-action; (reversed) impatience, failure, or incubation, action-in-inaction.***"

Image: A farmworker contemplates gloomily six pentacles on a vine, apparently nearly ripe, and a seventh at his feet.

Traditional: Success unfulfilled, delay but with growth, failure, blight. **"If you are patient in a moment of anger, you will escape a hundred days of sorrow"** (Chinese Proverb).

Spectrum of Possibility: [**Patience**] delay/ripen, failure/frustration, incubate/vegetate.

8 of Pentacles

Phrase: "***Apprenticeship, 'turns things out like hotcakes'; disciplined spontaneity, developing mastery; (reversed) rebelliousness, lethargy, mechanicality or inner study, spiritual practice, meditation.***"

Image: A woodworker chiseling out a pentagram within a circle. Five of them hang beside him, a seventh rests against his bench and the eighth on the ground beside him.

Traditional: Skill, artfulness, prudence, craftsmanship, ambition, preparation. **"Employ thy time well if Thou meanest to get leisure"** (Benjamin Franklin).

Spectrum of Possibility: [**Discipline**] study/practice, expediate/rebel, differentiate/repeat.

9 of Pentacles

Phrase: "***Refinement and cultivation; happy leisurely accomplishment; fine things; quality and natural aesthetics, the beautiful garden; (reversed) instinctual gratification, perfectionism, imitation, or aesthetic appreciation, psychological differentiation.***"

Image: A woman seen in her vineyard of ripe grapes. On her upraised left hand she holds a bird. Her gown is patterned with flowers in the form of the planetary sign for Venus.

Traditional: Discretion, prudence, accomplishment, worldly achievement. "**Get what you can and keep what you have; that's the way to get rich.**" (Scottish Proverb).

Spectrum of Possibility: [**Cultivation**] abundance/simplicity, nature/instinct, nurture/refine.

10 of Pentacles

Phrase: "***Marriage and Family; security in the community/stability in the home; accumulated wealth, investment in the future; (reversed) family crisis, divorce, fear of commitment, or inner stability, self-esteem, self-nurturance.***"

Image: A patriarch seated before his gate. Near him are his dogs, his children and his grandchild. Ripe grapes and crescent moons also figure in this card.

Traditional: Family matters, riches, stable home, prosperity, satisfaction, success. "**The woman cries before the wedding and the man after**" (Polish Proverb)

Spectrum of Possibility: [**Embodiment**] prosperity/security, conformity/dissipation, commitment/investment.

Page of Pentacles

Phrase: "***Student of science, objectivity, observes what's out there, seeks unbiased factual information; (reversed) materialistic, superficial, mechanistic, or self-reflection, sensory awareness.***"

Image: A young man stands in a field of flowers holding a pentacle.

Traditional: Application, study, reflection, diligence, business management. "**When you go to buy, use your eyes, not your ears**" (Czech Proverb).

Spectrum of Possibility: [**Objectivity**] dissect/analyze, reify/compartmentalize, separate/reduce.

Knight of Pentacles

Phrase: "***Conservative, very trustworthy, somewhat 'square' knight. Laborious, patient, grounded, dull; seeks practical feet; (reversed) dense, expedient, overidentified with appearance, money grabber; or naturalist, physician, master of the body.***"

Image: A knight on a black horse bears a pentacle before him. His helmet is crowned with oak. A partially visored knight, his armor has pentacles upon it.

Traditional: Utility, responsibility, trustworthy, man, upholder of the establishment. **"First secure an independent income, then practice virtue"** (Greek Proverb)

Spectrum of Possibility: [**Practicality**] economy/utility, density/compulsivity, account/contain.

Queen of Pentacles

Phrase: "***Goddess of the home, mature sensuous nurturer of ordinary magic, self-trust and earthly splendor; lover of children, animals, plants and trees; physical consciousness; (reversed) agoraphobic, lethargic, over-parental, insecure; or self-healing, communion with nature.***"

Image: A queen, seated upon a ram's head throne. She sits in a flowery field beneath roses. Near the throne is a rabbit.

Traditional: Opulence, generosity, intelligence, greatness of soul. **"If you are a host to your guest, be a host to his dog also"** (Russian Proverb).

Spectrum of Possibility: [**Ordinary Magic**] home/happiness, phobic/carelessness, sensuous/wholesome.

King of Pentacles

Phrase: "***Business magnate, ground-breaker, wheeler/dealer, worldly leader, wealth-maker, earthly power, natural integrity; (reversed) corruption and avarice; over-ambition, arrogance, hubris, or great inner strength, confidence, rootedness.***"

Image: A king on a bull's head throne. In his right hand he holds the scepter with orb at its end. His left rests upon a pentacle. In the background is a stone castle. His robe is decorated with a pattern of grape vines and ripe grapes.

Traditional: Solidification, business strength, practicality, perseverance. **"A rich man has no need of character"** (Hebrew Proverb).

Spectrum of Possibility: [**Responsibility**] achievement/enterprise, corruption/failure, integrity/increase.

THE MAJOR ARCANA

LEXICON

No.	Arcanum	**Agency** (intention)	**Coherence** (organization)	**Continuity** (process)	**Emotional Arousal** (motivation)
1	**MAGICIAN**	Will	Power	Transformation	Mastery
2	**PRIESTESS**	Insight	Penetration	Intuition	Mystery
3	**EMPRESS**	Nurturance	Love	Healing	Creation
4	**EMPEROR**	Order	Structure	Construction	Authority
5	**HIEROPHANT**	Guidance	Ethics	Learning	Understanding
6	**LOVERS**	Relationship	Harmony	Accommodation	Union
7	**CHARIOT**	Attainment	Action	Pursuit	Challenge
8	**STRENGTH**	Confidence	Endurance	Acceptance	Self-esteem
9	**HERMIT**	Wisdom	Retreat	Introspection	Soul
10	**WHEEL OF FORTUNE**	Change	Timing	Flow	Opportunity
11	**JUSTICE**	Equanimity	Balance	Adjustment	Equality
12	**HANGED MAN**	Awareness	Suspension	Surrender	Transcendence
13	**DEATH**	Metamorphosis	Dissolution	Dying	Life
14	**TEMPERANCE**	Transmutation	Integration	Blending	Refinement
15	**DEVIL**	Separation	Opposition	Deception	Domination
16	**TOWER**	Destruction	Resistance	Evacuation	Liberation
17	**STAR**	Luminosity	Inspiration	Emergence	Hope
18	**MOON**	Psyche	Imagination	Fluctuation	Emotion
19	**SUN**	Consciousness	Energy	Activity	Awareness
20	**JUDGMENT**	Resolution	Completion	Awakening	Accountability
21	**WORLD**	Wholeness	Universality	Participation	Celebration
0	**FOOL**	Possibility	Openness	Discovery	Play

MAJOR ARCANA

Phrases and Proverbs 0-22

[Note: Images describe the standard Waite/Smith Tarot images and traditional descriptions are taken from Butler's *Dictionary of the Tarot* (1975). Meanings, however, are applicable to all decks. Phrases are those of the author. Reversals suggest compromised and/or 'inner' aspect of card. Spectrums of possibility are taken from the lexicons in this book.]

0 The FOOL

Phrase: ***"The Trickster; spirit in search of experience; total potentiality; open space; undifferentiated spirit; freedom to make mistakes, without situational karma; beginner's mind; crazy wisdom; divine child archetype; freedom; inventiveness and eccentricity; (reversed) foolishness, menace, or 'inner child'."***

Image: A young man poses on the edge of a precipice. In his left hand he carries a white rose. His dog barks with joy .

Traditional Meaning: Folly, mania, extravagance, anarchy, thoughtlessness, chaos, ether, alpha and omega, beginning and end. **"Never squat with your spurs on"** (Texan Proverb).

Spectrums of Possibility: Possibility, Openness, Discovery, Play.

I The MAGICIAN

Phrase: ***"The magician in the lab of life, he transforms darkness into light, difficulty into ease, chaos into form, the ideal into the material; inspired communication; right speech, skillful means; associated with Hermes or Mercury; quickness of mind; (reversed) magical (infantile) thinking, powerlessness, or 'alchemist of the soul'."***

Image: A magician stands behind a table. In his upraised right hand is a wand. His left hand is extended downward pointing towards earth. Above his head is the lemniscate. On the table before him are the symbols of the four suits: pentacle, wand, cup, sword. Red roses bloom over him, red roses and lilies bloom before him.

Traditional: Communication skills, willpower or the exercise of will, self-confidence, beginning of consciousness; weakness of will, cunning and guile. **"It is not a fish until it is on the bank"** (Irish Proverb)

Spectrums of Possibility: Will, Power, Transformation, Mastery.

II The HIGH PRIESTESS

Phrase: "***Inner goddess of the psyche; keeper of the subtlest knowledge and impressions of past experience (the Akashic records of ancient Egypt); deep intuitive knowing; she equalizes opposites; (reversed) blocked psychic channels.***"

Image: A priestess of Isis, the solar cross upon her breast. The waxing crescent beneath her left foot. She sits between the pillars Boaz and Jachin and before a screen decorated with pomegranates. In her lap is a rolled scroll of the Torah. On her head is a crown signifying waxing, waning and full Moon and probably The Triple Goddess as well.

Traditional: Spiritual bride and mother, destiny, path of secrecy, psychic abilities, memory, and the subconscious. "**Don't think there are no crocodiles because the water is calm**" (Malayan Proverb).

Spectrums of Possibility: Insight, Penetration, Intuition, Mystery.

III The EMPRESS

Phrase: "***The anima or feminine principle; the divine mother principle of nature, nurture, the womb, fertility, mother earth; universal love; associated with Venus, Demeter, Ishtar, Tara; self-acceptance/healing; (reversed) smothering, infertility, or deep self-soothing.***"

Image: An empress, seated and wearing a gown decorated with pomegranates. On her head a crown of stars. She holds a rod raised in her right hand. A device on the symbol for Venus with a heart. Ripe wheat in the foreground.

Traditional: Fruitfulness, fertility, action, universal love, beauty, happiness, warm mother goddess. "**God could not be everywhere and therefore he made mothers**" (Jewish Proverb)

Spectrums of Possibility: Nurturance, Love, Healing, Creation.

IV The EMPEROR

Phrase: "***The leader, captain, explorer, father; animus figure or 'golden man within'; the masculine principle: logos, structure, order, organization; maintainer of the status quo; four-square reality; thought control; associated with Aries, ruled by Mars; (reversed) imperious, controlling, or inner law, the dharma.***"

Image: Seated on a throne embellished with rams' heads. He holds the orb, without the cross, in his left hand. In his right hand the scepter which terminates in the Crux Ansata.

Traditional: Virility, stability, power, protection, patriarchy, vigilance, temporal power and strength. "**To know and to act are one and the same**" (Samurai Proverb)

Spectrums of Possibility: Order, Structure, Construction, Authority.

V *The* HIEROPHANT

Phrase: **"*The spiritual teacher and teachings; particularly concerned with the worldly realms of human ethics, values, spiritual needs; guru, psychologist, spiritual authority; the capacity 'to walk the mystical path with practical feet'; a bit cloistered and dependent upon family, flock, or following; (reversed) pontifical, overbearing, self-righteous, or inner guidance and inner authority.*"**

Image: A seated pope, bearing the keys of Saint Peter. The pose seen wearing a stylized version of the triple crown. In the left foreground are the crossed Keys of St. Peter. In the right foreground is the Papal Cross.

Traditional: External religion, orthodox doctrine, mercy, kindness, goodness, occult knowledge, bridgemaker (Pontiflex), one who links the outer world of the flesh and substance with the inner one of spirit and transubstantiality. **"Call on God, but row away from the rocks"** (Indian Proverb).

Spectrums of Possibility: Guidance, Ethics, Learning, Understanding.

VI *The* LOVERS

Phrase: **"*The art of relationship; integration of opposites; true context for wholeness and intimacy; union of masculine and feminine; passion and compassion; (reversed) self love or hate, apathy, or psychological 'combination'.*"**

Image: An angel blessing Adam and Eve. Eve stands before the Tree of Knowledge of Good and Evil, on which is wrapped the smiling snake. Adam stands before a tree of flames.

Traditional: Human love, wisdom versus pleasure, attraction, love, beauty, choice, sacred vs. profane love. **"A heart in love with beauty never grows old"** (Turkish Proverb).

Spectrums of Possibility: Relationship, Harmony, Accommodation, Union.

VII *The* CHARIOT

Phrase: **" *Taking action, challenge; change and variety; victory over obstacles; master of language and communication; political power; speaks to the masses, great expanse; triumphal nature; (reversed) ruthlessness and aggression, or inner journey.*"**

Image: A king borne in a triumphal car. The car is drawn by sphinxes, the canopy is embellished with stars, a lingam and yoni appears on the front of the chariot. On the king's breast is a radiant square. An eight-pointed star on the crown.

Traditional: Influence, conquest, victory, overcoming obstacles, triumph over nature, speech. **"Vision without action is a daydream. Action with without vision is a nightmare"** (Japanese Proverb).

Spectrums of Possibility: Attainment, Action, Pursuit, Challenge.

VIII STRENGTH

Phrase: "***Spiritual strength; the feminine taming the instinctive; beauty and the beast myth; gentle mastery; courage to take risks; vitality and wholesomeness; yogin or bodhisattva; overcoming obstacles and patience, (reversed) psychic weakness, machismo, or inner strength.***"

Image: A woman with the lemniscate above her head opening the jaws of a lion. A stern knight with his dog.

Traditional: Inner strength, friendship, consolidation of energy, force, firmness, spiritual strength, vitality. "**When you have no choice, mobilize the spirit of courage.**" (Jewish Proverb).

Spectrums of Possibility: Confidence, Endurance, Acceptance, Self-esteem.

IX The HERMIT

Phrase: "***Wisdom seeker/spiritual journey; fiercely independent and determined; archetype of The Wise Old Man; cares little for outside approval; values aloneness; 'seeks his own salvation with diligence (Buddha)'; life purpose; path of individuation; introspection and self-containment, strong sense of self; (reversed) isolation, paranoia, antisocial, or inner guidance.***"

Image: A monk carrying a lantern.

Traditional: Attainment, pilgrimage, loneliness, inner wisdom, hidden cosmic mind, the inner life. "**If you wish good advice, consult an old man**" (Romanian Proverb).

Spectrums of Possibility: Wisdom, Retreat, Introspection, Soul.

X The WHEEL OF FORTUNE

Phrase: "***The secret of right timing; The Wheel of Life, knowing when to make your move, when to stay pat; knowledge of the laws of change, cycles, seasons, and all circular patterns; the wheel of dharma; unexpected opportunities; destiny; occult powers (siddhis); (reversed) stagnation, grasping, hesitation or inner certainty.***"

Image: A wheel surmounted by a smiling sphinx (holding a drawn sword over her left shoulder. On the wheel are the letters T-A-R-O; interspersed between these letters are the Hebrew letters Yod-Heh-Vau-Heh, or Jahweh, Jehovah (the tetragrammaton or unmentionable name of God). Additionally the symbols for mercury, sulfur, salt and water. At the four corners of the card are the four Apocalyptic Beasts, the Cherubs of the Four Elements. On the right, Anubis rising. On the left Typhon descending the form of a snake.

Traditional: Fluidity of human life, fortune (good or bad), evolution, change, benefits, money, destiny. "**No call alligator long mouth till you pass him**" (Jamaican Proverb).

Spectrums of Possibility: Change, Timing, Flow, Opportunity.

XI JUSTICE

Phrase: "***Balance, alignment, adjustment, equality, discriminating mind; poetic justice; taking control of karma; simplifying; sword of discrimination (Prajna); scales of balance; divine retribution; (reversed) one-sidedness or inner balance.***"

Image: Justice seated, scales in left hand, upraised sword in her right; a square device ornaments her crown and further square, enclosing a circle, is used to fasten her cloak.

Traditional: Equity, rightness, karma, law, balance, equilibrium, fairness, cosmic law, dharma. "**In case of doubt it is best to lean to the side of mercy**" (Legal Proverb).

Spectrums of Possibility: Equanimity, Balance, Adjustment, Equality.

XII The HANGED MAN

Phrase: "***Suspended mind; breaking patterns, 'turning it over'; detachment; turning the world upside down, and temporarily stepping off; stopping the world; witness consciousness, visualization, meditation; other ways of knowing; seeking options; (reversed) aloofness, dissociation or self-observation.***"

Image: The hanged man dangles from a Tau Cross of living trees, his head surrounded by a beatific penumbra. In either case it is important to note that the man is not suffering but seems to be having some beatific vision; also that his legs form the number four when the card is reversed.

Traditional: Wisdom, circumspection, intuition, voluntary sacrifice, punishment, occult wisdom, prophetic power. "**No one can see their reflection in running water. It is only in still water that we can see**" (Taoist Proverb).

Spectrums of Possibility: Awareness, Suspension, Surrender, Transcendence.

XIII DEATH

Phrase: "***Universal principle of detachment and release; Thanatos, transformation; death/rebirth; completion; reincarnation; extinction, the end of the line; (reversed) lethargy, petrifaction, sleep or ego death.***"

Image: Death in black armor riding a white horse. He carries in his left hand a flag on which is a white rose on a black field. In the field through which he rides are a dead king, a curious child, a despairing woman and a praying bishop. The sun is rising.

Traditional: Change, transformation, passage from lower to higher, ending, destruction, literal death, disaster, death and resurrection, rebirth, dark night of the soul. "**Life is not separate from death. It only looks that way.**" (Native American Proverb/Blackfoot).

Spectrums of Possibility: Metamorphosis, Dissolution, Dying, Life.

XIV TEMPERANCE

Phrase: "***The Middle Path; tempering the fires; patience; artistic pursuit; alchemy; blending and matching energy; synthesis and synergy; one foot on land, one foot on water; working with paradox; preparing, pacing, (reversed) intemperance or incubation.***"

Image: An angel stands beside a pool, one foot in the water. From the pool a path leads to the mountains and the sunrise. Beside the pool are yellow irises. On her breast a triangle within a square. On her head is a solar symbol.

Traditional: Economy, moderation, accommodation, combination, reconciliation, modification, mixing of opposite ingredients in proper proportions. **"When you want to test the depths of a stream, don't use both feet"** (Chinese Proverb).

Spectrums of Possibility: Transmutation, Integration, Blending, Refinement.

XV *The* DEVIL

Phrase: "***Bondage and duality, deception and delusion; humor and mirth; the shadow side: chaos and demons; not the Christian devil but associated with Pan (Greek God of Merriment and Sensuality); "living it up"; sensuality; intoxication; consciously courting the senses (Tantra); (reversed) shadow projections, the power shadow, evil, or occult experimentation.***"

Image: A claw-footed devil perched on a black pedestal. His right hand raised, the first and second fingers together as are the third and fourth. The sign of Saturn is his palm. Goat's horn, between which is an inverted pentagram. His left hand holds a torch, inverted, which has fired the tail of his male captive. On the right of the Devil is the woman, whose tail incorporates the pomegranate as part of its design. Both captives are loosely chained and horned. Waite has intended an obvious connection between this card and VI, the Lovers.

Traditional: Evil, fear, fate, misery, adultery, Pan, instinctive behavior, Siva, limitation, bondage to material things. **"Speak of the devil and he appears"** (Italian Proverb).

Spectrums of Possibility: Separation, Opposition, Deception, Domination.

XVI *The* TOWER

Phrase: "***Need for radical and immediate change; sudden awakening (satori); attack from outside, crumbling within; time to abandon ship; 'ivory tower'; restructuring as former position no longer tenable; laser intensity; (reversed) shake-up of core values, self-imprisonment or radical deconstruction.***"

Image: A tower struck by lightning. It is aflame from the upper windows and standing beside the sea.

Traditional: Unpleasant transitional condition, ruin, disruption, punishment of pride, downfall, mental obstruction, fall due to misuse of the intellect. **"He**

who puts up with insult invites injury" (Jewish Proverb).

Spectrums of Possibility: Destruction, Resistance, Evacuation, Liberation.

XVII *The STAR*

Phrase: "***Emergence, coming out, self-esteem, becoming a star; phoenix rising out of the ash; the guiding light; alchemy between the light above reflected off the pool of emotions (below) producing beautiful winged creature; purification, healing; (reversed) stagefright, or ceremonial magick.***"

Image: A naked woman kneeling on the shore. She pours one vase into water, one on to land. Behind her are eight stars, each having eight points. Seven are white and the eighth and central is yellow.

Traditional: Hope, immortality, inner light, possibilities.

Spectrums of Possibility: Luminosity, Inspiration, Emergence, Hope.

XVIII *The MOON*

Phrase: "***The unconscious, the non-rational, magic; the universal feminine principle (the yin); nighttime and moonlight, the dream world; fantasy, romance, emotion and intuition; pulls inward, irritability; (reversed) 'lunacy', emotional flooding or the psychic muse.***"

Image: An equatorial crescent. Below it are two dogs, one of them howling. A lobster emerging from a pool at the bottom.

Traditional: Darkness, deception, error, illusion, intuition, feelings and sentiments, mystery, romance, water and the female element in general, soul. **"After dark all cats are leopards"** (Native American Proverb/Zuni).

Spectrums of Possibility: Psyche, Imagination, Fluctuation, Emotion.

XIX *The SUN*

Phrase: "***Consciousness; the light of day, the rational and visible; vitality and life force; the yang; teamwork and partnership; daytime activity, vibrancy, creativity, play; radiant light, healing, energy; masculinity, heroism, the ego; (reversed) egotism, burnout, or agni (fire) yoga.***"

Image: A naked child smiling from the back of a white horse. He carries in his left hand a long banner on a pole. Behind him is a walled garden with sunflowers visible above it. Above, the sun in glory.

Traditional: Consciousness, super-rational, willpower, joy, universal radiance, splendor of the material world, enlightenment, happiness. **"Turn your face to the sun and the shadows fall behind you"** (Maori Proverb).

Spectrums of Possibility: Consciousness, Energy, Activity, Awareness.

XX *JUDGMENT*

Phrase: "***Finality; proclamation, coming to completion; the actualization of deep discrimination; ability to give birth to new forms; sounding your horn, taking a stand; choice and responsibility; outcome and resolution; (reversed) judgmentalness, self criticism or self-actualization.***"

Image: Angel seen blowing the last trumpet. The dead rise from the grave. The Angel only, blowing a trumpet.

Traditional: Judgment, choice, resurrection, outcome, completion, the last judgment, accomplishment. "**Man has responsibility, not power**" (Native American Proverb/Tuscarora).

Spectrums of Possibility: Resolution, Completion, Awakening, Accountability.

XXI *The* WORLD

Phrase: "***The Universe, integration of the whole, the great mandala; the dance of life, bringing spirit into the material world; the principle of wholeness and individuation; the final trump, completion; perfection and the absolute; (reversed) introversion, withdrawal, or mysticism, samahdi.***"

Image: A woman holding a piece of cloth strategically. She is surrounded by a wreath of leaves and berries. At the top of the wreath is an eagle, below left is a bull, below right is a lion.

Traditional: Completion, perfection of man, travel, cosmic consciousness, the reward, uroborus, Brahma, assured success. "**No need to teach an eagle to fly**" (Greek Proverb).

Spectrums of Possibility: Wholeness, Universality, Participation, Celebration.

Appendix B

Composite Tarot Voices

A Dialogue between Recovering Perpetrator and Victim

[Note: This dialogue is based strictly from card interpretation of composite spread positions found on pages 222 and 235. These prototypes are not meant to be interpersonally related, but speak individually as if in soliloquy]

(1) *THE PRESENT SITUATION*:

He: **(The Hermit reversed)** *I am an isolated, lonely man. I struggle to be self-reliant and true to my convictions. I'm kind of a loner, but ironically, I hate to be alone. I entertain private thoughts about other's motivations. I am uncomfortable disclosing, I trust no one, and care little for other's approval. I am not a follower, I go my own way.*

She: **(5 of Pentacles)** *I'm out in the cold now, looking in at the warmth and coziness I once enjoyed. My former sanctuary has failed me. It's time now to pay my dues, and I sense there's some lesson here for me as well. But with the scant resources I now have, I must fend for myself and my children just to survive. I am homeless, betwixt and between. It's cold out here and I'm starting to shiver.*

(2) *THE OBSTACLE*:

He: **(10 of Swords)** *I resist the call to surrender the war I've waged my whole life, the war with myself. They tell me I must grieve the pain and mental struggle that's in my heart. That I must release the huge negativity that stands at the core of my being. But this I can't do or won't do. I fear annihilation by my own mental demons, that is, if I give in to them, and then nothing will be left of me.*

She: **(Knight of Wands)** *I tend to be drawn to charismatic, aggressive men and I suppose I attract them as well. My husband was very passionate but also quite impulsive with a great need to control me and everyone else. He'd get frustrated easily when he didn't get what he wanted, he'd storm the house filled with pent-*

up emotions and then explode, sometimes violently, without warning, often after too much alcohol. I think I have the same potential myself. I have a love-hate relationship with this passionate aggressive energy, and I'm vulnerable before it.

(3) THE FOUNDATION:

He: (2 of Swords) *The foundation of my struggle now is to establish a sense of trust, friendship, and mutual respect in my relationships. This is all very new for me. These conditions must be present first before I can even consider emotional intimacy again.*

She: (The World reversed) *The foundation of my world has been turned upside down. I feel groundless and disoriented. My efforts to get back into the 'pulse of life' feel muted and lackluster. I want to become whole again, I want to be free, and dance with life, but I can't get myself moving. I have so much to put back together now yet I feel stagnant and disconnected.*

(4) PAST CAUSE:

He: (The Empress reversed) *As a child, I dreamed of some all-loving, sensuous, and nurturing goddess figure who would comfort and protect me from my father's abuses, as my real mother was inconsistent and couldn't be counted on. I became blocked off from all feeling, mistrusting offers of love and kindness from others. In relationships, my search for a true nurturer has been my secret motivation ever since.*

She: (9 of Swords) *I was very depressed in the past. When the relationship became insufferable, my worry and negativity really began to affect my thinking. I was convinced of my own worthlessness as a person and tended to see the darkness in everything. My depressive tendencies probably started well before I met my husband.*

(5) GOALS AND IDEALS:

He: (Queen of Cups) *My perfect picture is for some soft, caring woman to understand me and nurture me. Someone who knows intuitively what I am needing and have needed ever since I was a boy. My ideal woman, maybe not a perfect goddess as before, is a person who is warm and nurturing, who teaches me how to feel and have feelings for others, who knows what I am thinking, and who wants to make love to me.*

She: (6 of Wands) *My goal now is to mobilize all my resources, both inner and outer, to hold my head up high, and march off into whatever new struggles and challenges that lie ahead, filled with a strong sense of renewed confidence in my abilities to withstand whatever difficulties await me. I believe I will be successful.*

(6) COMING SOON: (future effect)

He: (King of Cups, reversed) *Soon I will yearn to become that mature man of compassion and good-will I have often admired. King of the heart. But he seems such a great mystery to me. Truth be told, I sense my tendencies towards the opposite are more likely to prevail, that is, domination, deceit, manipulation, keeping others away, and trickery. Unless, of course, I can truly make that great surrender to the 10 of Swords. Open my heart to the pain. I don't know if I have the courage.*

She: (8 of Swords) *With my depressive tendencies from the past, particularly if I continue to replay my relationships patterns around those fiery Knights, those charming and adventurous control freaks that I attract, I will soon return to another state of depression and paralysis, knowing full well this time that I've once again played with fire and gotten burnt, and I have only myself to blame…which I'm sure I will do rather well.*

(7) EGO IDENTITY:

He: (Judgment) *I see myself at major crossroads, a time now to 'make it or break it', a call to take the moral highground or be damned. I tell myself, daily, that I must make a firm resolve to be truthful—to myself, to my recovery program, and to my family. I must proclaim this commitment publicly and forthrightly if I am to restore my accountability.*

She: (Death reversed) *I am a woman struggling with the total loss of her former identity. Everything I thought I was—is now over. My marriage, my home, my innocence, my reputation—now gone. But strangely, I feel in some state of shock over it, I'm lethargic and numb and I feel almost unreal. They say that after a death comes 'new beginnings,' but so far inside me I feel mostly tremendous loss and disorientation.*

(8) OTHERS: (the object)

He: (Queen of Pentacles reversed) *I see my wife has lost a lot of confidence and trust in herself. She seems weakened and this frankly frightens me. She doesn't trust her instincts anymore and is out of sorts. She used to be really so connected to things, our home and children, our animals, her many physical activities, etc. But now she seems to have lost her rhythm. I'm sure I've played a large part in messing her up and I feel guilty about it. If only she could understand why I've done the things I've done.*

She: (7 of Wands) *I see my husband as defensive and combative as ever, but now he's digging in and trying to reclaim some of his power and control over me. It's subtler now, to his credit—he is asserting himself better without forcing his opinion like before, but I can still feel the stubbornness and need for control as he now positions himself in relation to me.*

(9) ANTICIPATION:

He: (7 of Wands reversed) *I fear I will continue to be defensive and combative like before. It's the way I protect myself. I become intractable. But I realize any replay of the past and I'm a goner. I desperately hope I can hold strong to my new skills, practice assertiveness and express my needs verbally and tactfully. And I hope I can rise above the conflict when she starts pushing my buttons with her emotional demands. I expect she will really test me this time. I can only hope to be ready for the attack.*

She: (Page of Wands) *My hope is to find a younger, 'kinder and gentler' version of my ex-husband. A man who is also strong-willed and charismatic, adventurous and very sexy in his own right, but not so controlling, impulsive, and domineering as my violent husband was. I'm just not attracted to boring guys. But my fear, of course, is that this made-to-order young Page is fated to evolve into the same fire-breathing dominant male that my husband was. That I'll get burnt again, maybe even killed this time (it must be my karma or something?), and I will end up once again depressed, disoriented, homeless, or dead.*

(10) OUTCOME:

He: (The Tower reversed) *The forces of destiny suggest I will no longer be able to live with the beliefs and behaviors of my past iron-clad 'ivory' tower. My house will indeed crumble if I cannot make a swift and radical departure from my violent, shutoff, defunct self. Should I fail, I will be condemned to suffer a harsh imprisonment within the walls of my own defective personality. I will become my own persecutor and victim.*

She: (7 of Cups) *The forces of my future destiny suggest great uncertainty up ahead. There will be many different options and possibilities of direction and it's likely that I will be vulnerable to indecision, rumination, and emotional seduction. I will need to make good choices and be quick to relinquish bad ones, or else find myself paralyzed and overwhelmed by confusion.*

(11) GIFT AND GUIDE: (The Oracle speaks)

To The Hermit Reversed: **(Ten of Cups)** ***Reflect on these words for they offer you a gift***—*"Love, imagination, and joy all come to us as gifts. Life brings happiness, not just an absence of pain. Domestic happiness is based on the recognition of the valuable qualities in a situation."* [As quoted from Rachel Pollack]

To The Lady of the Knight: **(The Emperor) Reflect on these words for they offer you a guide**—*"Follow the established structures of healthy society, and stability and benevolence will come. Seek a firm understanding of reality and create order and kindness in your affairs."* [Ibid.]

Thus spoke The Hermit Reversed and The Lady of the Knight.

Bibliography

Ammann, R (1991). *Healing and Transformation in Sandplay*; [in foreword by Donald Sandner], Open Court, La Salle, IL.

Anonymous (1985). *Meditations on the Tarot;* Element Classic Editions, MA.

Atamanspacher, H and Primas, H (1996). *The Hidden Side of Wolfgang Pauli* [*Journal of Consciousness Studies,* Vol. 3, No.2]; Imprint Academic, USA.

Arrien, Angeles, (1987). *The Tarot Handbook: Practical Applications of Ancient Visual Symbols;* Arcus Publishing Company, Sonoma, CA.

______. (1993). *The Four Fold Way: Walking the Paths of the Warrior, Teacher, Healer and Visionary;* Harper, San Francisco.

Bakan, David (1958). *Sigmund Freud and the Jewish Mystical Tradition;* D. Van Norstrand, Princeton, NJ.

Bowker, John (editor) (1997). *The Oxford Dictionary of World Religions;* Oxford University Press, Oxford, U.K.

Buryn, Ed (1995). *The William Blake Tarot;* Harper, San Francisco.

Butler, Bill, (1975). *Dictionary of the Tarot;* Schoken Books, New York.

Callahan, Roger J. and Callahan, Joanne, (1996). *Thought Field Therapy*^{Tm}; Indian Wells, CA.

Chalmers, David J. (1996). *The Conscious Mind: In Search of a Fundamental Theory;* Oxford University Press, New York.

Cirlot, J. E.(1962). A *Dictionary of Symbols* (Second Edition); Routledge & Kegan Paul, London.

Corbett, Lionel, (1996). *The Religious Function of the Psyche;* Routledge, London.

Crowley, Aleister, (1969) [Originally published in 1944]. *The Book of Thoth: A Short Essay On The Tarot of the Egyptians;* Samuel Weiser, York Beach, ME.

Diagnostic and Statistical Manual of Mental Disorders [Fourth Edition] (1994); American Psychiatric Association, Washington, DC.

Dunne, J.W. (1927). *An Experiment with Time;* Faber and Faber Ltd., London.

DuQuette, Lon Milo, (1997). *Angels, Demons & Gods of the New Millennium: Musings on Modern Magick;* Samuel Weiser, Inc., York Beach, ME.

Edinger, Edward F.(1984). *The Creation of Consciousness: Jung's Myth for Modern Man*; Inner City Books, Toronto.

Ethnographic Portraits: The Inupiat Eskimo of Arctic Alaska; Internet:http:www.lib.uconn.edu/Arctic Circle/Cultural Viability/Inupiat/ 1800s.html.

Fairbairn, W. R. D. (1952). *Psychoanalytic Studies of the Personality*; Tavistock Publications and Kegan Paul, Trench, & Trubner, London.

Fairfield, Gail (1985). *Choice Centered Tarot*; Newcastle Publishing Co., North Hollywood, CA.

Feng, Gia-Fu, and English, Jane (1972). *Lao Tsu: Tao Te Ching*; Vintage Books, New York.

Frank, J.D. (1973, 2nd edition). *Healing and Persuasion*; Johns Hopkins University Press, Baltimore.

Freud, S. (1964) [Original work published 1933]. *New Introductory Lectures* (Standard Edition), Hogarth, London.

Fishman, D. B., & Franks, C. M.(1992). *Evolution and Differentiation Within Behavior Therapy: A Theoretical and Epistemological Review.* In D. K. Freedheim (Ed.), *History of Psychotherapy: A Century of Change*; American Psychological Association, Washington, DC.

Fortune, Dion (1977) [Original published in England, in 1935]. *The Mystical Qabalah*, Samuel Weiser, Inc., York Beach, ME.

Gallagher, Shaun (1997); [Editor's Introduction] *Journal Of Consciousness Studies*; Vol 4, No. 5-6 *(Models of the Self)*, pp.399-405, World Copyright, Imprint Academic, Thoverton, U.K.

Getting, F. (1980). *Fate & Prediction: An Historical Compendium of Palmistry, Astrology, and Tarot*; Exeter, New York.

Giles, Cynthia, (1992). *The Tarot: History, Mystery, and Lore*; Simon and Schuster (Fireside) New York.

Greer, Mary K. (1988). *Tarot Mirrors: Reflections of Personal Meaning*, Newcastle Publishing Co, North Hollywood.

______. (1995)*Women of the Golden Dawn: Rebels and Priestesses*; Park Street Press, Rochester, Vermont,

______. (1987) *Tarot Constellations: Patterns of Personal Destiny*; Newcastle Publishing Co, North Hollywood.

______. (1984)*Tarot for Yourself: A Workbook for Personal Transformation*; Newcastle Publishing Co, North Hollywood.

Hall, James A. (1986). *The Jungian Experience*; Inner City Books, Toronto, Canada

______. "Religious Images in Dreams" (1979). *Journal of Religion and Health* [18(4); 327-335].

Hillman, James (1995). "A Psyche the Size of the Earth" in Roszak, Theodore, Gomes, Mary E., Kanner, Allen D., *Ecopsychology: Restoring the Earth/ Healing the Mind;* Sierra Club Books, San Francisco.

______, and Ventura, Michael (1992). *We've Had A Hundred Years Of Psychotherapy and the World's Getting Worse;* Harper, San Francisco.

Jahn, Robert, and Dunne, Brenda (1987). *Margins of Reality: The Role of Consciousness in the Physical World;* Harcourt, Brace, Jovanovich, New York.

Johnson, Cait and Shaw, Maura D. (1994). *Tarot Games: 45 Playful Ways to Explore Tarot Cards Together: A New Vision for the Circle of Community;* Harper San Francisco.

Johnson, Robert A (1986). *Innerwork: Using Dreams & Active Imagination for Personal Growth;* Harper & Row, New York.

Jung, C. G. (1953-1979). *The Collected Works* (Bollingen Series XX, 20 Volumes); Trans. R.F.C. Hull, Trans; H. Read, M. Fordham, G. Adler, & W. McGuire, Eds.; Princeton University Press, Princeton, NJ.

______. Volume VI: *Psychological Types* ((1921).

______. Volume VII (Part 1): *Two Essays on Analytical Psychology* (1926, 1928).

______. Volume VIII: *The Structure and Dynamics of the Psyche* (1947/54, 1952).

______. Volume IX: (Part 1): *The Archetypes and the Collective Unconscious* (1934/1950).

______. Volume XI: *Psychology and Religion: West and East* (1938, 1943, 1944, 1950).

______. Volume XV: *The Spirit in Man, Art, and Literature* (1930).

Jung, C. G. (1973). *Letters: 1906-1950.* Princeton University Press, Princeton, NJ.

Jung, Carl G., *(1964). Man and His Symbols;* Doubleday & Company Inc., Garden City, NY.

Jung, C. G. (1961). *Memories, Dreams, Reflections;* Vintage Books, Random House, New York.

Jung, C. G. [edited by Joseph Campbell] (1975). *The Portable Jung;* Viking Penguin, New York.

Karasu, T.B. (1986). "The Specificity Versus Nonspecificity Dilemma: Toward Identifying Therapeutic Change Agents." *American Journal of Psychiatry,* 143, 687-695.

Kalff, Dora, M.(1980). *Sandplay: A Psychotherapeutic Approach to the Psyche;* Sigo Press, Boston.

Kellog, Joan, (1978). *Mandala: Path of Beauty ;* ATMA, Inc., Belleair, FL.

Kendall, P. C., & Bemis, K. M.(1983).*Thought and Action in Psychotherapy: The Cognitive Behavioral Approaches.* [In M. Hersen, A. E. Kazdin, & A. S. Bellak (Eds.), *The Clinical Psychology Handbook* (pp. 565-592); Pergamon Press, Elmsford, NY.

Konrad, Sandor (1985). *Classic Tarot Spreads;* Whitford Press, Atglen, PA.

London, P. (1986). *The Modes and Morals of Psychotherapy* (second edition); Hemisphere, Washington D.C.

Mansfield, Victor (1995). *Synchronicity, Science, and Soul-Making,* Open Court, La Salle, IL.

Metzner, Ralph (1971). *Maps of Consciousness;* Collier Books, New York.

Mitchell, Stephen (1991). *The Enlightened Mind;* Harper Perennial, New York.

Needham, Rodney (1987). *Counterpoints;* University of California Press, London.

Newman, Kenneth, D. (1983). *The Tarot: A Myth of Male Initiation;* A Quadrant Monograph [published by the C.G. Jung Foundation for Analytical Psychology, New York.

Nichols, Sallie (1980). *Jung and Tarot: An Archetypal Journey;* Samuel Weiser Inc, York Beach, ME.

Ogden, C.K. (1967). *Opposition: A Linguistic and Psychological Analysis* ; Indiana University Press.

O'Neill, Robert V. (1986). *Tarot Symbolism;* Fairway Press, Lima, OH.

Otto, Rudolf (1917, 1923). *The Idea of the Holy;* Oxford Press, London.

Ouspensky, P. D. (1976). *The Symbolism of Tarot: Philosophy of Occultism in Pictures and Numbers,* Dover, New York.

Peat, F. David (1987). *Synchronicity: The Bridge Between Matter and Mind;* Bantam, New York.

Pollack, Rachel (1980). *Seventy-Eight Degrees of Wisdom* (Part 1): *The Major Arcana;* Aquarian Press Limited, Wellingborough, Northhamptonshire, U. K.

______. Part 2: *Seventy-Eight Degrees of Wisdom: The Minor Arcana* (1983).

Progoff, Ira (1973). *Jung, Synchronicity, and Human Destiny;* Delta Publishing Co., New York.

Reber, Arthur, S. (1985). *Dictionary of Psychology;* Penguin Books, London.

Riley, Jana (1995). *Tarot Dictionary and Compendium;* Samuel Weiser, York Beach, ME.

Ritsema, Rudolf and Karcher, Stephen [translators] (1984). *I Ching: The Classic Chinese Oracle of Change,* Element Books Limited, Great Britain.

Roberts, Richard, and Campbell, Joseph (1982). *Tarot Revelations;* Vernal Equinox Press, San Anselmo, CA.

Rohrig, Carl (1993). *The Rohrig Tarot Book;* Bluestar Communications, Woodside, CA.

Room, Adrian (1988). *Dictionary of Contrasting Pairs;* Routledge, London.

Rosengarten, Arthur, E. (1985). *Accessing the Unconscious, A Comparative Study of Dreams, The T.A.T. and Tarot* [doctoral dissertation]; University Microfilms International, Ann Arbor, MI.

Rosengarten, Arthur (1994). *Tarot as a Psychotherapeutic Tool;* self-published manual, Encinitas, CA [DrArt@electriciti.com].

Roszak, Theodore, Gomes, Mary E., Kanner, Allen D.(1995). *Ecopsychology: Restoring the Earth/Healing the Mind;* Sierra Club Books, San Francisco.

Samuels, Andrew, Shorter, Bani, and Plant, Fred (1987). *A Critical Dictionary of Jungian Analysis;* Routledge & Kegan Paul Ltd, New York.

Slife, Brent (1993). *Time and Psychological Explanation* ; SUNY Press, New York.

Snellgrove, D. L.(1959). *The Hevejra Tantra, Part 1*, Oxford University Press, London.

Streng, Frederick J. (1967). *Emptiness: A Study in Religious Meaning,* Abingdon Press, Nashville, TN.

Vaughan, Fraces, E. (1979). *Awakening Intuition.* Anchor Doubleday, New York.

Van Eenwyk, John (1997). *Archetypes & Strange Attractors: The Chaotic World of Symbols;* Inner City Books, Toronto, Canada.

Von Franz, Marie-Louise (1980). *On Divination and Synchronicity;* Inner City Books, Toronto, Canada.

Waite, Arthur Edward (1971). *The Pictorial Key to the Tarot;* Harper & Row [originally under Rudolf Steiner Publications], New York.

Wachtel, Paul L. and Messer, Stanley B. (1997). *Theories of Psychotherapy: Origins and Evolution;* American Psychological Association, Washington, D.C.

Watts, Allan [with collaboration of Al Chung-liang Huang] (1979). *Tao: The Watercourse Way;* Pantheon Books, New York.

Wilhelm, Richard, and Baynes, Richard (1950). *I Ching or Book of Changes;* Bollingen Series XIX, Princeton University Press, NJ.

Weinrib, Estelle, L. (1983). *Images of the Self; The Sandplay Process;* Sigo Press, Boston.

Young-Eisendrath, Polly, and Hall, James A, (1991) *Jung's Self Psychology: A Constructivist Perspective;* The Guilford Press, New York.

Index

Page numbers for charts and illustrations are in *italics*.